SPECULUM INCLUSORUM
A MIRROR FOR RECLUSES

A late-medieval guide for anchorites and its Middle English translation

The solitary life of the recluse or enclosed anchorite was one of the most extreme, and remains one of the most fascinating, forms of religious life of the Middle Ages. Leaving the world behind, anchorites submitted themselves to a life of perpetual enclosure, locked – or even walled – into a small cell, usually attached to a church. They were enclosed to the accompaniment of the Office of the Dead, and they expected to die and to be buried in their cells. Why did people choose to become anchorites? What did they do all day? What rewards did they hope for, in return for the sacrifice they had made? These are the questions addressed and answered in the *Speculum Inclusorum*, a 'rule' for male anchorites dating from the early years of the fifteenth century, and its English translation, designed for an audience of women anchorites, *A Mirror for Recluses*.

– *from the Introduction*

This edition prints the Latin *Speculum Inclusorum* in parallel with the English *Mirror*, and supplies a modern English translation for those parts of the *Speculum* that are (whether by accident or design) absent from the Middle English. It offers the first edition of the Latin since the 1930s, and the only available translation of the entire text. A substantial introduction places the *Speculum* in the context of late-medieval English anchoritism, orthodox reform, and constructions of masculinity, and considers the circumstances of its translation into Middle English.

E. A. Jones is Senior Lecturer in English Medieval Literature and Culture at the University of Exeter. He works on the non-regular or semi-religious vocations in the late Middle Ages, and the literature produced by and for the men and women who followed those vocations. He has previously edited the Middle English compilation *Disce Mori* in the series Middle English Texts (2006). He organises the Exeter Symposia on the Medieval Mystical Tradition in England, and edits their proceedings (volume VIII appeared in 2013), and is also engaged in an ongoing revision of Rotha Mary Clay's *Hermits and Anchorites of England*.

EXETER MEDIEVAL TEXTS AND STUDIES

Series Editors: Vincent Gillespie and Richard Dance

Founded by M. J. Swanton
and later co-edited by Marion Glasscoe

Speculum Inclusorum

A Mirror for Recluses

*A late-medieval guide for anchorites
and its Middle English translation*

Edited by
E. A. Jones

LIVERPOOL UNIVERSITY PRESS

First published in 2013 by
Liverpool University Press
4 Cambridge Street
Liverpool
L69 7ZU

Copyright © 2013 E. A. Jones

The right of E. A. Jones to be identified as author of this book has been asserted by him in accordance with the Copyright, Designs and Patents Act 1988.

All rights reserved. No part of this book may be reproduced, stored in a retrieval system, or transmitted, in any form or by any means, electronic, mechanical, photocopying, recording, or otherwise, without the prior written permission of the publisher.

British Library Cataloguing-in-Publication data
A British Library CIP record is available

ISBN 978 0 85989 885 0

Typeset by Carnegie Book Production, Lancaster.
Printed by CPI Group (UK) Ltd, Croydon CR0 4YY

Contents

Preface	vii
Abbreviations	ix
List of Illustrations	xi

Introduction

General introduction	xiii
Rules for anchorites	xiii
Men, masculinity and the anchoritic vocation	xxi
Editorial and critical history	xxxv
Manuscripts	xxxviii
Descriptions of extant manuscripts	xxxviii
Lost manuscripts	xlvii
Relationship of manuscripts	xlix
Author and readers	li
Speculum Inclusorum	li
A Mirror for Recluses	lxviii
A Mirror for Recluses as translation	lxxiv
This edition	lxxvii

The Texts

Notes to the Texts	117
Appendix to the Notes to the Texts: annotations to base manuscripts	143
Bibliography	147

Preface

Interest in the anchoritic life in medieval England has never been greater, and yet discussion of English anchorites has a tendency to circle back to the same individuals and the same texts. We are fortunate now to have excellent editions and translations of the key early texts, Ailred of Rievaulx's *De institutione inclusarum* in Latin and the English *Ancrene Wisse*, but there are half a dozen other works of advice and guidance for English anchorites that have still barely been explored. This edition of the fifteenth-century Latin *Speculum Inclusorum* and its Middle English translation for female anchorites, *A Mirror for Recluses*, is a step towards remedying that lack.

Both the *Speculum* and the *Mirror* have been edited before, though neither entirely satisfactorily. Livarius Oliger produced a careful edition of the Latin *Speculum* in the 1930s. Most of his editorial decisions hold good today, but the contextual scholarship is inevitably very dated. (Nor does it help the text's accessibility that Oliger's book is now difficult to get hold of, and that his introduction and commentary are written in Italian.) The English *Mirror* has been edited more recently, by Marta Powell Harley in 1995. It was chancing on her book in the British Library bookshop that first introduced me to these works. Harley produced a good, accurate, and usually judicious text of the *Mirror*, but did not provide many of the things that one expects from a critical edition: a full discussion of the manuscripts, a consideration of the text's date, its author or its audience. In response, I began what I thought would be a review article, but turned into my 1999 essay 'A New Look into the *Speculum Inclusorum*', and eventually became this edition.

The *Mirror* is not a complete translation of the *Speculum*. (Whether this is a matter of accident or design is something I consider in my Introduction.) Where one of its chapters has been left incomplete, Harley provided a modern English translation to fill the gap. But she did nothing with those chapters of the *Speculum* (its Prologue and five of its fourteen chapters) that the *Mirror* omits altogether. Would-be readers of the *Speculum* for whom Latin is a struggle (that is, most of us) have been left with an incomplete impression of a fascinating text, and careless readers have sometimes assumed that the *Mirror* represents all that there is.

This volume provides the first critical edition of the Latin *Speculum* since 1938. It also offers in parallel with the Latin text the first English translation of the whole work, in which a new edition of the Middle English *Mirror* is supplemented where necessary by a modern English translation. A substantial introduction places the *Speculum* in the context of other works of guidance for English anchorites, and of the anchoritic vocation in late-medieval England, especially among men. New arguments are advanced for the work's date and first audience that situate it squarely in the orthodox reform movement of the early fifteenth century. The *Speculum* and *Mirror* should prove of interest to historians of the anchoritic vocation and students of English anchoritic literature, but also to anyone interested in fifteenth-century spirituality and religious reform, as well as providing a useful case-study in Middle English translation.

I am indebted to the series editors at Exeter Medieval Texts and Studies for accepting the book into their series, and to the two editors I have worked with: Anna Henderson, whose enthusiasm and meticulous advice helped me to complete the edition, and Helen Gannon, who has seen it through to publication. I was very fortunate to have Bella Millett as the reader for the press. Her support, her minute attention to detail, and her very helpful suggestions have all been invaluable.

I am grateful to the staff of the British Library and the library of St John's College, Oxford, for their assistance with the manuscripts of the texts. In particular, Stewart Tiley at St John's has dealt swiftly and patiently with a stream of last-minute queries and requests. Thanks too to Cate Gunn for her essential assistance in the early stages of preparing the editions.

Finally, it is many years now since Godfrey Bond first taught me the rudiments of Latin and, though the fruits of his kindness have been a long time coming, it is a pleasure now to acknowledge it.

Abbreviations

DMLBS   *Dictionary of Medieval Latin from British Sources* (London, 1975-)

EETS   Early English Text Society

Harley   Marta Powell Harley, ed., *The Myrour of Recluses: A Middle English Translation of* Speculum Inclusorum (Madison, 1995)

Hogg   James Hogg, ed., *The Speculum Inclusorum, Vol. 2: St. John's College, Oxford, Ms. 177 of the Speculativum Clausorum*, Analecta Cartusiana 59:2 (1981)

Jones 'New Look'   E. A. Jones, 'A New Look into the *Speculum Inclusorum*', in *The Medieval Mystical Tradition: England, Ireland and Wales*, Exeter Symposium VI, ed. Marion Glasscoe (Cambridge, 1999), pp. 123–45

McAvoy, *Anchoritic Traditions*   Liz Herbert McAvoy, ed., *Anchoritic Traditions of Medieval Europe* (Woodbridge, 2010)

MED   *Middle English Dictionary*. Online edition, University of Michigan, 2006, at http://quod.lib.umich.edu/m/med/

NIMEV   *A New Index of Middle English Verse*, ed. Julia Boffey and A. S. G. Edwards (London, 2005)

ODNB   *Oxford Dictionary of National Biography*. Online edition, Oxford University Press, September 2012, at http://www.oxforddnb.com/

OED   *Oxford English Dictionary. OED* Online. Oxford University Press, September 2012, at http://www.oed.com/

Oliger   Livarius Oliger, ed., *Speculum Inclusorum Auctore Anonymo Anglico Saeculi XIV*, Lateranum n. s. iv/i (Rome, 1938)

PL	*Patrologia Latina cursus completus*, ed. J.-P. Migne, 221 vols (Paris, 1844–65)
STC	*A Short-Title Catalogue of Books Printed in England, Scotland and Ireland, and of English Books Printed Abroad 1475–1640*, ed. A. W. Pollard and G. R. Redgrave, 2nd ed. rev. W. A. Jackson, F. S. Ferguson and K. F. Pantzer (London, 1976–91)
Warren	Ann K. Warren, *Anchorites and their Patrons in Medieval England* (Berkeley, 1985)

List of Illustrations

Plate 1   British Library, MS Royal 5 A v, fol. 40v.

Plate 2   St John's College, Oxford, MS 177, fol. 36v.

Plate 3   British Library, MS Harley 2372, fol. 17r.

Plate 4   Reconstructed Plan of Sheen Charterhouse.

Introduction

General introduction

The solitary life of the recluse or enclosed anchorite was one of the most extreme forms of religious life of the Middle Ages, and remains one of the most fascinating.[1] Leaving the world behind, anchorites submitted themselves to a life of perpetual enclosure, locked – or even walled – into a small cell, usually attached to a church. They were enclosed to the accompaniment of the Office of the Dead, and they expected to die and be buried in their cells. Why did people choose to become anchorites? What did they do all day? What rewards did they hope for, in return for the sacrifice they had made? These are the questions addressed and answered in the *Speculum Inclusorum*, a 'rule' for male anchorites dating from the early years of the fifteenth century, and its English translation, designed for an audience of women anchorites, *A Mirror for Recluses*.

Rules for anchorites

The anchoritic life is usually, for obvious reasons, associated above all with constraint. But in some ways it offered freedom. Anchorites inhabited the liminal, grey areas that lay between many of the categories that defined medieval religious identity: they had set themselves apart from the laity, but were not (at least *ipso facto*) clergy; they had taken a vow, but were not (necessarily, or usually) professed members of a religious order; they lived a life of regularity, but were not bound by a formal rule. They are thus to be classed among the 'semi-religious' vocations that were expanding in number, range and importance during the Middle Ages, and that could claim in many ways to be the source and focus of the greatest spiritual energy in late-medieval

---

[1] By the late Middle Ages, the terms *recluse* and *anchorite* are synonymous, at least in English usage. Although my texts use *recluse* (Latin *inclusus*, Middle English *recluse*), I will generally prefer *anchorite* since this has become the standard term in contemporary scholarship.

religion.[2] The category (though by definition it is fuzzy) might be taken to include hermits, anchorites, vowesses, beguines, tertiaries, and those laypeople attempting to live a 'mixed life'. Of these, the life of the anchorite was probably the most strictly controlled and structured, but anchorites were never obliged to submit to a centralised rule, did not belong to a chapter or order, nor fit neatly into a hierarchical structure of obedience and command. Their arrangements were local, *ad hoc* and *ad hominem*.

They also sometimes left traces in text, and these we have come to call 'rules', though the term is problematic.[3] Among the sources from England, the earliest such document – and one whose influence is felt through all the others, including an explicit citation in the text edited here – is the *De Institutione Inclusarum* written c. 1160–2 by the Cistercian Ailred of Rievaulx for his sister.[4] Ailred calls his work a *formula*, a little outline, by which she can organise her mode of living (the very useful translation by Mary Paul Macpherson introduces the word 'rule' here in a way that is precisely inappropriate):

> Iam pluribus annis exigis a me, soror, ut secundum modum uiuendi quem arripuisti pro Christo, certam tibi formulam tradam, ad quam et mores tuos dirigere et necessaria religioni possis exercitia ordinare.
>
> [For many years now, my sister, you have been asking me for a rule [*sic*] to guide you in the life you have embraced for the sake of Christ, to provide spiritual directives and formulate the basic practices of religious life.][5]

---

[2] Kaspar Elm, 'Vita Regularis Sine Regula: Bedeutung, Rechtsstellung und Selbstverständnis des mittelalterlichen und frühneuzeitlichen Semireligiosentums', in *Häresie und vorzeitige Reformation im Spätmittelalter*, ed. František Šmahel (Munich, 1998), pp. 239–73; John van Engen, 'Friar Johannes Nyder on Laypeople Living as Religious in the World', in *Vita Religiosa im Mittelalter: Festschrift für Kaspar Elm zum 70. Geburtstag* (Berlin, 1999), pp. 583–615.

[3] For an excellent examination of the question of anchoritic 'rules', ranging much more widely than I do here, see Bella Millett, 'Can There Be Such a Thing as an "Anchoritic Rule"?', in *Anchoritism in the Middle Ages: Texts and Traditions*, ed. C. Innes-Parker and N. Kukita Yoshikawa (Cardiff, 2013), pp. 11–30.

[4] Ed. C. H. Talbot, in *Aelredus Rievallensis: Opera Ascetica*, ed. A. Hoste and C. H. Talbot (Turnhout, 1971), pp. 637–82. See also the life of Ailred by David N. Bell in *ODNB*. For the sake of this argument I am passing over a few earlier texts: Goscelin's *Liber Confortatorius* (which is nothing like a rule) and the brief epistles to anchorites written by Anselm. For a list of anchoritic rules and guides from medieval England, see Warren, *Anchorites and their Patrons*, pp. 294–8.

[5] Talbot, p. 637. 'A Rule of Life for a Recluse', trans. Mary Paul Macpherson, in *Aelred of Rievaulx: Treatises & Pastoral Prayer*, ed. David Knowles (Spencer MA, 1971), p. 43.

Even when, a little later, he does use the word 'rule' (*regula*), it is in a context dense with references to the personal, the occasional and the provisional:

> faciam quod hortaris, et ex diuersis patrum institutis, aliqua quae tibi necessaria uidentur excerpens, ad componendum exterioris hominis statum, certam tibi regulam tradere curabo, pro loco et tempore quaedam adiciens, et spiritualia corporalibus, ubi utile uisum fuerit, interserens.

> [I shall do as you ask then, and endeavour to draw up a definite rule for you, selecting from among the various regulations of the Fathers those that appear most useful in forming the exterior man. I shall add some details suited to your particular circumstances of time and place, and, wherever it seems helpful, blend the spiritual with the corporal.]⁶

Ailred thus exemplifies Rotha Mary Clay's observation that 'The recluse's Rule of Life consisted of friendly counsel rather than rigid regulations.'⁷ His words of guidance fall into three sections. He deals with the 'exterior' or 'outer man' first, offering advice on solitude, silence and poverty; the choice of servants and a confessor; visitors and other worldly engagements; routines for ordering the day, setting times for reading, meditation and prayer (though, he insists, the precise details 'should not be determined by vow or obligation but inspired by devotion'⁸), and appropriate food, drink and clothing. He then moves to an encomium of inner virtues (virginity and chastity, humility, and charity), before concluding with a model meditation that focuses in turn on the past (a series of powerfully affective meditations on vignettes from Christ's life), the present (the gifts received by himself and his sister, with her persistent virtue contrasted with his unworthiness), and the future (the prospect of the Judgement and heavenly bliss).

Ailred's distinction between the outer and inner man is taken up and becomes crucial for the best-known of medieval English guides to anchoritic living, *Ancrene Wisse*, written in the vernacular for three newly-enclosed sisters in the West Midlands in the 1220s.⁹ Its author opens, as Ailred had (and, as we will see, the author of the *Speculum Inclusorum* does too), with a petition: 'you,

---

⁶ Talbot, p. 637; Macpherson, pp. 43–4. Likewise, at the end of the text, Ailred describes its three parts as 'corporales institutiones', a 'formam praescriptam' and a threefold meditation (pp. 681–2): the word 'rule' is not used.
⁷ Clay, *The Hermits and Anchorites of England* (London, 1914), p. 96.
⁸ Macpherson, p. 56.
⁹ Ed. Bella Millett, *Ancrene Wisse: A Corrected Edition of the Text in Cambridge, Corpus Christi College, 402, with Variants from Other Manuscripts*, 2 vols, EETS, orig. ser. 325–6 (Oxford, 2005–6). Millett has also done a translation, *Ancrene Wisse: Guide for Anchoresses* (Exeter, 2009), and it is this that I quote.

my dear sisters, have been asking me for a long time for a rule.'[10] The whole of the 'Preface' then plays on this notion of *riwle*. The author distinguishes two kinds: the inner rule that 'rules the heart, and makes it even and smooth' and the outer, which 'is completely external and regulates the body and physical acts, giving directions on all outward behaviour, how you should eat, drink, dress, say your prayers, sleep, keep vigil' (§ 3–4). The outer rule is subservient to the inner, as a handmaid is to her lady. But the issue of 'rule', in the monastic sense that his petitioners seem to have wanted, is deftly sidestepped:

> Now you ask what rule you anchoresses should observe. You should in every way, with all your might, scrupulously observe the inner rule, and the outer for the sake of the inner. The inner rule is always the same, the outer varies; because everyone should observe the outer rule in the way that helps her best to follow the inner [...] This [inner] rule is not a product of human invention, but of divine precept; therefore it is always the same without any change, and everyone should always observe it in the same way.

The inner rule thus lies beyond the realm of competence of any human legislator. But, on the other hand, the outer rule is so specific as to be beneath the notice of centralising lawmakers:

> But not everyone can observe a single rule, and they need not and should not observe the outer rule in the same way [...] Therefore, the outer rule must be modified in various ways according to each individual's nature and her capacity [...] For this reason every anchoress should observe the outer rule according to her confessor's advice, and do whatever he asks and orders her to do in obedience, being familiar with her nature and knowing her strength. He can modify the outer rule at his discretion, as he considers that the inner rule can best be observed. (§ 5)

In other words, there are potentially as many outer rules as there are anchorites. As the author reiterates towards the end of his treatise, expressly dissociating himself from the role of monastic lawgiver, 'I am not writing [...] for anyone apart from you' (Part 8, § 1).

The rest of *Ancrene Wisse* is structured according to this opening distinction between inner and outer rules. It is framed by discussions of the outer rule, Part One dealing with liturgical and paraliturgical observances, and Part Eight concerning itself with practical arrangements for the cell, servants, and daily regimen, along the lines of the first part of Ailred's *De Institutione*, from which it borrows a number of suggestions. These material considerations enclose the

---

[10] Preface, § 2.

work's spiritual core, just as (in an analogy critics have been quick to notice) the anchorite's body is enclosed within the walls of her cell. This central part of the text begins by exploring how the anchorite should govern her relationship with the external world (through control of her five senses) and her own inward disposition; it then moves on to consider sin, confession and penance, before progressing to the love of God.

Later medieval works of guidance and instruction for anchorites have less to say about the 'outer rule', perhaps because of the continuing availability and relevance of texts like Ailred's, but perhaps also because, apparently over the course of the thirteenth century, many of the external aspects of the vocation became the subject, if not of universal legislation, then at least of established and recognised practice.[11] Anchoritic texts of this later period include some of the best-known and most celebrated works of fourteenth-century English religious literature. It is easy to forget that Richard Rolle's *Form of Living* and Walter Hilton's *Scale of Perfection* (its first book, at least) were originally addressed to female anchorites. In part this is because the texts themselves seem to have in mind a broader audience that may be looking over the shoulders of their anchoritic addressees. Rolle wrote the *Form* for Margaret Kirkby, a nun of Hampole with whom he appears to have had a long association, probably on the occasion of her enclosure as an anchorite at East Layton (North Yorkshire). Its first half examines 'how þou may dispose þi lyfe, and rewle it to Goddes will' (including material on fasting, temptations, and the avoidance of sins), before the treatise moves on to 'some special poynt of þe luf of Jhesu Criste, and of contemplatyf lyfe, þe whilk þou hase taken þe till at mens syght'.[12] This second part of the treatise comprises a mature statement of most of Rolle's characteristic mystical themes, including the 'three degrees of love' – heat, sweetness and song – and devotion to the Holy Name. Much of the general instruction on living well that is included in the first half of the *Form* would be equally applicable to a reader in the active life, whilst the more specialised material in the second half reached a wider lay and semi-religious audience through being quarried for fifteenth-century compilations and miscellanies.

Like Rolle in the *Form*, Hilton addresses Book I of the *Scale* to a female anchorite, though her identity is not known. She has 'forsaken the world like a dead man' and her body is 'shut up [...] in a house'. But, he argues, becoming

---

[11] For the beginnings of this process, see Tom Licence, *Hermits & Recluses in English Society, 950–1200* (Oxford, 2011), and, for its full late-medieval development, Warren, *Anchorites and their Patrons*, pp. 53–91.
[12] Part VI, lines 213–7, in *English Writings of Richard Rolle*, ed. Hope Emily Allen (Oxford, 1931), pp. 102–3.

an anchorite is only the start: 'the cause of your bodily enclosure is that you may the better come to spiritual enclosure; and as your body is enclosed from bodily association with men, just so should your heart be enclosed from the fleshly loves and fears of all earthly things.'[13] The disconnect that Hilton establishes between anchoritic spirituality and anchoritic practice clearly guards against complacency in his anchoritic reader. But it also opens the *Scale* up to a much wider audience. The heart of the treatise concerns itself with the image of God in man, lost through sin, but possible to recover through spiritual practices including contemplation. Much of this material could be applicable to a broader readership. Indeed, there is some overlap with another work that Hilton seems to have been working on simultaneously: his *Epistle on the Mixed Life*, designed to help a layman realise his spiritual ambitions, worldly commitments notwithstanding. But whereas that text allows its reader access only to an attenuated version of contemplative practice, the *Scale* hints at something more startling. As an anchorite, his initial reader can access the third and highest part of contemplation; but, Hilton argues, others can too:

> This part of contemplation God gives wherever he wills, to clergy or laity, to men and women occupied in prelacy and to the solitary as well; but it is a special gift and not a common one. Moreover, though a person in active life may have it by a special grace, I consider that no one can have the full use of it unless he is solitary and contemplative in life.[14]

Contemplation is particularly associated with the solitary life, but it is not restricted to it. Whereas the earlier texts worry that the world may be able to penetrate the reclusory walls and harm the anchorite inside, in the *Scale* anchoritic spirituality can leak out into the world and spread to a potential audience limited only by the operation of God's grace.

The *Speculum Inclusorum* shares with the *Form of Living* and the *Scale of Perfection* a general disregard for the 'outer rule' that had been a significant concern for Ailred and the author of *Ancrene Wisse*. The author can assume that his readers will be able to find such advice elsewhere. In fact, he is quite specific. At the end of the text, he exhorts recluses to persevere in their vocation and bring it to perfection, by continuing to live 'iuxta vestre professionis sacras obseruancias, & beati Alredi doctrina (*De Institucione reclusi*), atque aliorum deuotorum egregia documenta' (IV.iii.94–6) [according to the sacred observances of your profession, and the teaching of Saint Ailred ('The Rule of Life for a Recluse'), and the excellent teachings of other devout

---

[13] *Scale* I.1, in *The Scale of Perfection*, trans. J. P. H. Clark and R. Dorward (New York, 1991), pp. 77–8.
[14] *Scale* I.10, p. 83.

people].¹⁵ (Note that Ailred continues to be available, and to be considered relevant.) On the other hand, there is more in the *Speculum* than in Rolle or Hilton that is exclusively anchoritic, and the content as well as the language of the rest of the treatise hold it back from the kind of cross-over appeal that those writers enjoyed.

After a brief Prologue, in which the author (like Ailred and the *Ancrene Wisse* author before him) recalls the requests which explain and justify the treatise's existence, and his hesitation and scruples in fulfilling them, the work is divided into four parts. The first is the most unremittingly anchoritic in character, examining the various motivations that can lead an individual to seek enclosure. Modern readers will be surprised to learn that some recluses apparently chose the life because it was easy, offering more freedom and less hard work than ordinary life in the world. There are details here of the testing of an anchoritic vocation, and also of formal arrangements for a period of probation. Parts Two and Three follow a parallel structure. Part Two encourages recluses to spend time in prayer, meditation and reading, whilst Part Three shows them how to analyse their performance in each activity. Although they describe their subject as 'exercicium uite contemplatiue' [þe exercise or vsage of contemplatyf lyf] (II.i.2), there is less in these chapters that is specifically anchoritic. The triad of reading, meditation and prayer was monastic in origin, but by the late Middle Ages it had become part of the vocabulary of lay devotion too, frequently in such cases, as here, in a modified order that denied primacy to reading.¹⁶ As often, the meditative focus is on the body of the crucified Christ. The final part of the treatise is again more specialised in its address, looking forward to the rewards that can be expected by 'relinquentibus temporalia propter Deum' [those who renounce the things of this world for the sake of God] (IV.i.4): union with the divine in heavenly bliss after death, and those fleeting, mystical foretastes of such union sometimes vouchsafed to contemplatives in this life.

In common with the other works briefly examined in this Introduction, the *Speculum* does not describe itself as a rule.¹⁷ The author starts by registering

---

[15] References to the *Speculum* are to the edition below, by Part, chapter, and line number in the Latin. I follow medieval usage by translating *Beatus* as 'Saint', though in fact Ailred has never been formally canonised.

[16] Vincent Gillespie, '*Lukynge in haly bukes: Lectio* in some Late Medieval Spiritual Miscellanies', *Spätmittelalterliche geistliche Literatur in der Nationalsprache* 2, ed. James Hogg, Analecta Cartusiana 106 (1984), pp. 1–27, at pp. 3–6. Gillespie considers the *Speculum* and *Mirror* alongside texts of Rolle and Hilton and the compilation *Gracia Dei*.

[17] It is partly for this reason that I have chosen to translate the work's title with the non-definitive *A Mirror for Recluses*.

his reluctance to take on the role of legislator: he did not wish to lay down the law ('legem statuere') for a life that he has not himself experienced (Prol. 5–6). Instead, he describes his composition as a 'work of exhortation' [opus [...] exhortatorium] (Prol. 11–12), or a mirror (*speculum*) in which recluses might examine how well they have lived up to their vocation (IV.iii.99–100). The author thus re-activates the old metaphor by which the Latin *speculum* had come to mean 'survey, compendium' and as such features in the title of no end of medieval works.[18] That visual metaphor runs through the text in the form of the biblical *thema* upon which the whole is ostensibly a commentary: 'Videte vocationem vestram' – 'See', or perhaps 'Look to your vocation' (1 Corinthians 1:26).

Unlike the other texts discussed above, which all address a particular individual or (in the case of *Ancrene Wisse*, at least in its original form) a narrowly defined group of individuals, personally known to the author, the *Speculum* is directed to recluses in general, making consistent use of the second-person plural ('o dilectissimi vos inclusi', I.i.2 and passim). More often, however, the *Speculum* steps back from the kind of direct personal address that gives works such as *Ancrene Wisse* or the *Form of Living* much of their warmth and immediacy. He prefers indirect modes of address: impersonal constructions ('Contra tales mentis multiplices euagaciones in orando remedium poterit esse aliquando' [Against these various wanderings of the mind during prayer, this can sometimes be a remedy], III.i.29–30) or rhetorical questions (I.ii.18–20). When certain anchoritic behaviours are to be praised or blamed, he projects them onto hypothetical recluses who need to change their ways (I.ii.24–9) or whose example is (by implication) worth emulating. Most strikingly, he warns his readers against the dangers of masturbation by recounting an *exemplum* of a hermit who indulged the vice, thus displacing his admonitions not only into the third-person but onto a specific individual pursuing a different (even if closely related) vocation.

Direct imperatives are few, and these tend to be exhortations to moral good conduct rather than specifically anchoritic practices or, when they do touch on matters that are part of the 'outer rule', to do so only in the negative (cf. I.ii.62–6, a list of things that do *not* pertain to the anchoritic state). Although he recommends spending time in reading, meditation and prayer, the *Speculum*-author does not provide a schedule for the recluses' daily devotions. He ostentatiously invokes the language of the lawgiver ('hec lex [...] statuatur', II.iii.6), but this 'lex' turns out to be nothing of the sort: it is entirely up to the readers themselves to decide when to leave off

---

[18] *DMLBS* SPECULUM 4b.

Introduction xxi

one activity and turn to another. In similar vein, the author counsels 'iuxta discrecionis arbitrium sic corpus castigetur alterius uicibus & alatur' [aftir þe doom & arbitrement of discrecion, chastise & nursche ȝoure body in diuerse tymes] (I.iii.102–3). It may have been this reluctance to 'lay down the law' that Charlotte D'Evelyn had in mind when she wrote appreciatively of the *Speculum*'s 'humane qualities'.[19]

Men, masculinity and the anchoritic vocation

All the other anchoritic texts introduced so far were written for female anchorites. So to what extent should we regard the *Speculum Inclusorum* as an anomaly?

The first point to make is that, in addressing itself to male anchorites, the *Speculum* is not unique. Alongside the well-known works for women mentioned in the preceding section, there are two or three substantial 'rules' for men from the thirteenth century, and two more from the fourteenth. Probably the earliest of them is the so-called *Dublin Rule* (named for the location of its principal manuscript, rather than any evidence of medieval provenance), which includes Ailred and *Ancrene Wisse* among its sources, alongside the *Rule of St Benedict* and the ninth-century continental rule for monastic recluses by Grimlaic of Metz. Its priority is the 'outer rule', incorporating material on the cell and silence, fasting and clothing, and liturgical observances (including, for the literate anchorite, recitation of the Divine Office); the author is also particularly concerned to warn against the dangers of an excess of alcohol. It seems to be closely related to the *Rule of Godwin of Salisbury*, recently identified by Colman O Clabaigh and still awaiting full analysis.[20] From later in the thirteenth century, apparently, we have the intriguing text known as *Walter's Rule*. Uniquely among our extant anchoritic rules, it was composed by an author who was himself a recluse. Now in his sixties (he tells us), he has been a solitary for almost ten years, having spent the previous thirty living in a regular community. (He was probably an Augustinian canon.) His sources include the monastic *Rule of St Augustine* and Ailred. The *Rule* begins with the 'inner man', a discussion built around an allegorical reading of the anchorite's cell – its walls, windows and enclosure – as the virtues and vices of the true and false anchorite. It

---

[19] D'Evelyn, 'Instructions for Religious', in *A Manual of the Writings in Middle English*, vol. 2, ed. J. Burke Severs (New Haven, 1970), pp. 458–81, at p. 480.
[20] The Dublin Rule was edited by Livarius Oliger, 'Regulae tres reclusorum et eremitarum angliae saec. xiii–xiv', *Antonianum* 3 (1928), pp. 151–90 and 299–320, at pp. 170–83. Colman O Clabaigh, 'Anchorites in Late Medieval Ireland', in McAvoy, *Anchoritic Traditions*, pp. 153–77, at pp. 169–71.

continues to concentrate on the 'inner rule', showing a particular interest in temptations and other diabolical attempts to deflect the solitary from his chosen course, before concluding with a long and impressive model meditation to be used at the side of the recluse's open grave.[21]

The fourteenth-century examples address themselves more directly to the needs and circumstances of particular individuals. The earlier, dating from the first part of the century, is the less ambitious. It goes by the somewhat unwieldy, though helpfully transparent, title of 'The Reply of a Fourteenth-Century Abbot of Bury St. Edmunds to a Man's Petition to be a Recluse'.[22] The identities of both the abbot and the recluse remain unknown, though it is clear that the petitioner was one of the monks of the abbey, and that his cell was apparently in or near its precincts. The abbot's 'Reply' is in fact a series of instructions designed expressly to supplement the *Rule of St Benedict*, from whose requirements the recluse's new vocation does not exempt him. Apart from a brief exhortation to 'reading, meditation, and fervent prayer', it is concerned entirely with the 'outer rule' and draws a number of its details from Ailred's treatment of the subject. Finally, there is Walter Hilton's short epistle *Ad quemdam solitarium de leccione, intencione, oracione, meditacione et aliis*.[23] Like the *Speculum*, it opens with an apostolic call to heed one's vocation, in this case Ephesians 4:1, 'ambules Deo vocacione qua vocatus es' [that you walk worthy of the vocation in which you are called by God].[24] But, Hilton says, it is not a rule: 'I tell you how this seems to me by way of example, and not so that you should keep to this particular method.'[25] Its editors have questioned whether the epistle was really intended for an anchorite, but (although the text is not

---

[21] Also ed. Oliger, 'Regula reclusorum angliae et quaestiones tres de vita solitaria', *Antonianum* 9 (1934), pp. 37–84 and 243–68, at pp. 53–84. The dating and ascription of the work to 'Walter' are open to question. See Richard Sharpe, *A Handlist of the Latin Writers of Great Britain and Ireland before 1540* (Turnhout, 1997), p. 740. There is a brief discussion of the closing 'Memoriale ante sepulcrum' in my 'Ceremonies of Enclosure: Rite, Rhetoric and Reality', in *Rhetoric of the Anchorhold*, ed. Liz Herbert McAvoy (Cardiff, 2008), pp. 34–49.

[22] Antonia Gransden, 'The Reply of a Fourteenth-Century Abbot of Bury St. Edmunds to a Man's Petition to be a Recluse', *English Historical Review* 75 (1960), pp. 464–7. For a recent discussion see Liz Herbert McAvoy, *Medieval Anchoritisms: Gender, Space and the Solitary Life* (Woodbridge, 2011), pp. 45–56.

[23] Ed. John P. H. Clark and Cheryl Taylor, in *Walter Hilton's Latin Writings* (Salzburg, 1987), pp. 213–43. Joy Russell-Smith printed a translation under the title 'A Letter to a Hermit', *The Way* 6 (1966), pp. 230–41.

[24] The verse is also used in the *Speculum*, at I.iii.49.

[25] 'Istud dico tibi ut uidetur michi exempli gracia, non ut hunc modum semper teneas'. Ed. Clark and Taylor, lines 422–3 (pp. 240–1); trans. Russell-Smith, p. 240.

generally interested in the 'outer rule' at all) there seems no compelling reason to take references to the addressee's bodily enclosure ('inclusionem corporis') in a cell ('habitaculum') as anything other than literal.[26] He was a priest who had fallen into some sort of error, and seems to have had himself enclosed as a response. Hilton writes as a friend and a straight-talking spiritual advisor, reminding him of the faults in his character and pointing out that anchoritic withdrawal is not in itself going to cure those faults, and indeed may provide new opportunities for them to manifest themselves unchecked. He writes on the image of sin and its reformation, with clear links to *Scale* I, and on the practice of prayer and meditation. On the former, he stresses the importance of the divine office and the prayers of the church, which must continue to take precedence over any personal prayers and devotions. In this, and in Hilton's concern over his addressee's 'causa […] inclusionis' (line 67), and the substantial treatment of discernment, the epistle has a number of features in common with the *Speculum*.

Although each of these texts (with the exception of the newly-identified *Rule of Godwin of Salisbury*) has been available in a modern edition or translation for upwards of forty years, they have attracted little or no significant discussion.[27] It is true that the evidence of manuscript survival and circulation suggests that none of these works could rival *Ancrene Wisse*, Rolle or the *Scale* for medieval popularity or relevance, but the thirteenth-century examples in particular do not lack literary interest, and in each case there is work to be done to identify their authors, intended recipients, and the networks of relationships that produced them.[28] One suspects that their almost total neglect in modern scholarship is chiefly down to their composition in Latin, and the fact (related, of course) that they were designed for readers who were men.

---

[26] Lines 60–1 and cf. 67 in Clark and Taylor's edition. For their reluctance to take such phrases at face value, see p. 215 and notes on pp. 392 and 396. Clark and Taylor's short title for the work is the *Epistola de leccione* (though it has precious little to say about reading), which renders invisible the 'solitarius' to whom it is addressed. But as it is the standard title, I have retained it in this discussion.

[27] They are absent, for example, from Mari Hughes-Edwards's recent study of works of guidance for English medieval anchorites, *Reading Medieval Anchoritism* (Cardiff, 2012), though she does include the *Speculum* and *Mirror*. See p. 9 and n. 66 on p. 115 for a discussion of the scope of her book.

[28] Although there are numerous copies of the other works of anchoritic guidance, in most cases where we can identify their owners and readers, they were not in fact solitaries, but the kind of spiritually-aspirant laypeople (especially laywomen) who come to especial prominence in the fifteenth and sixteenth centuries.

Much of the recent upsurge of work on the vocation has homed in on anchoritism as a 'specifically feminine' phenomenon.[29] Many aspects of the anchoritic life do indeed come from the repertoire of tropes that western culture habitually genders as feminine. We might think of the enclosure of the body, renunciation of an active sexuality, or exclusion from the Symbolic Order of language and power in a kind of ritual death. But it is sometimes rather carelessly assumed that the corollary of recognising the vocation as culturally feminine must be that it was always, or usually, or normatively, pursued by women. This is not self-evidently the case, at least in England, where significant numbers of male anchorites are recorded.[30]

The most recent review of the documentary evidence remains Ann Warren's study of 1985, in turn based largely on the researches of Rotha Mary Clay in the early years of the twentieth century.[31] Warren examined the records of 780 anchorites between the twelfth and sixteenth centuries. Four hundred and fourteen were women and 201 were men, leaving 165 individuals whose gender could not be determined (typically because they were referred to only by the Latin *anachorita*, which does not distinguish gender). The 'gender gap' was wider in some centuries than others. Thirteenth-century females outnumbered males by more than three to one (123 against thirty-seven, of those whose gender is indicated), whereas in the sixteenth century the thirty-seven women were run close by twenty-seven men. For the fifteenth century (to which the *Speculum Inclusorum* and *Mirror for Recluses* belong), Warren counted 110 women against sixty-six men (a ratio of 5:3), and there were twenty-eight further individuals whose gender was not recorded. So, throughout the period, whilst anchoritic men were always in the minority, they were never less than a substantial minority, and they demand somewhat more attention than they have hitherto received.

---

[29] Paulette L'Hermite-Leclercq, 'La réclusion volontaire au moyen âge: une institution religieuse spécialement féminine', in *La condición de la mujer en la edad media* (Madrid, 1986), pp. 135–54. See further Liz Herbert McAvoy and Mari Hughes-Edwards, eds, *Anchorites Wombs and Tombs: Intersections of Gender and Enclosure in the Middle Ages* (Cardiff, 2005), and McAvoy *Medieval Anchoritisms*. This section draws on a paper I wrote in 2002 for the conference that yielded the volume *Anchorites, Wombs and Tombs*. I was not able at the time to develop it for inclusion in the proceedings, though some of my arguments are alluded to in the introduction to that volume by McAvoy and Hughes-Edwards.

[30] See McAvoy, *Anchoritic Traditions*, for surveys of practice in a number of European countries.

[31] *Anchorites and their Patrons*, pp. 18–29, especially Table 1 on p. 20. Warren's figures are frequently cited: see most recently, Mari Hughes-Edwards, 'Anchoritism: The English Tradition', in McAvoy, *Anchoritic Traditions*, pp. 131–52, at p. 140.

Introduction xxv

To put some flesh on the figures, and to get a sense of the range of male anchoritic experiences, we may look in more detail at some of the men who were enclosed during the period in which the *Speculum* was written. I will suggest below that the text's composition should be dated to the first quarter of the fifteenth century, so these individuals will generally be younger contemporaries of Julian of Norwich, who was (so the manuscript of her Short Text tells us) 'ȝitt [...] on lyfe' in 1413, though probably nearing the end of her life.

The first and most obvious difference between male and female anchorites is that most of the men were priests. This would have implications for their sense of identity and their daily routine, the design of their cells and the spiritual support they required (they would have their own oratory and altar, for example), and the range of functions they could assume.

It also seems (though the sample is small) that more men than women moved on to the anchoritic life having previously spent some time living in community. A number of regulars were enclosed (like the Bury St Edmunds recluse who received his abbot's 'Reply') in a cell attached to their monastery. Most celebrated of these was John London, a Benedictine monk of Westminster Abbey who inhabited the reclusory there from around 1393 until his death in 1428. Henry V made his confession to him on the night his father died, prior to assuming the throne the next morning, and the new king seems to have kept in contact with him throughout his life.[32] There was also a cell attached to the Benedictine abbey of Sherborne (Dorset). William Whiting, monk of Sherborne, occurs as the recluse there in bequests made in 1405 and 1413.[33] Such a progression from the *coenobium* to the solitary life of the anchorite was envisaged, at least for some monks, by the *Rule of St Benedict*. But examples are not confined to the Benedictines. In 1402 the Dominican friar John Bourne, who 'after long remaining in his order' had been enclosed in a *reclusorium* or cell within his convent at Arundel, was allowed to transfer to another cell, 'on account of the inconvenience of the place where the said cell is situate, as also of the penury under which the brethren of the said house labour'.[34] In 1420 the Franciscan John Toker, 'having completed his fiftieth year, and having been a Friar Minor since he completed his thirtieth year', received a papal licence to be

---

[32] See the entry by Barbara F. Harvey in *ODNB*.
[33] *Somerset Medieval Wills. Second Series: 1501–1530*, ed. F. W. Weaver, Somerset Record Society 19 (1903), p. 304; *The Register of Bishop Stafford*, ed. F. C. Hingeston-Randolph (London, 1886), p. 402.
[34] *Calendar of Entries in the Papal Registers Relating to Great Britain and Ireland, Papal Letters, Volume 5: A.D. 1398–1404*, ed. W. H. Bliss and J. A. Twemlow (London, 1904), p. 470.

enclosed in a house near the church of the Knights Hospitaller at Minchin Buckland (Somerset).[35]

Other members of the religious orders were enclosed at parish churches. In 1402 Robert Cherde, a Cistercian from Forde Abbey in Somerset, was enclosed, with his abbot's leave, 'in a certain house near the parish church of Crewkerne [...] within the churchyard on the west side of the same church, constructed for such a person to dwell in for ever'.[36] (Crewkerne lies just to the south-west of Forde.) And in Shropshire Richard Goldeston, recluse at Priorslee in 1409, had previously been an Austin canon of Wombridge, a few miles to the west.[37] Both these men were enclosed at their nearest parish church, but monastic recluses could also be found a considerable distance from their monastery. In 1409 the Benedictine John Kyngston of Chertsey Abbey (Surrey) – probably, given his name, a local man – was enclosed at Broughton near Brigg, far away in Lincolnshire.[38] And Margery Kempe, we recall, has dealings with a 'monk of a fer cuntre', now living as an anchorite at the College of St Mary in the Fields, Norwich. He had once thought highly of her (she reports), but subsequently 'thorw evyl language that he herd of hir, he turnyd al ayens hir'. He may have been Thomas Brakleye, who died in 1417.[39] It is interesting to note that all these churches are situated in relatively small, rural communities: these are not the urban recluses of whom the *Speculum*-author is so suspicious, and who seem more often to have been women.[40]

Although Margery Kempe is forever seeking out recluses whom she can consult regarding her life and revelations, her 'principal gostly fader' was the anchorite at the Dominicans in Lynn. He was academically and spiritually accomplished: a doctor of divinity, known for a prophet, and Kempe showed her revelations to him and no-one else 'for he cowde most skyl in swech

---

[35] *Calendar of Entries in the Papal Registers Relating to Great Britain and Ireland, Papal Letters, Volume 6: A.D. 1417–1431*, ed. W. H. Bliss and J. A. Twemlow (London, 1906), p. 180.

[36] *The Registers of Walter Giffard, Bishop of Bath and Wells, 1265–6, and of Henry Bowett, Bishop of Bath and Wells, 1401–7*, ed. T. S. Holmes, Somerset Record Society 13 (1899), pp. 36–7.

[37] H. Owen and J. B. Blakeway, *A History of Shrewsbury*, 2 vols (London, 1825), i.315.

[38] Anon., 'Anchorites in Faversham Churchyard', *Archaeologia Cantiana* 11 (1877), pp. 24–39, at pp. 36–7.

[39] *The Book of Margery Kempe*, ed. Barry Windeatt (London, 2000), lines 3388–93 and notes.

[40] Even the Norwich example was, as the name suggests, outside the city. See I.ii.47–59 for the comment about urban anchorites. The implicit gendering of the *Speculum*'s attitude is noted by McAvoy, *Medieval Anchoritisms*, pp. 64–5.

thyngys'.⁴¹ He was not the only anchorite to take on pastoral responsibility. William Tredewy, anchorite at Great Torrington (Devon), held the position of penitentiary in the deanery of Torrington for over thirty years, from 1395 to at least 1429.⁴² This was a role requiring significant public engagement: penitentiaries were 'clerics of usually high reputation who were granted special faculties by the bishop to hear confessions and absolve even in cases of reserved sins'.⁴³ Two more anchorites fulfilled prominent outward-facing roles in the same period. Henry V, whose connection with the anchorite of Westminster Abbey has already been noted, chose recluses to play key parts in his new foundation of Syon Abbey. William Alnwick oversaw spiritual matters during the process leading up to the first formal professions at the house, when he was succeeded by another former solitary, Thomas Fishbourne, who became Syon's first Confessor General in 1420.⁴⁴

Even if it was a minority of priest anchorites who held a pastoral role, their status permitted them a form of continued engagement with the world that was denied female recluses. William de Salle, anchorite at Wendling (Norfolk), received bequests to say masses and to pray for testators' souls in 1418 and 1424.⁴⁵ In 1428 William Bowdler of Chirbury (Shropshire) left 10s to the unnamed anchorite of Maelienydd (just over the border in Wales) to say mass for his soul.⁴⁶ The recluse at Kexby (near York) who was left 13s 4d in the will of Henry Lord Scrope, executed for treason in 1415, may have been the priest Thomas Coke who occurs there in 1398.⁴⁷ John, recluse of Welbeck (Notts.),

---

⁴¹ Ed. Windeatt, lines 1396, 528, 1612. On this anchorite, see further Windeatt's note to lines 528–30 on pp. 73–4.
⁴² *Register of Bishop Stafford*, p. 352; *The Register of Edmund Lacy: Bishop of Exeter, 1420–1455. Registrum commune, Vol. I*, ed. G. R. Dunstan, Canterbury & York Society 60 (1963), p. 217.
⁴³ William J. Dohar, '"Since the Pestilence Time": Pastoral Care in the Later Middle Ages', in *A History of Pastoral Care*, ed. G. R. Evans (London, 2000), pp. 169–200, at p. 181. For some further examples of anchorite-confessors and penitentiaries, see my 'Vae Soli! Solitaries and Pastoral Care', in *Texts and Traditions of Medieval Pastoral Care*, ed. C. Gunn and C. Innes-Parker (Woodbridge, 2009), pp. 11–28, at pp. 22–3.
⁴⁴ The best single account of the foundation of Syon remains F. R. Johnston, 'Syon Abbey', in *The Victoria History of the County of Middlesex*, vol. 1 (Oxford, 1969), pp. 182–91.
⁴⁵ Wills registered in Norwich Consistory Court: Norfolk Record Office, NCC Hyrning, fols 32r and 148v.
⁴⁶ *The Register of Thomas Spofford, Bishop of Hereford (1422–1448)*, ed. A. T. Bannister, Canterbury & York Society 23 (1917), p. 107.
⁴⁷ Thomas Rymer, 'Rymer's Foedera with Syllabus: June 1415', *Rymer's Foedera Volume 9*, pp. 258–83 (at p. 275), online at http://www.british-history.ac.uk/, and *Testamenta Eboracensia*, vol. 1, ed. James Raine, Surtees Society 4 (1836), p. 244.

was left 20s by Elizabeth, widow of Philip Lord Darcy, in 1412. He is identified as a priest only by the honorific *Dominus*.[48] So too Roger, anchorite attached to the Benedictine nunnery of Carrow (in Norwich), who appears alongside Julian of Norwich in the will of the chantry priest Thomas Emund (Roger got 20 pence to Julian's 12).[49]

We have a little more information about William Bolle, rector of the parish church of Aldrington in Sussex, who in 1402 resigned his church in order to live as an anchorite attached to Chichester Cathedral. He was granted a plot adjoining the north side of the cathedral that measured 24 x 29 feet, upon which he might build, at his own expense, a dwelling where he would pursue the life of an anchorite or recluse until the end of his life.[50] The measurements sound generous compared to other examples that we know about, though the implication may be that the cell would occupy only a part of the site, the rest providing a small garden. The administrative process around these arrangements seems to have been somewhat complicated. The bishop's licence to erect the reclusory replaced a previous licence from the Dean and Chapter, which Bolle was required to surrender. It was similar in most particulars, but included an additional clause permitting Bolle to leave his cell in order to celebrate mass in the adjoining Lady chapel. This is interesting to read alongside a passage in the *Mirror for Recluses* (but not the *Speculum*) that may be interpreted to say that male anchorites were less strictly enclosed than their female counterparts.[51] It is not clear whether the clause's absence from the bishop's licence reflects a change of mind on this point, or simply a different set of priorities in drafting the document.[52] The bishop enclosed William Bolle in his cell on 20 December 1402. He remained there for at least another dozen years, being last recorded in 1414.[53]

---

[48] Alfred W. Gibbons, *Early Lincoln Wills*, Lincoln Record Series 1 (1888), p. 118.

[49] His will is printed in translation in Nicholas Watson and Jacqueline Jenkins, eds, *The Writings of Julian of Norwich: A Vision Showed to a Devout Woman and a Revelation of Love* (Pennsylvania, 2006), pp. 432–3.

[50] E. Turner, 'Domus Anchoritae, Aldrington', *Sussex Archaeological Collections* 12 (1860), pp. 117–39, at pp. 135–6. (Turner misread the document to make Bolle's place of enclosure Aldrington.)

[51] The syntax of the passage is, however, ambiguous, and I do not read it this way. See ME I.iv.48–51 and the discussion in the Notes to the Texts.

[52] The other differences are in the measurements of the plot, which are given more precisely in the bishop's licence, and (perhaps most importantly) a final clause in the latter which adds that the site and everything built upon it should revert to the bishop on Bolle's decease.

[53] 'Religious Houses: Introduction', in *A History of the County of Sussex: Volume 2*, ed. William Page, Victoria County History (London, 1973), pp. 45–7, at p. 47.

If priests, whether secular or regular, were the norm among fifteenth-century male anchorites, laymen were not unknown. Robert Riell or Ryhill, a recluse at Beverley (North Yorkshire), was another of the several anchoritic beneficiaries in the will of Henry Scrope in 1415. He must have been a layman because he had received a pension from the Duchy of Lancaster since 1397 to pay for a chaplain to celebrate divine service for him.[54]

Many of the functions of a fifteenth-century male recluse that have been explored above are exemplified in John Lacy.[55] He was a Dominican friar, initially at Newcastle under Lyme (Staffordshire), where he was ordained priest in 1397. By 1407, however, he had moved north and east to Newcastle upon Tyne, where he was enclosed in a cell at the convent of his order. He remained there until at least 1434. The *Speculum Inclusorum* suggests the copying of books as a suitable occupation for anchorites, and we know of several volumes connected with Lacy, who was an accomplished scribe and limner. He gave an English New Testament, now Bodleian Library, Oxford, MS Rawlinson C.258, to the church of St John in Newcastle upon Tyne, and made a copy of another work, probably Deguileville's *Pèlerinage de l'âme*. The third volume is more personal. St John's College, Oxford, MS 94 combines a Latin book of hours (an established staple of personal, para-liturgical devotion) with a number of English texts. These include summaries of catechetic material and several texts on the practice of confession, which perhaps indicate a role in the spiritual guidance of others. There is also a compilation formed from the Ps.-Jerome *Epistle to Demetrias* and some selections from Hilton's *Eight Chapters on Perfection*. Its focus is more on chastity and the love of God, and could perhaps be taken to reveal something of Lacy's spirituality. There are a few references to Lacy by name, chiefly requests for subsequent users of the book to pray for his soul. There is also a half-page self-portrait showing Lacy in his cell, looking out through his reclusory grille at an image of the rood (a crucifix flanked by Mary and John) and asking for mercy on his soul. It is all

---

[54] He acknowledged the pension for 'finding a chaplain to celebrate divine service before him the said Robert', British Library, Stowe Ch. 432: *Catalogue of Stowe Manuscripts*, 2 vols (London, 1895–6), i.775. For Scrope's will, see also the recluse at Kexby noted above.

[55] For Lacy, see Rotha Mary Clay, 'Further Studies on Medieval Recluses', *Journal of the British Archaeological Association*, 3rd ser. 16 (1953), pp. 74–86, at pp. 75–8; John B. Friedman, *Northern English Books, Owners, and Makers in the Late Middle Ages* (New York, 1995), p. 52; Ralph Hanna, *A Descriptive Catalogue of the Western Medieval Manuscripts of St John's College, Oxford* (Oxford, 2002), p. 129. The St John's manuscript is also listed as part of the 'Manuscripts of the West Midlands' project, http://www.hrionline.ac.uk/mwm/. I have discussed Lacy and his book in my 'Vae Soli'.

quite conventional: though the book may reflect what Lacy did as an anchorite, it rarely reveals what he thought or felt about it.

There is one possible exception. At the end of the book is a selection of quotations on a variety of devotional topics. They are headed by a pair of passages from Gregory on the active and contemplative lives, and I have suggested elsewhere that their inclusion might point to tensions in Lacy's conception of his vocation, and his embodiment of it.[56] Was he an active or a contemplative? Probably, as so often with the anchoritic vocation, he occupied a grey area between the two, whether or not he was comfortable with that position. But, this possibility aside, Lacy's is not an anxious book. In particular, there is no trace here of fraught masculinity, of an individual struggling to identify himself in a vocation that, though it was (as we have seen) pursued by a significant number of men, remained 'haunted by [...] femininity'.[57]

So how did anchoritic men conceive of themselves and their vocation? And did they suffer from 'gender trouble'? Gender studies over the past twenty years has turned its attention to the study of masculinity or masculinities, so that there is now a significant body of work on the range of gender identities within which medieval men could understand themselves, and be understood.[58] Medieval masculinities are complicated by the presence in the culture of a high-prestige group of men who had renounced most of their society's usual markers of masculine identity: active sexuality, the fathering of children, governing and providing for a family or household, and engaging in warfare and other kinds of violence. That group, of course, is clerics in general and, in the earlier period, particularly monks and anchorites.

The most long-standing model of monastic masculinity was the *miles Christi*, or warrior for Christ.[59] The Prologue to the *Rule of St Benedict* interpellates its reader in a number of masculine guises – as labourer, son, brother, a runner and a scholar – as well as a soldier 'armed with the strong and noble weapons of obedience to do battle for the true King, Christ the Lord'.[60] But this was

---

[56] 'Vae Soli', p. 27.
[57] McAvoy, *Medieval Anchoritisms*, p. 7.
[58] Key collections for orientation are *Medieval Masculinities: Regarding Men in the Middle Ages*, ed. Clare A. Lees et al. (Minneapolis, 1994); *Becoming Male in the Middle Ages*, ed. Jeffrey Jerome Cohen and Bonnie G. Wheeler (New York, 1997); *Masculinity in Medieval Europe*, ed. Dawn M. Hadley (London, 1999); *Holiness and Masculinity in the Middle Ages*, ed. P. H. Cullum and Katherine J. Lewis (Cardiff, 2005).
[59] For a good recent discussion, see Katherine Allen Smith, 'Saints in Shining Armor: Martial Asceticism and Masculine Models of Sanctity, ca. 1050–1250', *Speculum* 83 (2008), pp. 572–602.
[60] Prologue 3 and cf. 40. See also 2.14; 1.5–7; 21–2, 44, 48–9; 45. *RB 1980: The Rule of St. Benedict*, ed. and trans. Timothy Fry (Collegeville MN, 1980).

the identification that caught the imagination. Militaristic imagery dominates in the *Rule*'s well-known characterisation of solitaries in its first chapter, where Benedict speaks of

> the anchorites or hermits, who have come through the test of living in a monastery for a long time, and have passed beyond the first fervor of monastic life. Thanks to the help and guidance of many, they are now trained to fight against the devil. They have built up their strength and go from the battle line in the ranks of their brothers to the single combat of the desert. Self-reliant now, without the support of another, they are ready with God's help to grapple single-handed with the vices of body and mind. (1.3–5)

This individualistic and pugilistic version of masculinity finds its way into many of the later texts addressed to male anchorites. Grimlaic warns the anchorite that 'we come not to rest or security here, but to battle, we advance to the contest, we hasten to make war against the vices.'[61] In the English *Walter's Rule*, the ascesis of the spiritual athlete is likened in some detail to the military training undergone as part of the formation of secular manhood:

> Someone who is going to fight in a duel is first taught to protect himself with his shield, then all the different ways he may get at his enemy, thrusting his sword-arm at that enemy fiercely and violently, now from below, now from above, now from the side, as he was first taught by his teacher. Anyone who defies the orders of his teacher will find his life in danger when battle begins, and when he is vanquished he will say: 'I performed badly, because I defied the orders of my teacher.' And so the contestant (*athleta*) will be disgraced and ashamed, unless he has paid attention to the instructions he received before.[62]

Hilton, too, declares in the *Epistola de leccione* that 'One must fervently desire purity of heart, like the end and reward due to veteran soldiers. To obtain it one must exert oneself like a man, with humility and wisdom, in steadfast effort

---

[61] 'Non utique ad requiem nec ad securitatem, sed ad pugnam huc venimus, ad agonem processimus, ad exercenda cum vitiis bella properavimus' (cap. 23).
[62] 'Qui vero pugnaturus est in duelli certamine primo instruitur scuto se protegere, deinde quot modis possit hostem appetere, nunc ab ymmo, nunc ab alto, nunc a transverso armatum brachium in ipsum hostem fortiter et acriter vibrare sicut instructus fuerat primo a doctore. Qui si docentis contempnat imperia, in periculo sui capitis exorta est pugna, qui cum victus fuerit dicet: Male feci, quia doctoris mei imperium contempsi. Ita degener et confusus erit athleta, nisi premissa attenderit precepta.' Ed. Oliger, pp. 75–6, my translation.

of body and spirit.'[63] Later the reader is told to 'take up [the] shield of faith', which must be bound to one's breast by 'the baldric of fear and humility', so that it can 'not only catch the shafts blessedly kindled by the love of Christ, but also "extinguish all the fiery darts of the most wicked one"'.[64]

The *Speculum* participates solidly in this tradition. Its readers are addressed as 'pugiles Christi' (IV.ii.84) and 'generosi milites Iesu Christi [gentil kny3tes of Iesu Crist]' (I.ii.60), and are told 'forcius resumatis arma milicie spiritualis [my3tyly resumeþ and takeþ agayn þe armes of spiritual kny3thode]' (I.iii.106–7). More extensively, its author demands:

> 'Quis coronabitur nisi prius legittime certauerit?' Quis certabit nisi pugnam habuerit? Et quis pugnam habens vincet, nisi fortis perseuerauerit usque in finem? Presertim in pugna spirituali, vbi mors ipsa vincit aduersarium, & nichil militem captiuat nisi fuga, desidia uel consensus uoluntarius inimico. O spiritualiter pugnantis consolacio plenissima graciarum, vbi Deus continue, cum omnibus sanctis, angelis & animabus beatis, suos milites respicit contra temptaciones uarias dimicantes, vincentibus congratulans & eis coronam glorie preparans; fatigatis autem & eius auxilium corditer inuocantibus statim (supra quod credi potest) graciose succuret Omnipotens in uirtute. (III.iii.60–9)

> ['Who shall be crowned, except he first strive lawfully?' Who shall strive unless he joins battle? And which of those who join battle shall have the victory, unless he remains strong until the end? And especially in spiritual battles, where death itself overcomes the adversary, and nothing can take the soldier captive except for flight, idleness or his voluntary consent to his enemy. Oh it is a comfort full of grace for those engaged in spiritual battle to see that God, together with all the saints, angels and blessed souls, continuously watches over his soldiers as they struggle against various temptations, congratulating the victors and preparing for them a crown of glory; and when they get tired and make a heartfelt cry for his help, at once the Almighty in his strength comes graciously to their aid, beyond anything you would believe.]

---

[63] 'Cordis namque puritas, tanquam finis et remuneracio militibus emeritis debita, feruide desideranda est, pro qua optinenda laborandum est viriliter, humiliter et prudenter per exercicium continuum corporis et spiritus'. Ed. Clark and Taylor, lines 15–18 (pp. 221–2); trans. Russell-Smith, pp. 230–1.

[64] 'Arripe ergo in tuo certamine hoc scutum fidei in quo non solum iacula amoris Christi succensa fauorabiliter excipies, sed eciam omnia tela nequissimi ignea poteris extinguere, dum tamen hoc scutum cingulo timoris et humilitatis tuo fuerit pectori tenaciter alligatum'. Ed. Clark and Taylor, lines 239–42 (p. 232); trans. Russell-Smith, p. 236.

Nothing could be easier than to contrast the encounter with the enemy envisioned by these texts with that experienced by the female anchorite Julian of Norwich:

> Ande in my slepe, at the beginning, methought the fende set him in my throte, putting forth a visage fulle nere my face like a yonge man, and it was longe and wonder leen. I saw never none such. The coloure was red, like the tilestone whan it is new brent, with blacke spottes therein like freknes, fouler than the tilestone. His here was rede as rust, not scored afore, with side lockes hanging on the thonwonges. He grinned upon me with a shrewde loke; shewde me whit teth and so mekille, methought it the more ugly. Body ne handes had he none shaply, but with his pawes he helde me in the throte, and would have strangled me, but he might not.[65]

For virile male we substitute vulnerable female, for active engagement passive resistance, and for the battlefield or arena the bedroom. This is the devil's assault experienced as rape, to be resisted passively, or even endured patiently.

Such an opposition would, however, tell only a part of the story. In the later Middle Ages, and particularly in the wake of the Gregorian reforms that enjoined celibacy on all clerics in higher orders, the old militaristic model of monastic masculinity lost ground. As sexual abstinence came to be the defining feature of clerical identity, so sexuality and the performance of sex acts (whether voluntary or involuntary) came to be the central issue in questions of masculine identity. In an essay published in 1999, Robert Swanson proposed that clerical men constituted a third gender, biologically male but culturally (performatively) not-masculine, that he labelled 'emasculinity'.[66] The term has not caught on, but it points usefully to the key problematic for late-medieval clerics: how to '*be* masculine without having *to act* masculine'.[67] As Jo Ann McNamara puts the question, 'Can one be a man without deploying the most obvious biological attributes of manhood? If a person does not act like a man, is he a man?'[68]

This is the context for the *Speculum Inclusorum*'s discussion of nocturnal

---

[65] Ed. Watson and Jenkins, p. 333.
[66] Swanson, 'Angels Incarnate: Clergy and Masculinity from Gregorian Reform to Reformation', in Hadley, *Masculinity in Medieval Europe*, pp. 160–77.
[67] Jacqueline Murray, 'Masculinizing Religious Life: Sexual Prowess, the Battle for Chastity and Monastic Identity', in Cullum and Lewis, *Holiness and Masculinity*, pp. 24–42, at p. 27.
[68] In the introduction to Lees et al., *Medieval Masculinities*, p. 5.

emission and masturbation in I.iv. The former, as later medieval monastic writings agreed, was a weakness of man's sinful nature rather than a sin in itself.[69] It was only when arousal continued after waking, with 'consensus [...] ad sic delectandum' [a consent to delyte in þat same] (I.iv.47), that mortal sin ensued. But the original arousal said something not only about the nature of male flesh, but specifically about the flesh of the *Speculum*'s readers. The author apologises for raising the subject at all, but argues that 'ubi temptacionis est possibilitas ibi est necessaria prudens informacio resistendi' [where is possibilite of temptacion, þer ys a prudent enformynge of resistence or wiþstondynge ful necessarie & meedful] (I.iv.53–4). But the 'temptacionis [...] possibilitas' matters. It shows that the recluses' abstinence is grounded in force of will, not physiological necessity. They can, but choose not to, perform their biological maleness. Murray argues that the late Middle Ages saw the development of the 'myth of ungovernable male sexuality', in order to provide a new adversary for the *miles Christi*, to replace the demons of the desert tradition. The 'battle for chastity' was a discourse that 'reaffirmed to celibate men that they were not a third gender nor were they effeminate or emasculinized'.[70] In such terms, to succumb to an occasional defeat could provide some reassurance of biological maleness, as well as the opportunity to perform clerical masculinity in its traditional guise: 'si (quod absit) vnquam ceciderint, digne peniteant, sicque per grauissimi spiritualis belli uictoria coronabuntur' [ʒif þei falle at any tyme in suych caas (as God kepe hem þerfro) to be sory and repentaunt þerof, and so for þe victorie of a scharp & greuous spirituel bataylle þei may aftir þis lyf be coroned in ioye] (I.iv.60–1).

The *Speculum* will, then, have a contribution to make to ongoing discussions of anchoritism and gender, and in particular to the neglected question of anchoritic masculinity. But I conclude this section with a reminder that gender is only one of several intersecting variables that we need to take into account. In his *Provinciale* (completed by 1434), William Lyndwood, the leading canon lawyer of his day, noted the requirement for a bishop to consider carefully the status of any candidate for the anchoritic life. In his gloss, he expanded on the kinds of thing such consideration should cover: 'That is, whether [the candidate] is religious or secular, cleric or layperson, man or woman, someone who has prior experience of austerity of living or someone without

---

[69] See Dyan Elliott, *Fallen Bodies: Pollution, Sexuality, and Demonology in the Middle Ages* (University Park PA, 1998); Conrad Leyser, 'Masculinity in Flux: Nocturnal Emissions and the Limits of Celibacy in the Early Middle Ages', in Hadley, *Masculinity in Medieval Europe*, pp. 103–20.
[70] 'Masculinizing Religious Life', p. 37.

that experience, young or old, and so on.'[71] By this reckoning, our task of understanding anchoritic identities has only just begun.

Editorial and critical history

The earliest modern notice of the *Speculum Inclusorum* or *Mirror for Recluses* came in Rotha Mary Clay's monumental *Hermits and Anchorites of England*, published in 1914. Clay knew only the English text, which she calls the 'Book for Recluses'. She gives a single-paragraph summary of its contents, noting in particular the fourfold analysis of the would-be anchorite's motives in Part I, and commenting somewhat whimsically on the

> pathos in the suggestion made to one so straitly shut up that she might stir her heart to praise by thinking upon the merry noise of birds in their sweet song, the delight of flowers and fruits, the usefulness of beasts, which follow without fail the law of nature and are every year marvellously renewed to the behoof of man.[72] (For the passage to which she refers, see I.ii.71–8.)

The *Mirror* also found an editor before the *Speculum*. Lilian Rogers edited it under the title 'Advice to Recluses' for an Oxford B. Litt. in 1933. As well as a careful edition of the text from its unique manuscript, Rogers provided a substantial introduction that described the manuscript, identified the William Browne to whose hospital in Stamford it was given in the fifteenth century (discussed further below), and analysed its language. Not unlike the present edition, she also included a detailed consideration of English anchoritic rules, placing the *Mirror* in the context of Ailred, *Ancrene Wisse*, the *Form of Living* and the *Scale of Perfection*, as well as, less obviously perhaps, the *Cloud of Unknowing* and Marguerite Porete's *Mirror of Simple Souls*. A few years after completing her thesis, Rogers submitted the edition to the Early English Text Society. By then, however, the *Mirror*'s connection to the *Speculum Inclusorum* had become apparent; the Society would not consider the edition unless it was revised to take into account the text's relation to the Latin, and the project lapsed.[73]

The Latin *Speculum* received its first mention in Louis Gougaud's

---

[71] '*Personarum.* Utrum sc. sit Religiosus vel Saecularis, Clericus vel Laicus, Vir vel Mulier, austeritatem vitae prius expertus, vel non expertus, Juvenis vel Senex, vel alia hujusmodi.' William Lyndwood, *Provinciale (seu Constitutiones Angliae)* (Oxford, 1679), iii.20.2 at p. 214.
[72] *Hermits and Anchorites*, pp. 99–100.
[73] Letter to Rogers from Mabel Day, Secretary of the Society, 4 Jan. 1939. This letter, and Lilian Rogers's copy of her thesis, are now among the papers of Rotha Clay: University of Bristol, Special Collections, DM 1590/I–III.

wide-ranging study of hermits and anchorites in medieval Europe in 1928, with a reference to the Royal manuscript, though he was unaware of the *Mirror*.[74] The relationship between the two texts was established definitively ten years later, when the Latin *Speculum* was edited by Livarius Oliger, from photographs supplied by Hope Emily Allen.[75] Oliger is remembered chiefly as a historian of the Franciscan order to which he himself belonged, but he also produced editions of a number of English works for anchorites and hermits during this period.[76] He was alerted to the English *Mirror* by Lilian Rogers, and included a brief account of it and its relation to the Latin *Speculum* in the introduction to his edition (pp. 23–31).[77] He bases his text of the *Speculum* on the Royal manuscript, as I do, and supplements this with a commentary that is chiefly theological (and still very useful); and an introduction that incorporates fairly brief treatments of codicology, sources and style, preceded by a wide-ranging but rather general discussion of the anchoritic life in medieval Europe.

The works remained neglected, however, in studies both of the history of late-medieval religion and spirituality, and its literature.[78] In 1970, Charlotte D'Evelyn (as we have already seen) included the *Speculum* as the final entry in her bibliographic survey of 'Instructions for Religious' in the second volume of the *Manual of the Writings in Middle English*. Though strictly speaking it was beyond her remit, she provided a brief account of the *Speculum*, which she describes as 'a borderline rule more concerned with the inner than with the outer life', before moving on to the English *Mirror*. The latter is left nameless, though an edition is identified as a *desideratum*:

> A full appraisal of the translator's ability to match the literacy and humane qualities of his Latin original must await the publication of the English text, desirable in spite of its damaged state.[79]

The *Mirror* was also listed in another bibliographic aid from this period, P. S. Jolliffe's invaluable *Check-List*, where it is listed as item H.28, in the

---

[74] Louis Gougaud, *Ermites et recluses* (Vienne, 1928), p. 65.
[75] Allen and Oliger began a long and productive correspondence in the 1920s. See John C. Hirsh, *Hope Emily Allen: Medieval Scholarship and Feminism* (Norman OK, 1988), pp. 66–8.
[76] See the appreciation by Eustace J. Smith, 'In Memoriam: Livarius Oliger, O. F. M., 1875–1951', *The Americas* 7 (1951), pp. 475–480.
[77] Rogers and Oliger's correspondence, and the copy of his edition that Oliger presented to her on completion, are also among the Clay papers.
[78] The *Speculum* was not used, for example, in Francis D. S. Darwin's generally very useful *English Mediaeval Recluse* (London, n.d., c. 1944).
[79] Charlotte D'Evelyn, 'Instructions for Religious', p. 480.

section on 'Growth in the spiritual life', and O.40, among treatises 'For those living under rule'.[80]

In the early 1980s James Hogg projected editions of both the Latin *Speculum* and the Middle English *Mirror for Recluses*, but in the event he produced only a facsimile of the later and inferior of the *Speculum*'s two extant copies (the St John's manuscript, described below), with a very brief introduction. His facsimile would have been available to, but was not used by, Ann Warren in her study of *Anchorites and their Patrons*, still the most important book on late-medieval English anchorites. She includes the *Speculum* and *Mirror* (in Rogers's unpublished edition) in an appendix listing English anchoritic rules, but makes scant use of it in her text.[81]

The Middle English *Mirror* was finally published in 1995, in a new edition by Marta Powell Harley. With minimal discussion of the manuscripts, nothing on author, audience or date, and no sense of the anchoritic context which produced the *Mirror* and *Speculum*, and which they served, the edition has its shortcomings; but its more accessible text has been the catalyst for critical interest in both the English and Latin texts, initially in the form of my own essay 'A New Look into the *Speculum Inclusorum*'. Since then, I have included discussions of the *Speculum/Mirror* in several essays.[82] The works have also featured in studies by Liz Herbert McAvoy and Mari Hughes-Edwards, and are included in Hughes-Edwards's recent examination of anchoritic guidance writing, *Reading Medieval Anchoritism*.[83]

---

[80] Jolliffe, *A Check-List of Middle English Prose Writings of Spiritual Guidance* (Toronto, 1974).

[81] Warren, p. 297. The only substantive use she made of the *Speculum* was its strictures in I.ii against urban anchorites whose primary motivation was the garnering of alms. See pp. 39–40 and 43.

[82] Most fully in 'Hermits and Anchorites in Historical Context', in *Teaching Anchorites and Mystics*, ed. Roger Ellis, Dee Dyas, Valerie Edden (Cambridge, 2005), pp. 3–18; and 'Anchoritic Aspects of Julian of Norwich', in *A Companion to Julian of Norwich*, ed. Liz Herbert McAvoy (Cambridge, 2008), pp. 75–87.

[83] See also her 'Hedgehog Skins and Hairshirts: The Changing Role of Asceticism in the Anchoritic Ideal', *Mystics Quarterly*, 28:1–2 (2002), pp. 6–26; '"Wrapt as if to the Third Heaven": Gender and Contemplative Experience in Late-Medieval Anchoritic Guidance Writing' in *Anchorites, Wombs and Tombs*, pp. 131–41; '"How Good it is to be Alone"? Sociability, Solitude and Medieval English Anchoritism', *Mystics Quarterly*, 35:3–4 (2009), pp. 31–61. And see McAvoy's '"Neb [...] sumdeal ilich wummon & neddre is behinden": Reading the Monstrous in the Anchoritic Text' in *The Medieval Mystical Tradition in England*, Exeter Symposium VII, ed. E. A. Jones (Cambridge, 2004), pp. 51–67; 'Gender, Rhetoric and Space in *Speculum Inclusorum*, *Letter to a Bury Recluse* and the Strange Case of Christina Carpenter', in Liz Herbert McAvoy (ed.), *Rhetoric of the Anchorhold: Space Place and Body within the Discourses of Enclosure* (Cardiff, 2008), pp. 111–26; and her *Medieval Anchoritisms*.

Manuscripts

Descriptions of extant manuscripts

R   London, British Library, MS Royal 5 A v

Previous descriptions
G. F. Warner and J. P. Gilson, *Catalogue of Western Manuscripts in the Old Royal and King's Collection*, 4 vols (London, 1921), i.95–6; the British Library online Manuscripts Catalogue at http://www.bl.uk/catalogues/manuscripts/INDEX.asp; Oliger, pp. 15–19; Michael G. Sargent, *James Grenehalgh as Textual Critic*, 2 vols (Salzburg, 1984), pp. 520–6.

Physical description
Two modern paper flyleaves + i + 135 parchment leaves + 1 early-modern paper endleaf + 2 modern paper endleaves. Leaves typically 147 x 223 mm. Modern pencil foliation (the leaf between fols 133 and 134 has been omitted from the foliation, and is referred to here as fol. 133*). Collation: fols 1, 2 are singletons, $1-2^8$, 3^{8-1} lacks fifth (fols 19–25), $4-14^8$, 15^6 (fols 114–19), 16^6 (fols 120–5), 17^8, 18^2 (fols 133*–134). Quires 8 and 10 are misbound; contemporary notes at the end of each leaf guide the reader through the correct sequence. (Quire 8 affects the *Speculum*: see notes and apparatus to IV.iii.30 and 103 in the edition, and p. xlix below.)

Signatures in black ink in a single sequence a-p (though occasionally lost to cropping, including all signatures in quire 12) on quires 1–15; catchwords on all quires except 10, 12, 13, 15–17. The absence of signature and catchword evidence, and the fact that the manuscript is very tightly bound, makes collation of the last three quires uncertain. The last word on fol. 125v (deuo/tor*um*) has been hyphenated and its second half bracketed beneath the last ruled line, as if squeezing it in before the end of a quire.

Written space 91 x 152 mm approx., pricked and ruled in 30 long lines, quires 1–8 faintly in black ink, quires 9–18 in brown crayon (the change in practice evidently related to the change in hand noted below).

Written in two hands, the change occurring in mid-sentence on fol. 64v, towards the end of quire 8.[84] Hand 1 writes items 1–5 (including the whole of the *Speculum*) and the beginning of item 6 in Bastard Anglicana, using

---

[84] Not noted by Sargent in his description.

Introduction   xxxix

unusually black ink. See Plate 1. Hand 2 employs a dark brown ink, using a Bastard Secretary of somewhat larger proportions than Hand 1, although the ruling remains unaltered. Decoration is in a single style throughout the book. Each new text has initial capital 3–4 lines high in blue with red flourishing. Chapter initials thereafter two lines high, similarly decorated. Chapter rubrics, some paraph marks, and some underlining in red. At head of fol. 40v (the beginning of the *Speculum*) 'ihc maria' in red.

A little contemporary annotation and correction. Also annotated by the sixteenth-century Carthusian James Grenehalgh. His annotations are discussed further below.

The volume was half-bound in black morocco, stamped with the royal arms and the date 1757 (the date of acquisition), in 1917.[85]

Secundo folio: si*quidem omn*i op*er*i

Contents

fol. 1v	*Ownership inscription and contents list in a sixteenth-century hand*
	'Hic liber est domus sancte Anne ordinis cartusien' iuxta Couentriam ex prouidencia et dono domini Roberti Odyham. Contenta in hoc libello.' *A contemporary list of contents follows.*
	Three sententiae in the hand of James Grenehalgh
	'Cassiodorus. Nichil potest esse forcius, nichil egregius [...]' Exposition of Psalm 70 (*PL* 70.276).
	Then an unidentified sentence: 'Multo enim melius est vnam grauem iniuriam sustinere sine murmure propter amorem dei, quam pascere centum pauperer, & quam ieiunare vsque ad celum stellatum tempore longum.'
	'Gregorius. Nulla sunt bona que agimus [...]' In fact from one of Bede's homilies (lib. III hom. 35), *PL* 94.347.
fol. 2r	*Ownership inscription in a seventeenth-century hand*
	John Theyer.
1 (fols 3r–17v)	'Liber Augustini beati de spiritu et anima.'

---

[85] Information from Charmaine Fagan at the British Library.

Speculum Inclusorum / A Mirror for Recluses

	PL 40, 779–832. Incomplete: ends with c. 33. The attribution to Augustine was doubted already in the Middle Ages.
2 (fols 17v–21r)	'Liber Hugonis de Sancto Victore de laude caritatis.' *PL* 176, 969–76; also in *L'œuvre de Hugues de Saint-Victor, I: De institutione novitiorum; De virtute orandi; De laude caritatis; De arrha animae*, ed. P. Sicard et al. (Turnhout, 1997).
3 (fols 21r–31v)	'Soliloquium H[ugonis de S. Victore] de arra anime.' *PL* 176, 951–70; and in Sicard et al.
4 (fols 31v–40r)	'Tractatus de peccato originali editus a fratre Egidio Romano.' No. 1886 in Morton W. Bloomfield et al., *Incipits of Latin Works on the Virtues and Vices, 1100–1500 A.D.* (Cambridge MA, 1979).
5 (fols 40v–60r)	'Tractatus qui vocatur Speculum Inclusorum.' A further portion of the text is copied out of sequence on fols 61r–v (see below).
6 (fols 60r–133v)	'Incipit tercia pars libelli qui intitulatur Formula Nouiciorum. De profectibus religiosorum.' Book 3 of David of Augsburg, *De exterioris et interioris hominis compositione libri III* (Quaracchi, 1899). Described in the colophon (fol. 133v) as 'Formula Nouiciorum, secundum Hubertum magistrum theologiae, ordinis Predicatorum.' The *Formula novitiorum* was sometimes attributed to Humbert of Romans (d. 1277); for another fifteenth-century English example see Bodleian Library, Oxford, MS Rawlinson C. 72, fol. 33r.
fol. 134r	*Various notes and inscriptions* *Ownership inscription in a sixteenth-century hand* Edwardus Aglionby. *Four lines of English verse in a sixteenth-century hand, perhaps Aglionby's* inc. 'At meat feare & thank god tak tyme hear su*m*thing redd.' *NIMEV* 1694; see also 2233. A translation of the Latin lines from *Stans puer ad mensam* that appear below, distinct from the published translations listed in *NIMEV*.

Note in a fifteenth-century hand
'5 gen*er*a sompniorum Augustin*us* de sp*iri*tu & A*ni*ma. cap. 19.'

Four lines of Latin verse in a fifteenth-century hand
inc. 'Sit timor in dapibus.'
Lines found at the end of some texts of *Stans puer ad mensam*, the original of which was attributed to Robert Grosseteste. Lines 53–6 in the edition by Servus Gieben, 'Robert Grosseteste and Medieval Courtesy Books', *Vivarium* 5 (1967), pp. 47–74. As four lines standing alone, also no. 29881 in H. Walther, *Proverbia sententiaeque Latinitatis Medii Aevi: Lateinische Sprichwörter und Sentenzen des Mittelalters in alphabetischer Anordnung* (Göttingen, 1963).

Ownership inscription in a sixteenth-century hand
'Constat domui / cartusie iux*ta* coue*n*tria*m*.'
'deo gr*a*ci*a*s.'

Provenance
Robert Odyham (or Odiam), originally professed at the London Charterhouse, was appointed prior of the Priory of St Anne, Coventry in 1457. He was relieved of office in 1467, and his death was notified to the General Chapter of the order in 1480.[86]

It was most likely at Coventry that the book was annotated by James Grenehalgh. A monk of Sheen Charterhouse by 1499, he developed an inappropriate attachment to a novice of Syon Abbey, Joanna Sewell, to whom he had been acting as spiritual adviser in the lead-up to her profession. As a punishment – not necessarily for incontinence, but perhaps for an obstinate refusal to take correction – he was removed to Coventry in 1507 or 1508, and may have been moved on to another house of the order between 1512 and 1516.[87] He died at the charterhouse of Hull in 1529 or 1530. He is well-known as a textual critic, especially of Walter Hilton, but more so for the personal annotations that he added to a number of manuscripts and printed books. These include his own monogram, J. G., but also a variant version in which his own initials appear 'eloquently overlapping' with those of Joanna Sewell:

---

[86] *The Heads of Religious Houses: England and Wales, III. 1377–1540*, ed. David M. Smith (Cambridge, 2008), pp. 356–7.
[87] Sargent, *James Grenehalgh*, p. 80. The whole of this paragraph is based on Sargent, pp. 75–109.

J. G. S.[88] In addition to the monograms, both their full names appear in **R** at the foot of fol. 47v.

All but one or two of Grenehalgh's annotations in **R** are to the *Speculum*. They include a couple of textual corrections, but also some important personal annotations. The majority of those passages that he highlighted with a monogram concern tribulations and the rewards for those who withstand them; on fol. 53v recluses are encouraged to remember in their prayers 'miserias exulum & incarceratorum' [the myseries & wrecchidnesses of outlawed folk and of hem þat bien in prison] (III.i.95–6).[89]

Coventry charterhouse was dissolved in 1539.

Edward Aglionby (1520–91?) was a Cambridge MA (1544), MP for Carlisle and later, through Dudley's influence, for Warwick, and recorder of the latter town under Elizabeth.[90] He translated 'A notable and marueilous epistle […] concernyng the terrible iudgemente of God' from a work of the Paduan antitrinitarian Matteo Gribaldo.[91]

John Theyer (c. 1598–1673), the antiquary and bibliophile, amassed a collection of some 800 manuscript books. I have not, however, been able to match this volume with those that were seen by Edward Bernard at the end of the century.[92] More than 300 of Theyer's manuscripts were bought by Charles II in 1678. The Royal collection came to the British Museum in 1757.[93]

Date

There is no strong evidence to date the manuscript very precisely. The latest text included is the *Speculum* itself, which (I will argue below) probably dates to c. 1417. The death of Robert Odyham provides a *terminus ante quem* of 1480. The handwriting is consistent with a mid-century date.

---

[88] The phrase is Lee Patterson's. See *Negotiating the Past: The Historical Understanding of Medieval Literature* (Madison, 1987), p. 144.

[89] A full list of the passages annotated by Grenehalgh is given in the Appendix to the Notes to the Texts.

[90] Stephen Wright in *ODNB*.

[91] *STC* 12365

[92] Bernard, *Catalogi librorum manuscriptorum Angliae et Hiberniae in unum collecti cum indice alphabetico* (Oxford 1697/8), nos 6371–6682 at II.i.198–203.

[93] Charlotte Fell-Smith (rev. Robert J. Haines) in *ODNB*.

Introduction xliii

J Oxford, St John's College, MS 177

Previous descriptions
H. O. Coxe, 'Catalogus codicum MSS. Collegii S. Johannis Baptistæ', p. 58, in *Catalogus codicum MSS. qui in collegiis aulisque Oxoniensibus hodie adservantur*, 2 vols (Oxford, 1852), vol. II; Oliger, pp. 19–22; Hogg, pp. 3–5; most fully, Hanna, *Manuscripts of St John's College, Oxford*, pp. 247–8.

Physical description
iii (modern) + 104 + iii (modern) paper leaves. Leaves 195 x 140 mm. Modern pencil foliation. A collation is impossible: the book is made up of individual leaves, stab-bound. Catchwords on verso of some leaves, especially in the final third of the book, but they seem designed to link leaves, rather than quires.

Written space typically 140 mm × 90 mm, unruled, no pricking, bounded in dry-point. Lines per page vary between 13 and 27, though 20–22 is usual.

Written in secretary of widely varying degrees of formality, 'probably not a single hand'.[94] See Plate 2. Headings in text hand. A 2-line initial, undecorated, to the heading and incipit of the *Speculum* (fol. 38v; see Plate 2). Space for similar initials has been left at the opening of Parts II–IV, but these were not executed. Swag initials begin texts and sections within texts in the rest of the book.

Modern binding of leather on millboards.

Secundo folio: lium quod et

Contents

1 (fols 1–16v)   'Incipit prologus pontii diaconi carthaginensis in librum de gestis et passione beati cypriani episcopi carthagine[n]sis et martyris.'
Life of Cyprian by Pontius of Carthage (*PL* 3.1481–98). Imperfect: breaks off in cap. 15, to be followed without a break by another account of Cyprian's passion (*PL* 3.1498–1506). A note at the foot of fol. 14v highlights the lacuna, and suggests a missing leaf in the exemplar, which is plausible.

2 (fols 16v–23v) 'Hic subsequuntur annotamenta quedam valde necessaria et

---
[94] Hanna, p. 247.

qui voluerit proficere in virtutibus iuxta votum sue professionis autore dionisio cartusiano De modo dicendi pater noster.'
Three excerpts from Denys of Ryckel: arts 4, 7, 6 of *De fructuosa temporis deductione*. Noted Kent Emery Jr., *Dionysii Cartusiensis opera selecta* (Turnhout, 1991), p. 190. Printed *Doctoris ecstatici D. Dionysii Cartusiani Opera Omnia*, vol. 40 (Montreuil, 1911), pp. 51–71.

3 (fols 24r–37v) 'Sanctus pater climacus.'
A series of brief excerpts on the solitary or monastic life, the first (fols 24r–25r) from John Climacus's *Scala paradisi*.

4 (fols 37v–104r) 'Incipit prologus cuius deuotissimi patris scribentis ad inclusos de ipsorum vocatione sancta.'
At end: 'Explicit speculatiuum clausorum'.

(fol. 104v) *Devotional fragment added in sixteenth-century hand inc.* Wherffor cam I out of my mothres uome [...] Breaks off incomplete at foot of page.

Provenance

There are no contemporary marks of ownership. J's other contents include excerpts from the fifteenth-century Dutch Carthusian Denys of Ryckel. On this evidence, coupled with the codicological and palaeographical characteristics of the manuscript, Hogg proposed that

> we are faced, in all probability, with a Carthusian manuscript, whose provenance cannot be exactly established, written by a monk for his private usage or for the library of his house, rather than a professionally produced text from a large scriptorium.[95]

This hypothesis will be strengthened by the arguments for the Carthusian origins of the *Speculum* presented below. Note further that J's erroneous title for the work, 'speculatiuum clausorum', is shared by one of the lost manuscripts that is of certain Carthusian provenance (below, p. xlviii).

Date

Handwriting and watermark evidence place the manuscript in the sixteenth century. Principal watermark a gloved hand with five-pointed star above, identified by Hanna as Piccard XVII, nos 1306, 1318 and 1350–70, in use

---

[95] Hogg, p. 4.

1517x1536.⁹⁶ Hanna also found a mark resembling Piccard XVII, nos 1476–82 on fols 72 and 78 (in the *Speculum*), with the anomalous date after 1540. The mark is indistinct, however, and the identification is not certain.

H   London, British Library, MS Harley 2372

Previous descriptions
A Catalogue of the Harleian Manuscripts, 2 vols (London, 1808–1812), ii.672; Oliger, pp. 23–4; Harley, pp. xxvii–xxviii; British Library online Manuscripts Catalogue at http://www.bl.uk/catalogues/manuscripts/INDEX.asp (catalogued as part of the Harley Medieval Medical Manuscripts Project (2007)).

Physical description
Two modern paper flyleaves + 1 contemporary parchment flyleaf (numbered 1*) + 37 parchment leaves + 2 modern paper flyleaves. Leaves 227 x 155 mm, modern ink foliation.

Collation: 1^{8-2} (lacks first and second), $2-4^8$, 5^{8-1} (lacks fourth). Catchwords on all quires except quire 5 (the foot of whose final leaf is damaged), viz. fols 6v, 14v, 22v, 30v. The catchword on fol. 30v does not match the opening of fol. 31r, indicating the loss of some material at this point (and see below ME II. ii.235). This is confirmed by the signatures. These are visible only in quires 4 and 5 (quires designated by a letter in red, leaves by roman numerals in brown ink). Quire 4 is designated 'c' and (the present) quire 5 'e', implying the loss of one quire after fol. 30v.

Written space typically 146 x 90 mm, ruled in brown ink in 23 long lines, plus an unruled outer margin of 22 mm for notes.

The main text hand is a Bastard Secretary of the mid-fifteenth century.⁹⁷ See Plate 3. Running titles ('Prima pars', 'Secunda pars', 'Tercia pars') in red. Large initials 3–4 lines high at opening of I.v, II.i and II.ii (fols 13v, 17r, 22r): gold on blue and pink backgrounds with white tracery. Other initials touched in yellow; paraph marks in alternating red and blue with contrasting decoration; rubrics and running titles in the main hand in red ink. Marginal *notae* (typically one or two per page) and a few other annotations, the latter listed below in the Appendix to the Notes to the Text.

---

⁹⁶ I have used the online version: Landesarchiv Baden-Württemberg, Hauptstaatsarchiv Stuttgart, J 340 (http://www.piccard-online.de).
⁹⁷ So dated by Harley (p. xxviii) with the assistance of Malcolm Parkes.

Binding identified by the Harley Medieval Medical Manuscripts Project as 'mottled brown leather over pasteboards with gilt- and blind-tooled decoration, possibly attributable to Christopher Chapman.' Chapman (fl. 1704–56) was one of the two binders (the other was Thomas Elliott) responsible for most of the Harleian bindings.[98]

Secundo folio: of oure lord. (The original first quire has, however, been lost.)

Contents

(fol. 1*r)   *Medicinal recipes, in a sixteenth-century hand*
               'Thes be good medesens for the gowtt that doues folwy.'
               Included in the list given by R. H. Robbins, 'Medical Manuscripts in Middle English', *Speculum* 45 (1970), pp. 393–415, at p. 403 n. 28.

(fol. 1*v)   *Ownership inscription, in a sixteenth-century hand*
               'Thys ys a good bok ffor holy men or wemen the whyche bok bylongeth to the almos howse off wyll*i*am Brown' in stawnford in the dyocesse off lyncoln' By the gyft off s*er* Iohn trvs chapleyn' to the seyd wyll*i*am Brown' su*m* tyme and prest in the seyd beyd howse.'
               'Orate q*ue*so legentes p*ro* a*n*i*m*a dicti d*omi*ni Ioha*nn*is.'
               The inscription is in the hand of John Taillour, Warden of Browne's Hospital 1497–1503.[99]

1 (fols 1r–37v)   *Mirror for Recluses*
               Imperfect at beginning and end, and with lacuna in II.iii–III.i.

Language
H was analysed as Linguistic Profile no. 9430 in *The Linguistic Atlas of Late Medieval English*.[100] Its language was identified as Hertfordshire, and localised to grid reference 530 209, a few miles south-west of Hertford.

---

[98] H. M. Nixon, *Five Centuries of English Bookbinding* (London, 1978), pp. 138–42.
[99] Information from Alan Rogers. See further below, pp. lxx–lxxi.
[100] Angus McIntosh, M. L. Samuels, Michael Benskin, *The Linguistic Atlas of Late Medieval English* 4 vols, (Aberdeen, 1986), i.111 and iii.181.

Provenance
There is no indication of the manuscript's provenance before its donation to Browne's Hospital, Stamford. The latter was first founded in 1475. The founder William Browne of Stamford died in 1489. The donor John Trus is otherwise unknown: he is not recorded as a member either of Browne's household or his hospital (its accounts from 1494 are extant). John Taillour, who wrote the donation notice, was Warden of Browne's Hospital 1497–1503. H therefore came to Browne's Hospital between 1489 and 1503, and probably between 1489 and 1494. See further the discussion below.

The John Roonling whose name appears in an early-modern hand on fol. 13v has not been identified. He may be responsible for a roughly-drawn astrological chart on fol. 14r.

It is not known how the manuscript came into the collection of Edward Harley (1689–1741). Harley's manuscript books were sold to the nation by his widow and daughter in 1753 to form part of the founding collection of the British Museum.

Date
The only evidence for a *terminus a quo* is provided by the composition of the *Speculum Inclusorum*, from which the *Mirror* is translated. Arguments for dating the *Speculum* c. 1417 will be presented below. The *terminus ante quem* is the donation to Browne's Hospital, probably by 1494. Palaeographical dating of the manuscript to the mid-fifteenth century is consistent with such a range of dates.

Lost manuscripts
In addition to the extant manuscripts of the *Speculum* and *Mirror*, there is evidence in medieval library catalogues and booklists of a further four copies of the Latin text. Because in each case the *secundo folio* of the volume was recorded, it is possible to distinguish these from the surviving manuscripts. (In two instances, the *secundo folio* also helps to confirm the identification of the lost text.) Two belonged to the Bridgettine Syon Abbey, while two were in Carthusian ownership.

1. Item M.35 in the Syon brothers' library was a volume containing a variety of contemplative texts (headed by the ps.-Bonaventure *Meditationes*, and including a number of other Bonaventuran works) and some forms of living. It included also the three *Meditations* of William of Rimington, which are addressed to an anchorite. The fifth item in the book was a 'Speculum inclusorum habens 4^{or}

partes', occupying fols 45–70.[101] Title, description and length leave little doubt that this was a copy of the text edited here. The book came to Syon from Symon Wynter, an early brother of the house first recorded in 1423. He was granted leave to transfer to a house of a less strict observance in 1429, though it is not clear whether he did in fact leave; he died in 1448. If he brought the book with him when he came then this gives a *terminus ante quem* for the *Speculum* that is consistent with the arguments for dating the text that will be presented below.

2. The first item in Syon M.56 was a 'Speculum edificatorium tam religiosorum quam Reclusorum'; the next item (a *Speculum peccatoris*) began on fol. 48. Vincent Gillespie suggests several possible identifications for the text, including the *Speculum*. This is made virtually certain by the *secundo folio* of the volume, 'ria vide', which appears (twice) early in Chapter 1:

> O benignissime Iesu, o singularis custos hominum & saluator eorum, uide captiuorum tuorum suspi**ria**, **uide** electorum tuorum deside**ria**, **uide** temptacionum pericula, & reuela mihi quod eis proferam […] (Prol. 10–13)

The volume was a donation of Thomas Lay, priest, who died in 1477.[102] The catalogue's recognition that the *Speculum* might be of interest to a wider audience than anchorites alone ('edificatorium tam religiosorum quam Reclusorum') is worthy of note.

3. A list of twenty-four books conveyed from the London Charterhouse to Hull Charterhouse by John Spalding includes a 'paruus liber qui dicitur speculum inclusorum'. The list includes two printed books of c. 1493; Spalding died as vicar of Hull before 1528.[103]

4. Among the sixty-eight books given between 1463 and 1474 to Witham Charterhouse by John Blacman, a *clericus redditus* of the house, was a 'Speculatiua clausorum'. It appears to be one of Blacman's final two donations to Witham, made in 1474. The title given the text is very close to that of J, and is confirmed as a *Speculum* by its *secundo folio*, 'lacione: aggredior', which occurs in the Prologue: 'Ex hac ergo igitur confidencia sumpta conso**lacione aggredior** opus istud exhortatorium ad inclusos' (Prol. 11–12).[104]

---

[101] SS1.768 in Vincent Gillespie, *Syon Abbey*, Corpus of British Medieval Library Catalogues 9 (London, 2001), pp. 231–2. For Wynter, see pp. 593–4.
[102] SS1.789 in Gillespie, p. 238; for Lay, see p. 583.
[103] C2.15 in A. I. Doyle, *The Libraries of the Carthusians*, printed with Gillespie, *Syon Abbey*, p. 618. The list was first printed by Margaret Thompson, who dated it incorrectly c. 1400: E. M. Thompson, *The Carthusian Order in England* (London, 1930), p. 324.

Relationship of manuscripts
There are two extant copies of the *Speculum*, but they represent a single textual tradition: **J** is in a direct line of descent from **R**. The misbinding of **R**'s quire 8 (noted above) has affected the text towards the end of the *Speculum*, so that the sequence of IV.iii is disrupted. The error was noticed by James Grenehalgh who, in a note at the foot of fol. 59v, instructs the reader to turn over two leaves to continue reading in sequence. The *Speculum* continues on fols 61r–v. Another note at the foot of the latter then sends the reader back to fol. 60r, where the *Speculum* concludes. (See the notes and apparatus to IV.iii.30 and 103.) The scribe of **J**, or of an intervening copy, did not notice the error.[105] **J**'s text runs on from fol. 59v to fol. 60r, apparently unaware that the text that results is nonsense: 'secure comprehendet in futuro misericordialem[106] [*sic*] glorie coronam habebitis'.

As already noted, it is possible that the error was not introduced by **J**, but inherited from an ancestor. The nature of the oversight, however, would be entirely in keeping with the profile of **J**, which is generally a careless and inaccurate witness to the text. It is characterised by a large number of morphological variants, many of them manifest errors, and numerous omissions of one or two words at a time. These regularly result in bad grammar, bad sense, or both. **J**'s erroneous readings include the work's title (given in the explicit as *Speculatiuum clausorum*) and the text on which the whole treatise is a commentary, omitting 'vestram' from 'Videte uocacionem vestram' at I.v.75. Most of the readings from **J** recorded in the Apparatus are likewise clear errors. Genuine variant readings are few (see e.g. I.ii.74, I.iv.42). The text edited here has been emended to the reading of **J** in fewer than a dozen instances, and (since **J** is descended from **R**) these must simply be fortunate coincidences where **J**, or an intervening copyist, has corrected **R**'s reading independently.

R has a number of contemporary corrections, mostly inserted above the line in the main text hand. These have occasionally been incorporated into **J**'s text (see II.iii.17, III.ii.56), but more often **J** transmits the uncorrected reading of **R** (see I.ii.12, I.iii.73, I.v.4, IV.ii.68). If **J** did indeed copy directly from **R** then this adds weight to the circumstantial evidence presented above that it, like **R**, was a Carthusian book.

---

[104] C9.68 in Doyle, p. 651. For Blacman and his donations, see pp. 630–3.
[105] See below for evidence that **J** or its exemplar was copied before a number of corrections were made to **R**. **J** may not have had the benefit of the instructions described above.
[106] The word, though rare, is recorded (*DMLBS* gives a single, twelfth-century example with the sense 'merciful').

l   *Speculum Inclusorum / A Mirror for Recluses*

The translator of the Middle English *Mirror for Recluses* worked from a *Speculum* closer to **R** than **J**. None of **J**'s errors is present in the *Mirror*, and in those places where the two witnesses each provide viable readings, the *Mirror* follows **R** rather than **J** (see I.iii.16, II.i.68, III.ii.37, III.ii.55). In two places the *Mirror* appears to be based on a Latin reading superior to that of the extant manuscripts. At I.iii.22 I have used the Middle English 'And it is no wonder' as the basis for an emendation of **R**'s and **J**'s 'ubi nimirum' to 'nec uero mirum', and at I.v.45 the Middle English 'vsage' must derive from Latin 'usus' rather than the erroneous reading 'uisus' shared by **R** and **J**. This could imply the *Mirror*'s descent from a *Speculum* superior in that text's history, though in both these cases it is not inconceivable that the translator spotted and corrected the error in his archetype independently.

Even if the translator of the *Mirror* had access to a good copy of the *Speculum*, however, H is generally rather a careless witness to it, being especially prone to the omission of short words. Two errors indicate that H was copied from an English exemplar.[107] Neither 'deceyuyd' for 'decernyd' (ME I.i.40) nor 'dalyaunce' for 'Dalyda' (I.iv.21) is easily explained as an error in Latin transmission.

---

[107] They were noted by Harley, p. xiii. She cites two further examples, but these are not convincing.

Author and readers

Speculum Inclusorum

All the external evidence situates the *Speculum* in a Carthusian environment. The earlier of the surviving manuscripts, **R**, belonged to the Coventry charterhouse. The provenance of **J** is unknown, but there are several reasons to identify it, too, as a Carthusian book. Two of the lost manuscripts were in Carthusian ownership. The other lost copies of the work so far identified belonged not to the Carthusians but to the Bridgettines of Syon, but the close literary connections between Syon and the neighbouring Charterhouse of Sheen are by now very well established.

A piece of internal evidence also points to a Carthusian origin. In Part Three the author recommends doing 'some suitable manual labour' ('aliquid honestum manibus operandum', III.i.3–4). When he comes to specify what kinds of manual work might be appropriate for recluses, he says only:

> Presertim autem scriptura sancte & edificatorie leccionis meritoria videtur que, post mortem scribentis, forsitan usque ad diem Iudicii ipsum quodammmodo uiuere faciet & mereri, in edificacione & profectu singulorum legencium uel audiencium scripta sua. (III.iii.84–8)

> [And in particular, the writing of material that is holy and edifying to read seems commendable, because, after the person that wrote it has died – and even perhaps right up until the Day of Judgement – it can make him live and gain merit in some way, by the edification and profit of each of those who read or hear what he has written.]

This undoubtedly recalls the Carthusian notion of 'preaching with the hands' first promoted by Guigo I in the silent and solitary order's *Consuetudines*, where he enjoins 'Since we cannot preach it with our mouths, let us preach the word of God with our hands,' continuing

> For as many books as we write, so many heralds of the truth does it appear that we make for ourselves, hoping for mercy from God for all who may be either corrected from error by them, or stronger in the catholic truth – for all, in fact, who may be either goaded from their sins and vices, or lifted up by the desire of our heavenly home.[108]

---

[108] 'Quia ore non possumus, Dei verbum manibus praedicemus' (cap. 28, PL 153.694). The translations are by Michael G. Sargent, from his 'The Transmission by the English Carthusians of Some Late Medieval Spiritual Writings', *Journal of Ecclesiastical History* 27 (1976), pp. 225–40, at p. 226. Quoted, together with the Adam of Dryburgh that follows, by Oliger, pp. 123–4 n. 4.

The passage is quoted by Adam of Dryburgh in chapter 36 of his *De Quadripertito exercitio cellae*, 'De opere manuum', where he says

> There is one work to the performance of which you ought especially to attend; that is either that you learn to write (if, of course, you can learn), or if you can and know, that you do write. This work is, as it were, immortal work; work, if one may say so, not passing but lasting; work certainly, may we say, and yet not work; the work, finally, which, among all other works is most fitting to literate religious men.[109]

The benefits and merits of the 'opus immortale' are similarly laid out in the conclusion of the Carthusian *Speculum Christiani*:

> Magnum enim meritum est illi & multum premium habebit in futuro, qui scribit uel scribere facit doctrinam sanam ea intencione, ut ipse querat in ea, quomodo sancte uiuat, & ut alii eam habeant, ut per eam edificentur.
>
> [Great is the merit, and great the reward to be had in the future, for the person who writes sound doctrine, or causes it to be written, with the intention that he might find in it how to live a holy life, and that others who possess it might be edified by it.][110]

Once again the assurance of present and future merit for one who writes holy material for the edification of readers now and to come recalls quite strikingly the *Speculum*'s endorsement of scribal labour.

That the *Speculum* is a Carthusian production thus seems highly probable. To pin its composition down to one particular charterhouse is, however, more difficult. Copies have been identified at Coventry, Witham (in Somerset), and en route from London to Hull; the Syon manuscripts might be taken to imply its presence at Sheen. That suggests a certain degree of continuing and widely-dispersed interest in the text, but not a place of origin.

It may be productive to change the angle of approach, and look not at where we know the *Speculum* to have been, but where we have evidence that it might have been needed. In broad terms, it is not difficult to see the attraction of a work like the *Speculum* to the Carthusians. As an order made up of communities of solitaries, they might be expected to take an interest in texts that addressed the ideals and the practicalities of the solitary life. And indeed their ownership and transmission of works like Rolle's *Form of Living* and Hilton's *Scale* is well

---

[109] Sargent, *loc. cit.*
[110] Quoted by Vincent Gillespie, '*Cura Pastoralis in Deserto*' in *De Cella in Seculum*, ed. Michael G. Sargent (Cambridge, 1989), pp. 161–81 at p. 181. My translation.

known.¹¹¹ Moreover, three of the six extant copies of Ailred's *De Institutione Inclusarum* are of Carthusian provenance, and one of the two Middle English translations of the work was copied by Stephen Dodesham, Carthusian of Witham and later (c. 1470) of Sheen.¹¹² The Carthusians were also interested in 'mystical' material. Several key works of late-medieval spirituality owe their preservation to the order, including the *Book of Margery Kempe* and the Short Text of Julian's *Revelations*.¹¹³ The Carthusians seem to have been attracted to a broad range of texts dealing with visionary experience including, alongside more theoretical treatments, narratives that provided them with some of 'the raw data of psychic phenomena'.¹¹⁴ The *Speculum* is generally happier discussing meditation than revelation, but parts of it could be seen to fall into this category too.

To gather in copies of works by and for solitaries is one thing; to compose a fairly substantial treatise of spiritual direction for an individual solitary is another, and is difficult to comprehend except where such a pastoral responsibility existed. Evidence for such relationships involving the English Carthusians are, however, rather few.¹¹⁵ An important early sixteenth-century example is reflected in Richard Methley's *Pystyl of Solytary Lyf Nowadayes* addressed to 'Hew Heremyte'. Methley became a Carthusian at Mount Grace (North Yorkshire) around 1476, and is known for a range of autobiographical spiritual writings as well as translations into Latin of the *Cloud of Unknowing* and *Book of Simple Souls* of Marguerite Porete.¹¹⁶ The Hugh to whom Methley

---

[111] Sargent, 'Transmission'; A. I. Doyle, 'Carthusian Participation in the Movement of Works of Richard Rolle between England and Other Parts of Europe in the 14th and 15th Centuries', in *Kartäusermystik und -Mystiker*, ed. James Hogg, Analecta Cartusiana 55 (Salzburg, 1981), ii.109–20.
[112] 'New Look', pp. 137–8. For Dodesham, see John Ayto and Alexandra Barratt, *Aelred of Rievaulx's De Institutione Inclusarum*, EETS orig. ser. 287 (1984), xxix–xxxi.
[113] The Short Text survives in the 'Amherst manuscript', British Library MS Add. 37790. For a detailed discussion of this manuscript, including its Carthusian character, see Marleen Cré, *Vernacular Mysticism in the Charterhouse*, The Medieval Translator 9 (Turnhout, 2006). It is less certain that the order was interested in disseminating this material.
[114] Vincent Gillespie, 'Dial M for Mystic: Mystical Texts in the Library of Syon Abbey and the Spirituality of the Syon Brethren,' in *The Medieval Mystical Tradition: England, Ireland and Wales*, Exeter Symposium VI, ed. Marion Glasscoe (Cambridge, 1999), pp. 241–68 at p. 244.
[115] The rider here must be that the surviving evidence for medieval English solitaries is scarce and fragmentary. See most recently my 'Hidden Lives: Methodological Reflections on a New Database of the Hermits and Anchorites of Medieval England', *Medieval Prosopography* 29 (2013, at press).
[116] See his life by Michael Sargent in *ODNB*.

addressed his *Pystyl* lived at a 'place or the chapel of owr blessed lady', probably the Chapel of Our Lady that stands on the hill, a short but steep walk above Mount Grace Priory, where there are some suggestive architectural features.[117] He was not, however, a recluse or anchorite, but a hermit. By the late Middle Ages, this had become a significant distinction. Hermits were not enclosed, they were more likely to be involved in public works (such as road-mending or bridge-keeping) than advanced spiritual exercises and contemplation, they were rarely priests and often illiterate. Methley's brief epistle instructs Hugh 'How thou shuldest pleas god to his worship & profight to thy selfe', reminding him of his commitments to obedience, poverty and charity, and exhorting him to guard his sense of sight, keep to his cell as much as possible, and to maintain silence.[118]

The *Speculum* plainly addresses itself to a reader of greater *clergie* and spiritual ambition than Hugh Hermit. Its composition in Latin, and the range of 'edifying reading' recommended in II.iii, would suggest a clerical audience, and this is confirmed by the opening of the latter chapter, which stipulates that its suggestions for holy reading should only be explored 'postquam diuini seruicii debitum completum est' [after you have fulfilled the requirements of divine service] (line 1), including explicitly the canonical hours. If he is to perform manual labour, then (as we have seen) the writing of books is most appropriate for him. And in Part IV he is offered spiritual rewards that include the fire of devotion and a momentary forestaste of the sweetness of Heaven.

Moreover, the *Speculum*'s usual address to 'reclusi' – anchorites in the plural – seems to imply something more substantial or long-lasting than Methley's *ad hominem* advice to Hugh. We are looking, then, for a fifteenth-century priest-anchorite, or group of priest-anchorites, with connections to the Carthusian order. The only candidates known to fit that description occupied the reclusory at Sheen.

The Charterhouse of Jesus of Bethlehem was part of Henry V's ambitious plans for a complex of religious foundations clustering around his newly-rebuilt palace of Sheen beside the Thames.[119] He planned houses of three of the newer

---

[117] See Anthony Storey, *Mount Grace Lady Chapel: An Historical Enquiry* (Beverley, 2001).
[118] Quotations from 'Richard Methley: To Hew Heremyte: A Pystyl of Solytary Lyfe Nowadayes', ed. James Hogg, in *Analecta Cartusiana* 31 (1977), pp. 91–119.
[119] Jeremy Catto, 'Religious Change under Henry V,' in *Henry V: The Practice of Kingship*, ed. G. L. Harriss (Oxford, 1985); Neil Beckett, 'St. Bridget, Henry V, and Syon Abbey', in *Studies in St Birgitta and the Brigittine Order*, ed. James Hogg, 2 vols, Analecta Cartusiana 19 (Salzburg, 1993), pp. 125–50.

orders, each of them associated with the late-medieval reform movement and characterised by an anchoritic spirituality. In the event, the projected house of Celestines came to nothing, but the Carthusians of Sheen and (on the Middlesex side of the river) the Bridgettines of Syon were soon among the richest and most important of late-medieval religious houses. Sheen's foundation charter was issued in 1414, and the monastery was probably functionally complete by 1417 when the General Chapter of the order recognised John Widrington as its first prior.[120]

The reclusory at Sheen dates from the monastery's earliest days. It was founded by Henry in 1417. The recluse was to be a priest and, in order 'that he and his successors might be provided with suitable food and clothing and a sufficient habitation and so be more free for orisons and divine praises and holy contemplation', maintenance for himself and two servants was to come from the monastery, which was also responsible for repairs to the reclusory. Rents of 20 marks per annum were assigned to meet this requirement in perpetuity.[121] The reclusory must have been a quite substantial building. In 1423–4, 436 lb of lead was brought from the demolished royal manor at Sutton in Chiswick for its roof.[122] Some time after the cell's foundation a garden was added, for which the recluse paid a rent of 8d to the Prior.[123] The site is described in the endowment documents as 'within the precinct' ('infra procinctum') of the monastery, but its precise location is not given. It was presumably separate from the cells of the professed monks of the house ranged around the great cloister. John Cloake, who has reconstructed the plan of the charterhouse, identifies it with a building that in 1649 was being used as a dovecote, and is also shown on a map of the area made by Moses Glover in 1635. It straddles the wall that divides the spiritual core of the monastery, the great cloister and priory church, from the inner court, where the domestic services would have been housed (see

---

[120] The best account is John Cloake, 'The Charterhouse of Sheen', *Surrey Archaeological Collections* 71 (1977), pp. 145–98, at p. 150. See also his *Palaces and Parks of Richmond and Kew*, vol. 1: *The Palaces of Shene and Richmond* (Stroud, 1995).

[121] The licence granting the prior permission to alienate these rents, and rehearsing the terms of the foundation, is recorded in Hampshire Record Office A1/14 (Register of William Waynflete II), fol. 37r and *Calendar of the Patent Rolls A.D. 1416–1422* (London, 1911), p. 114. No foundation charter as such is known to survive. The date of foundation is given incorrectly as 1416 in 'House of Carthusian Monks: Priory of Sheen', in *A History of the County of Surrey: Volume 2*, ed. H. E. Malden, Victoria County History (London, 1967), pp. 89–94 at p. 91. There is no suggestion that the recluse was to be a professed Carthusian, as is assumed by a number of authors.

[122] Cloake, p. 150.

[123] Thompson, *Carthusian Order*, pp. 241–2, from the late fifteenth-century inventory of Sheen muniments in British Library MS Cotton Otho B. XIV, fol. 100r.

Plate 4).[124] If Cloake is correct in identifying the building as the reclusory, then its site is symbolically appropriate, its liminal position reflecting the anchorite's semi-religious, peri-monastic status.

The first recluse was appointed at the time of the foundation: he was a priest named John Kyngeslowe. We do not know much about him, but we do know that he bequeathed a copy of *The Chastising of God's Children* to the priory library.[125] An important discussion of the discernment of visions and revelations, as well as other spiritual matters, the *Chastising* is notable for its use of continental writers including Alphonse of Pecha and, especially, Ruusbroec. Though adventurous in this respect, it exhibits a nervousness of visions that can be paralleled in the *Speculum*.

Subsequent occupants of the site seem to have shared these bookish interests. John Dygon became the fifth Sheen recluse in 1435. (That date implies that Kyngeslowe and three successors had come and gone within the reclusory's first eighteen years of existence: a fairly rapid turnover, perhaps suggesting that the cell was conferred only on maturer occupants.) Dygon had studied law at Oxford, was a bachelor of both canon and civil law by 1424, and held benefices in Salisbury diocese (where he had connections with the reformist circle around Bishop Robert Hallum) and later in London. Nineteen books now in the library of Magdalen College Oxford were either written by him or show signs of his ownership or use. A number contain preaching aids and other materials probably connected with his life before reclusion. Looking at these, Sheila Lindenbaum has noted an 'anti-heretical zeal and desire for spiritual purity' that makes Dygon very much of his time and milieu.[126] But there is also (as Ralph Hanna describes it) 'a heady group of texts on the solitary life', including the Latin translation of *Ancrene Wisse*, Walter Hilton's epistle *De Utilitate et Prerogativis Religionis*, an early Thomas a Kempis, and, in one particularly rich

---

[124] Cloake p. 175; the detail from Glover's map is Fig. 9 on p. 168.

[125] *The Chastising of God's Children and the Treatise of Perfection of the Sons of God*, ed. Joyce Bazire and Eric Colledge (Oxford, 1957), p. 8; N. R. Ker, *Medieval Libraries of Great Britain*, 2nd ed. (London, 1964), p. 305. A king's clerk of this name occurs in 1378, and was warden of the royal free chapel of St George by York Castle from 1382 until his resignation a year later (see *Calendar of the Close Rolls Preserved in the Public Records Office, A.D. 1377–1381* (London, 1914), p. 110; and for his resignation from York, *Calendar of the Patent Rolls A.D. 1381–1385* (London, 1897), p. 306), but after that he disappears. It is possible that, after a lifetime of unobtrusive royal service, the reclusory became his place of retirement (if he was already a priest in 1378 he would have been at least 63 in 1417); but the identification is far from certain.

[126] Sheila Lindenbaum, 'London after Arundel: Learned Rectors and the Strategies of Orthodox Reform', in *After Arundel: Religious Writing in Fifteenth-Century England*, ed. Vincent Gillespie and Kantik Ghosh (Turnhout, 2011), pp. 187–208 at p. 201.

volume, the Latin translation of Hilton's *Scale of Perfection*, *Walter's Rule*, and Petrarch's epistle *On the Solitary Life*. In these books, Hanna finds evidence of Dygon's 'apparent discovery and transmission of a sophisticated literature of the contemplative life'.[127]

A later recluse would probably also have appreciated such material. We do not know his name, but he too seems to have had good academic connections. In 1461–2 Hugh France, a fellow of Queen's College Oxford, gave British Library MS Harley 3820 to the reclusory. Alongside devotional works ascribed to Augustine and Bernard, the volume includes the *Stimulus Peccatoris* or *Meditations* of the fourteenth-century Cistercian William Rymington. The *Meditations* are written in the effusive Anselmian manner, and were often attributed to Rolle; they were addressed to 'quemdam monachum anachoritam', though we know even less of that original recipient than we do of their later reader.[128] We have already seen that they appeared alongside the *Speculum* in one of the lost manuscripts from Syon.

It could, then, have been for men such as these that the *Speculum* was intended – having been either written in the first instance for a particular Sheen recluse, or in some other way connected with the foundation of the reclusory in 1417. The internal evidence fits rather precisely with this hypothesis.

It will be necessary first to re-examine the arguments for dating the *Speculum* advanced by Livarius Oliger, the text's previous editor, who thought that it was a work of the fourteenth century.[129] He noted that it drew on some sources from the first half of the century, Nicholas of Lyra and (probably) Richard Rolle.[130] He also knew of the *Speculum*'s inclusion in the list of books taken by John Spalding to Hull Charterhouse, which at that time was believed to date from the fourteenth century.[131] He therefore felt able to date the text

---

[127] Ralph Hanna, 'John Dygon, Fifth Recluse of Sheen: His Career, Books and Acquaintance', in *Imagining the Book*, ed. Stephen Kelly and John J. Thompson (Turnhout, 2006), pp. 127–41; quotations from pp. 134 and 141.
[128] For Harley 3820, see the British Library online Catalogue of Illuminated Manuscripts at http://www.bl.uk/catalogues/illuminatedmanuscripts. The *Meditations* have been edited by Robert O'Brien, 'The "*Stimulus Peccatoris*" of William of Rymyngton', *Cîteaux: Commentarii Cistercienses* 16 (1965), pp. 278–304; the quotation is from p. 284. O'Brien made no use of Harley in his edition, which is based only on selected manuscripts. For Rymington, see the entry by Jeremy Catto in *ODNB*.
[129] See Oliger, pp. 36–40. In her edition Harley does not discuss the date of either the *Speculum* or the *Mirror for Recluses*.
[130] For Lyra, see note to II.i.60–1. The passage reminiscent of Rolle is discussed later in this Introduction.
[131] See above, p. xlviii and n. 103.

to the second half of the fourteenth century, further suggesting, tentatively, that its recommendation to the non-Latinate reader to carry out his devotional reading in French rules out a date after the Statute of Pleading of 1362 (which is taken for evidence that the language was no longer spoken in England by this date); and, with more confidence, that it must predate the Schism (which began with the election of the rival popes Urban VI and Clement VII in 1378) and the Wycliffite heresy (whose emergence Oliger dates to 1375–6), since he had not detected any echo of them in the treatise.[132]

The Spalding booklist is now known to date from around 1500 (see above), which rules it out as evidence for a *terminus ante quem* (the manuscripts **R** and **H** are both earlier than this). Oliger's invocation of the Statute of Pleading cannot stand up to current understanding of the continuing use of French in late-medieval England.[133] The questions of the Schism and Lollardy are, however, worth examining in more detail. Both are relevant to the dating of the *Speculum*, though not in the way that Oliger assumed.

In Part I the author discusses those anchorites who enter the vocation 'non primo & principaliter propter amorem Dei, sed propter uitam ducendam iuxta sue uoluntatis arbitrium' [nat fyrst ne principaly for þe loue of God, but for to leede her lyf aftir her lust]. Some, he says,

> fugiunt ab ordine suo tanquam perdicionis filii, uel aliquam exempcionem non sine consciencie scrupulo procurant, utputa quod sint 'capellani pape', uel 'episcopi nullatenses', & sic libere uacare valeant suis illecebris. (I.ii.13–16)
>
> [fleen fro her ordre as children of perdicion, & procuren and suen an exempcion or sum oþer liberte and þat nat withouten scripule or wem of conscience – as to be 'þe Popes chapleyns' or 'byscopes *nullatenses*' – þat þei mowe in þat wyse frely & wilfully entende to her unliefful lustys.]

The reference to 'Popes chapleyns' is significant.[134] Papal chaplains, properly speaking, served in the papal curia and received certain privileges and exemptions in return. From the fourteenth century, however, clerics could be made honorary papal chaplains, receiving the benefits of the position without being required to perform its duties. In particular, appointment as a papal chaplain exempted a professed religious from regular life and obedience. The

---

[132] 'Di cui non si percepisce nessuna eco nel trattato', p. 40.
[133] For which, see the work being done under the umbrella of the 'French of England' project, at www.fordham.edu/frenchofengland/.
[134] For comment on 'episcopi nullatenses' in this passage, see the Notes to the Texts.

Introduction   lix

proliferation – and, apparently, straightforward sale – of papal chaplaincies is particularly associated with the period of the Schism (which ended with the Council of Constance, convoked in 1415, and the consequent election of Martin V as pope in 1417). At least 326 papal chaplains were appointed in England between 1390 and 1415.[135] In 1395, the minister of the Franciscans in England, with royal support, complained that

> an increasing number of members of the order in that province, without licence of their superiors, go or send to the Roman court, and get themselves received as papal chaplains, abuse the immunities, liberties, and privileges thereof, despise the obedience and correction of their superiors, and run about through the world.[136]

The reference to papal chaplains thus points towards quite a precise timeframe. F. Donald Logan writes that 'The window of opportunity was open for about twenty-five years. It had opened abruptly in the late 1380s and closed just as abruptly in 1415.'[137] For the *Speculum*'s comments to have topical resonance, they must have been written during the period this 'window' was open, or within a few years of its closing.[138]

To turn to the question of Lollardy: Oliger is certainly right that Wycliffite heresy is absent from the *Speculum*, but it seems more likely that the author has set out to make this a conspicuous absence. The fastidious precision of his discussion of the Eucharist in Part III chapter ii reads like a point-by-point profession of orthodoxy: although in the sacrament (he says) Christ's flesh appears under the likeness of bread, and his blood as wine, flesh and blood are equally present in both kinds; when a host is broken, each part contains Christ in his entirety, and every crumb of each host contains Christ. Most crucially, the author unequivocally states that, after the words of consecration, although the accidents (*accidentia*) of the bread and wine – their colour, taste and mass – remain, their substances (*substancia*) are no longer present, having been replaced by the substance of Christ's body and blood ('nec est ibidem panis, nec vinum, nec ulla substancia nisi substancia corporis & sanguinis Iesu Christi', III.ii.102–4). This last engages specifically with the technical language of transubstantiation in order to restate the orthodox position that Wyclif,

---

[135] F. Donald Logan, *Runaway Religious in Medieval England* (Cambridge, 1996), p. 51.
[136] *Calendar of Entries in the Papal Registers Relating to Great Britain and Ireland, Papal Letters, Volume 4: A.D. 1362–1404*, ed. W. H. Bliss and J. A. Twemlow (London, 1902), p. 508.
[137] Logan, p. 54.
[138] Oliger noticed the potential of these comments for dating the *Speculum*, but his discussion (pp. 37–9) is inconclusive.

unable to accept the annihilation of the substance of the bread and wine, rejected. The question whether 'aftir þe sacringe of [the] sacrament þere dwelliþ substaunce of breed or nay?' quickly became a litmus test for Lollardy.[139] As if to underscore his point, the author lards the passage with explicitly credal language: 'Credere [...] debetis firmissime' (86); 'firmiter credere debet quilibet christianus' (112); 'hec omnia firma fide credenda sunt' (121).[140]

It is not difficult to see why an author writing in the second decade of the fifteenth century should take extra care to spell out the orthodoxy of his eucharistic doctrine. This is, of course, the period of the first wave of Lollard persecutions, and the beginnings of orthodoxy's attempts to reassert and reinvigorate itself. Key events include the statute *De Heretico Comburendo* of 1401; the framing of Arundel's *Constitutions* in 1407, and their publication in 1409; the composition and official approval of Nicholas Love's *Mirror of the Blessed Life of Jesus Christ* 'around the year 1410';[141] the burning of John Badby as a heretic under the statue in the same year; the crushing of the 'Oldcastle Rebellion' in 1414, and its leader's execution in 1417, the year that the Sheen reclusory was founded. The *Speculum* demonstrably belongs to this cultural moment.

Although it is only on the Eucharist that it engages directly with the language of doctrinal controversy, the *Speculum* is anxious about the potential for heterodoxy more generally. Writing earlier in III.ii on the dangers that can be incurred during meditation, the author worries what might happen if the recluse's thoughts stray into speculation on matters of doctrine: 'si intellectus erret in fide catholica, seu in articulis fidei ab ecclesia determinatis' (59–60) [ʒif þe vndirstandynge or reson inwardly erre in the feyth of Holy Cherche, or in þe artycles of the feyth determynyd by Holy Cherche]. The solution to such a possibility is uncompromisingly straightforward:

> Sed pro intellectus errore possibili prodest quod articuli fidei, qui continentur in Symbolo Apostolorum & in Symbolo Athanasii, plenius intelligantur, firmiter credantur & memorie commendetur, nec aliquis

---

[139] This formulation of it comes from the 'Testimony' of William Thorpe, purporting to recount Thorpe's examination by Archbishop Arundel in 1407. See *The Testimony of William Thorpe, Two Wycliffite Texts*, ed. Anne Hudson, EETS, orig. ser. 301 (1993), lines 1024–5 (p. 55; I have supplied the word 'the' for clarity). Thorpe, dismissing the question as 'scole-mater', refuses to reply, at least in the terms that Arundel requires.
[140] *Firmiter credimus* was the first canon of the Fourth Lateran Council (1215), which enunciated a form of belief that featured newly refined definitions of both the Trinity and the Eucharist (including, for the first time in such a context, the term transubstantiation).
[141] Nicholas Love. *The Mirror of the Blessed Life of Jesus Christ*, ed. Michael G. Sargent (Exeter, 2005), p. 7 (translated p. xv).

pertinens ad fidem disputetur uel aliter credatur quam prius, sine consilio theologi sapientis, sed credulitati sancte matris Ecclesie firmissime quilibet adhereat sine hesitacione, quamuis in quibusdam non habeat euidenciam racionis. Quia, secundum beatum Gregorium, 'Fides non habet meritum vbi humana racio prebet experimentum.' (53–9)

[But for the errour þat may be of vndirstondynge, it profiteth þat þe articles of þe feyth þat ben conteynyd in the Byleve of þe Apostles and in þe Byleve of Athanasie be fully vndirstonden, beleued stedefastly, and taken vnto memorie or mynde; and þat nothing þat longiþ to þe feyth be disputyd, ne be othirwise beleeuyd þan was byforn, withoute conseyl of a wys devyn. But euery man knytte hym stedefastly & myȝtyly, wiþoute hesitacion or doute, to þe byleve of oure modyr of Holy Cherche, þouȝ he haue nat in some articules euydence or tokne of reson. For, after þe wordes of Seynt Gregory, 'Feyth hath no meryt where mannes reson ȝeueth experyment or preef.']

Gregory's dictum was a conservative favourite. It is also used by Thomas Hoccleve in his scornful *Remonstrance against Oldcastle* (1415):

> Lete holy chirche medle of the doctryne
> Of Crystes lawes & of his byleeue,
> And lete alle othir folke ther-to enclyne,
> And of our feith noon argumentes meeue.
> For if we mighte our feith by reson preeue,
> We sholde no meryt of our feith haue.[142]

This is the attitude identified above all with Nicholas Love, who advises, 'When þou herest any sich þinge in byleue þat passeþ þi kyndly reson, trowe soþfastly þat it is soþ as holy chirch techeþ & go no ferþer'.[143]

Love here is discussing (or, as it turns out, refusing to discuss) the Trinity, and the *Speculum* similarly identifies the two areas of doctrine 'que omnem hominis intellectum longe transcendunt' [þat passen ful feer the intelligence or reson of euery man] (III.ii.70–1) as the mysteries of the Eucharist and the Trinity. In the latter, the author declares, using scholastic language that he uncompromisingly refuses to gloss, 'Pater & Filius & Spiritus Sanctus sunt

---

[142] *Hoccleve's Works: The Minor Poems*, ed. Frederick J. Furnivall and I. Gollancz, rev. Jerome Mitchell and A. I. Doyle, EETS extra ser. 61+73 (rev. ed., Oxford, 1970), lines 137–42.

[143] Ed. Sargent, p. 23, lines 37–9. Love also quotes the line from Gregory in the 'Treatise on the Sacrament' that he appends to the *Mirror*: see p. 227.

tres persone distincte, quarum nulla persona est alia, & tamen he tres persone sunt substancialiter vnus & idem Deus' [þe Fadir & Sone and Holy Goost ben þre persones distynct, of þe wyche noon ys otheres persone, and ȝyt nathelees þo þre persones ben substancialy oon & þe same God] (III.ii.71–4).[144] As he puts it in an earlier discussion, 'ita quodammodo in diuinitate sunt tres persone, et hii tres sunt substancialiter vnus & idem Deus' [ryȝth so lyk in a manere þer bien thre persones in the Godhede, and þo þre ben substancialy on and þe same God] (II.ii.31–2). In both places, however, the opportunity for doctrinal enquiry is passed over, the author instead swiftly taking refuge in bland affectivity: 'Iste igitur Deus trinus & vnus est ab homine diligendus, iuxta primum & maximum mandatum, ex toto corde, ex tota anima, ex tota mente & ex tota uirtute' [Þerfore this God that ys þre and oon ys to be louyd, aftir þe firste & grettest commaundement, of al þin herte, of al þi soule, of al þi mynde and of al thi vertu] (32–4).

In a manner that we have learnt to associate with Arundel's *Constitutions* and their aftermath, the *Speculum* repeatedly pushes its reader away from theological speculation and into affectivity. Whilst acknowledging that meditation can lead in some cases to 'ipsius Omnipotentis aliquali uisione et ineffabili consolacione' [a kind of vision of the Almighty himself and his ineffable comfort] (III.ii.12–13), the author catalogues its more usual effects as:

> Dei timorem peccatoribus incutit, eius amorem in tepidis & in indeuotis accendit, deuocionis lacrimas prouocat, laudes Dei multiplicat, generat odium peccati, & auget desiderium honeste uite, atque in celestibus mentem figit. (III.ii.4–7)

> [it strikes the fear of God into sinners, inflames the lukewarm and the impious with his love, provokes tears of devotion, increases God's praises, produces a hatred of sin, and increases the desire to live a virtuous life, and fixes the mind on heavenly things.]

Naturally, the most suitable object of meditation is the passion, and the author misses few opportunities to recommend such activity, the best example being a long and thoroughly representative passage in the affective mode in II.ii:

> Sed inter cetera maxime stimulat peccatorem ad cordis compunccionem, prouocat deuocionis lacrimas, mouet ad paciendum aspera propter amorem

---

[144] For the scholastic origins of this language, see the Notes to the Texts. The English phrasing is reminiscent of Love, who states that in the Trinity 'þo þre persones ben on substance & on god, & ȝit is þere none of þees persones oþer' (Sargent, 23/27–8). The resemblance is probably coincidental, though conceivably it might not be.

Dei, fortificat & confirmat ad resistendum singulis temptacionibus, frequens memoria gloriosissime passionis. (lines 65–9)

[But among alle oþer þinges ofte to remembre hertly on þe glorious passion of oure Lord Iesu moost prikkeþ and sterith þe synful man to compunccion of herte; it prouoketh a man to teres of deuocion, it sterith a man to suffre paciently scharpe þinges for þe loue of God, and strengtheth a man to withstonde alle temptacions.]

The narrative of Christ's passion is therefore, just as it is in Love's *Mirror*, affective and exemplary rather than analytical or speculative. The same qualities are emphasised in the recluses' choice of reading matter. They are encouraged to select from 'sacras litteras, sanctorum uitas, martirum passiones, deuotorum meditaciones' [holy literature, saints' lives, the passions of the martyrs, devout meditations] (II.iii.32–3); but in particular they should choose reading that, in their experience, 'tends most to increase [their] devotion' ('inter hec omnia, frequencius illud legas quod per experienciam tuam deuocionem magis accendere consueuit', 33–5). They should read, in other words, not to engage their intellects, but to stir up their affects. And similarly the lessons they are to draw from their reading are not doctrinal but moral:

> In leccione siquidem percipies quod semper, a mundi principio, superbi & impenitentes abiecti fuerunt a Deo finaliter & reprobati, contriti & humiles per penitenciam sunt saluati, iusti & pacientes penalia propter Deum eternaliter premiabantur, obedientes & in pugna spirituali contra temptaciones viriliter perseuerantes ad celestis glorie coronam immarcessibilem diuinitus sunt uocati. (II.iii.35–41)

> [By reading you will certainly see that, ever since the beginning of the world, the proud and impenitent have been cast out by God and finally condemned, the contrite and humble are saved by penitence, the just and those who suffer hardships on God's account have been given eternal reward, the obedient and those who have persevered courageously in the spiritual battle against temptations receive the divine call to an imperishable crown of heavenly glory.]

From the evidence of his own reading, the author seems to share with Arundel's *Constitutions* a suspicion of the *moderni*.[145] His most frequent

---

[145] Article 6 of the *Constitutions*, noting that 'a new way doth more frequently lead astray, than an old way', ordained 'that no book or treatise made by John Wickliff, or others whomsoever, about that time, or since, or hereafter to be made, be from henceforth read in schools, halls, hospitals, or other places whatsoever' in the province, unless it had first

references by an appreciable distance are to the Bible, which he mines for literal and historical examples, rather than allegorical narratives. His favourite *auctores* are the Fathers, above all Augustine and Gregory. The most recent authors to whom express citation is made are the twelfth-century Bernard and Ailred. When he uses a more modern author (Nicholas of Lyra's *Postilla*, completed 1331), he does so without identifying him.[146] And his fullest account of a mystical *excessus* comes not from one of the English or continental contemplative authors of the thirteenth or fourteenth centuries, but in an anecdote borrowed from Ailred.[147]

There is, however, at least one allusion to an English 'mystic', though he goes unnamed. In Part IV, the author considers the rewards that recluses might receive in this life. There are some, he says

> (vel saltem fuerunt) quibus legentibus, orantibus siue meditantibus velut inestimabilis odoris suauitas, omnium possibilium specierum fragrancia exsuperans, per nares influebat, atque per os infundebatur quasi celestis manna dulcedo, omne delectamentum in se habens; que, ad interiora tam anime quam corporis profluens, utrumque homines tam interiorem quam exteriorem inenerrabili dulcore perfudit, quadamque suaui iocunditate & iocunda suauitate arras celestis glorie contulit pregustandas. Hos autem omnes non extra corpora raptos, sed in corporibus, estimo talem consolacionem diuinitus habuisse. (IV.i.77–86)

> [(or at least there were) into whose noses, while they were reading, praying or in meditation, there streamed a sort of immeasurably sweet odour, surpassing all possible varieties of fragrance, and a sweetness like the manna of heaven, holding all delights within it, was poured into their mouth; and, flowing deep into the soul and the body, it filled both the inner man and the outer with an indescribable sweetness, and in sweet joy and joyful sweetness allowed them to experience a foretaste of heavenly glory.]

---

note 145 continued been examined and approved. Quoted by Nicholas Watson, 'Censorship and Cultural Change in Late-Medieval England: Vernacular Theology, the Oxford Translation Debate, and Arundel's Constitutions of 1409', *Speculum* 70 (1995), pp. 822–64, at p. 827 n. 13. A preference for more traditional *auctores* was, however, part of a broader shift in the intellectual climate of late-medieval Europe. See Jeremy Catto, 'After Arundel: The Closing or the Opening of the English Mind?', in *After Arundel*, ed. Gillespie and Ghosh, pp. 43–54, at pp. 45–7. Oliger has a consideration of the *Speculum*'s sources, pp. 33–6.

[146] See II.i.60–1. His reference to the 'glossa' obscures the fact that he is using Lyra, rather than the older *Glossa ordinaria*. As it happens, the material he has taken from the *Postilla* is thoroughly traditional.

[147] See IV.i.87–94.

This sounds like nothing so much as Richard Rolle's *dulcor*, and the *Speculum*'s immediately succeeding words of caution chime exactly with the usual orthodox response to Rolle's enthusiastic promotion of his experiences:

> Hos autem omnes non extra corpora raptos, sed in corporibus estimo talem consolacionem diuinitus habuisse. (85–6)
>
> [But I think that all these people had such divine comforts in their bodies, not ravished out of their bodies.]¹⁴⁸

All this seems to point unerringly to 'the constrained circumstances under which fifteenth-century theology was composed'.¹⁴⁹ Just about all the discussion of this period hitherto, however, has focused on the constraints placed upon theological writing *in English*, and therefore open to the laity. But in the Latin *Speculum*, written for a priest-anchorite, the vernacular is not at issue. Rather, perhaps, it is the recluse's ambiguous location in the 'semi-religious' grey area between clergy and laity, professed and secular, that has led to some of the same anxieties, and similar responses to those anxieties, that we see in the domain of 'vernacular theology'. It may be sufficient explanation to suggest that a text written (as the *Speculum* seems to have been) in the eye of the anti-Lollard storm – and for readers dwelling within a stone's throw of a royal palace – might be expected to show an exaggerated level of nervousness over such matters, and to exercise self-censorship where perhaps none was needed.

But there does seem to have been some concerted attention directed at the semi-religious vocations in this period, of an intensity that looks out of proportion to their numerical significance and that still awaits full analysis and explanation. Considerable efforts seem to have been initiated to regularise hermits, whose lives had always been more unstructured than those of

---

¹⁴⁸ Hilton, the *Cloud*-author and the Carthusian against whom Thomas Basset wrote his *Defensorium* all suggest Rolle's sensations of *calor*, *dulcor* and *canor* were physical rather than spiritual. For a useful summary, see Michael Sargent, 'Contemporary Criticism of Richard Rolle' in *Kartäusermystik und -mystiker*, i.160–205, esp. pp. 177–80 and 184. Just before this evocation of Rollean *dulcor*, the author alludes to another variety of mystical transport:

> Quidam enim, in deuotis precibus coram ymagine crucifixi, uel in meditacione sue gloriosissime passionis, tanta cordis dulcedine perfunduntur & tanta delectactione diuini amoris inebriantur, quod pro tocius mundi deliciis illo spirituali gaudio non carerent. (IV.i.70–4)

Perhaps it is fanciful to hear in this a reminiscence of Julian of Norwich's revelations, but if we know that the Short Text at least was in Carthusian hands pretty early on, the Amherst manuscript preserving a text that was written in 1413, while Julian was still alive, then it is not impossible.

¹⁴⁹ Watson, 'Censorship and Cultural Change', p. 852.

recluses, and not only in the obvious matter of stability.[150] Hermits and other semi-religious, and in particular anchorites, are a concern for Nicholas Love. In the little treatise on the active and contemplative lives that he inserts into his account of Jesus at the house of Martha and Mary, he expresses some reservations about those non-regular contemplatives who may not have been adequately prepared in the active life for their more advanced form of living:

> Many þer bene boþe men & women in þe state of contemplatif life, as specyaly ankeres & recluses or hermytes þat witen litel as in effecte trewly what contemplatif life is by defaut of exercise in actife life as it is before seide. And þerfore it is ful perilous & ful dredeful to be in astate of perfection & haue a name of holynes: as hauen specialy þees Recluses, bot þe lyuyng & þe gostly exercise of hem be acordyng þerto.[151]

The same point is made a few years later by William Lyndwood. He stipulates that before agreeing to enclose someone, a bishop should consider carefully her or his character:

> That is, whether the person is notoriously vicious, or virtuous. Also whether they are steadfast or easily changeable, for it is necessary for everyone who desires to live devoutly in Christ to be steadfast in adversity [...] Also whether they are perfect in the Active Life, and established in virtue, because someone less than perfect, or otherwise unsuited to the perfection of the Active Life, will not readily bring profit to himself or to others in the Contemplative Life. And so the Active Life is preparatory to the Contemplative Life; as Isidore says, 'The person who initially succeeds in the Active Life ascends from it to contemplation.' Therefore, so long as a man has not reached perfection in the Active Life, there can be within him nothing more than as it were the beginning of the Contemplative Life.[152]

This stricter line runs through everything that Lyndwood has to say about anchorites. He is glossing a statute that he identifies as thirteenth-century (presumably in good faith, though it is now thought to be spurious), which lays

---

[150] For a preliminary discussion, see my 'Langland and Hermits', *Yearbook of Langland Studies* 11 (1997), pp. 67–86. I have a book-length study of this process in preparation.
[151] Ed. Sargent, 119/24–31.
[152] '*Moribus. Sc.* an sit flagitiosus, vel virtuosus. Item an sit constans, vel ciro mutabilis. Nam omnibus in Christo pie vivere volentibus, necessaria est constantia in adversis [...] Item an sit in Vita Actiba perfectus, & virtuose confirmatus, quia minus perfectus, vel alias indispositus ad perfectionem Vitae Activae, non est de facili, nec sibi, nec aliis profectus allaturus in Vita Contemplativa. Est namque Vita Activa dispositiva ad Contemplativam: unde dicit *Isid. de Summo bono*. qui prius in Vita Activa proficit, inde ad Contemplationem

down that no-one should be enclosed without the specific licence of the local diocesan bishop, who shall first have considered the 'location, the character and status of the people, and how they will be maintained'.[153] These kinds of preliminary questions are also given prominence in a newly revised and expanded version of the order for the enclosing of anchorites that was produced under the auspices of Archbishop Henry Chichele (who had succeeded Arundel in 1414), apparently as part of his project to establish the Use of Sarum as standard for the province of Canterbury.[154] His version of the enclosure rite is much the fullest and most detailed of those extant, and is notable in particular for the way in which it tries to approximate the anchoritic life to the regular religion of the monastic orders. It includes an important preamble that seems to be designed especially for someone charged with assessing the suitability of a candidate for enclosure. He is to examine the candidate,

> enquiring carefully whether he seeks this strict life out of good intentions or bad; and whether he desires to please God, or to gain material reward or people's praise; and also whether he has sufficient strength to fight with a constant mind against the tricks and blandishments of the wicked Enemy, and (as he wants and intends to do) effectively to spurn and despise the countless troubles of the world, and the various unreliable impulses that pertain to human fragility; and, as well as despising them, to resist every one of them with all his heart.[155]

The currency of these questions perhaps lies behind one of the most interesting

---

conscendit. Ideo quamdiu non pervenit homo ad perfectionem in Vita Activa, non potest esse in eo Vita Contemplativa, nisi secundum quandam inchoationem' (*Provinciale*, iii.20.2 at p. 214; my translation). See also above.

[153] Interestingly, under 'location' Lyndwood suggests that it is often better for an anchorite to be enclosed in an urban location, 'since a recluse's needs can more easily be looked after in a town, where there are lots of people, than in the country, where there are few, and the greater part of them poor people who are unable to help them' (*ibid.*). On this at least he is less conservative (or more realistic) than the *Speculum*, which is suspicious of urban anchorites, and appears to believe that the proper place for solitaries is the desert. See I.ii.47–52.

[154] See my 'Rites of Enclosure: The English *Ordines* for the Enclosing of Anchorites, s.xii–s.xvi', *Traditio* 67 (2012), pp. 145–234.

[155] 'requirens sollicite vtrum bona intensione vel mala hanc strictam appetit vitam; & vtrum si Deo placere, aut lucrum siue laudem humanam acquirere, affectat; ac eciam si vires eius in constancia mentis suppetant contra maligni hostis versucias & incitamenta militare, atque ut velit & perficere proponat huius mundi innumerabiles molestias, ac fragilitatis humane motus lubricos & diuersos, effectualiter spernere & calcare, & calcando singulis cordialiter resistere.' 'Rites of Enclosure', pp. 182–3.

passages in the *Speculum*: the detailed consideration in Part I of the reasons (both commendable and specious) that people seek the anchoritic life, and especially the thoughtful treatment of discernment and *probatio* in I.iii, which includes provision for a formal period of probation before the final, irrevocable vow is made.

A Mirror for Recluses

We do not know who translated the *Speculum* into English as *A Mirror for Recluses*, or when or where the translation was done, or for whom it was intended.[156] Translation into the vernacular suggests that the new reader was either a lay male anchorite or a woman. As we have seen, some examples of the former are known, though the majority of male anchorites were priests.[157] Textual evidence, however, demonstrates that the *Speculum* was translated into English in order to adapt it for a female readership. Nonetheless, the full extent of that adaptation remains unclear.

The Latin *Speculum* addresses its readers throughout as *inclusi*, singular *inclusus*, a masculine form for a way of life that (at least as it is imagined in this text) will be pursued by men. The *Mirror* almost always renders the Latin *inclusus* with ME *recluse*, a noun used for both genders. In one passage, however, the translator uses the alternative term, *anker/ankress*, which does distinguish gender. Perhaps not irrelevantly, the context is a discussion of sin, and the sins in question are the two that the Middle Ages most routinely gendered feminine: the 'sins of the tongue' – including 'songes & karoles of love, foul & vnclene speches, streyve, accusacions, blamynges; wordes of detraccion or bacbytynge; wordes of envye, pride, auarice, glosynges and lesynges' (ME I.iv.36–8) – and lechery. Solitaries are protected from most species of lechery by virtue of their solitude, of course: 'Swych ancres & ankeresses ben more sekyrly conseruyd & kept from þe peryls of þe bodyly wyt of touchynge, by þe which entriþ þe lust of lecherie in sondry wyse.' And then, more particularly, 'Alle suych spices of lecherie ben fer from an ancresse' (ME I.iv.52–4, 57–8).[158] Just before this, the

---

[156] Several modern sources include a reference to a second reclusory at Sheen, occupied by a female recluse (see e.g. Warren, *Anchorites and their Patrons*, p. 182 n. 98). She sounds like a possible recipient, but unfortunately the reference is a 'ghost', based on Coxe's misreading of the donation notice of Oxford, Magdalen College, MS 77: the book was given *by* its female donor *to* the recluse of Sheen (who was John Dygon). See Coxe, 'Catalogus codicum MSS. Collegii B. Mariae Magdalenae', p. 44, in *Catalogus*, vol. II.
[157] See above, p. xxix.
[158] The Latin here reads 'Tales enim securius conseruantur a periculis sensus tactus, in quo contingit uoluptas uenerea [...] Ab omnibus huiusmodi luxurie speciebus longe subtrahitur inclusus' (I.iv 41–5).

Speculum argues that the sins of the tongue are most effectually avoided by somone who 'a cunctis mundi uanitatibus elongatur' [kepith hym afeer from alle worldly vanytes], primarily (of course) recluses: 'prout patet euidencius de inclusis viuentibus sicut debent'.[159] In a rare expansion of its source, the *Mirror* renders this as follows:

> as yt schewith by euydence & tokne of recluses – & naamly of anchoresses – þat bien more streytly closed þan oþer religious men & wommen enclosed, enclosyd in her houses be leue of her souereyns, and in alle tymes at her souereyns wyl. (ME 48–51)

The *Mirror* is addressing itself, therefore, specifically ('naamly') to the particular circumstances of anchoresses.[160]

Whether or not these minor textual changes are part of a much larger programme of adaptation of the *Speculum* to a female readership is, due to the unfortunate state of the only extant manuscript, impossible to say. A quick comparison of the *Mirror* with the *Speculum* seems to reveal a definite pattern. Although the Prologue is missing, the whole of Part I (on the various reasons people decide to become recluses) is included. In Part II, which examines the practice of the contemplative life, the discussions of prayer and meditation are present, but reading is absent. Similarly in Part III's further consideration of these topics, prayer and meditation are there, but reading is not. And Part IV, which anticipates the possibility of mystical rapture, and the bodily and spiritual joys of heaven, is also missing. It looks like a case of a text being 'dumbed down', or perhaps censored, for a female audience better suited to listening than reading for themselves, and whose susceptibility to visions and unschooled speculation were causes for clerical concern. But here codicology urges caution. The manuscript has a number of lacunae. In particular, a quire has been lost after the end of the fourth quire (fol. 30v), towards the end of II.ii (on meditation). A close translation of *Speculum* II.iii, the discussion of reading, would have occupied about one quire in H, which resumes a little way into the next chapter, III.i. Similarly, the manuscript currently ends at the foot of fol. 37v, the text breaking off towards the end of III.ii. Whether III.iii, with its discussion of reading, once followed there is now no way of telling, and Part IV might (or might not) also have been included. The *Speculum*'s Prologue, which outlines the author's fourfold division of his topic, ought to have given an indication whether or not Part IV was included in the *Mirror*, but it too has been lost.

---

[159] 'As is shown very clearly by those recluses who live as they should' (I.iv.39–40).
[160] Harley interprets this passage differently: see the Notes to the Texts for details.

If the chapters on reading were once included in the *Mirror*, they would have required some modification. The reference in II.iii to the 'requirements of divine service' ('diuini seruicii debitum' (II.iii.1)) would not have been relevant to a female reader. Similarly the invitation to read holy scripture on the one hand, and on the other the suggestion that a non-Latinate reader might read instead in the vernacular (II.iii.78–80), would both seem equally out of place in the new context. Likewise, the recommendation discussed at the beginning of this section, that manual work should consist in the copying of manuscript books, would probably not have been made. That at least the first of the two treatments of reading was originally included, but that it had undergone some alteration, is suggested by the opening of Part II, which establishes the traditional *distinctio* of the contemplative life into the triad of prayer, meditation and reading:

> uocati estis ad exercicium uite contemplatiue, que in tribus precipue consistit, videlicet in oracione feruida, in meditacione deuota, & in edificatoria leccione. (2–4)

In the English *Mirror*, however, the third of these terms has been significantly altered:[161]

> For ȝe ben callyd to þe exercise or vsage of contemplatyf lyf which standiþ namly in þre thinges, þat is to seyn in feruent preiere, in deuout meditacion, and in edificatyf *spekynge, þat is to sey in speche strecchinge vnto vertu*. (ME lines 2–6, emphasis added)

Speaking, not reading, is what women do, and insofar as they engage with the literature – 'speche strecchinge vnto vertu' need not involve books at all – they engage with it by hearing it read, or having it mediated it to them by a clerical reader.

Readers of the Mirror
The only identified medieval owner of the *Mirror* was a man. John Trus, as we have seen, gave H to Browne's Hospital in Stamford, probably between 1489 and 1494. The donation notice identifies him as a 'prest in the seyd beydhowse' having formerly ('sum-tyme') been chaplain to William Browne, the hospital's eponymous founder, who died in 1489. Nothing else is known of Trus.[162]

---

[161] The opening of Part III is missing from H, as part of the lacuna that means it also lacks II.iii, so we are not able to see whether the translator dealt similarly with its statement that recluses are called 'ad iugiter orandum, meditandum, legendum, uel aliquid honestum manibus operandum' (III.i.3–4).
[162] Alan Rogers suggests that Trus might be an alias for John Taillour, who was a clerk in Browne's household in 1488 and warden of his hospital 1497–1503; he died c. 1524. As

Browne and his hospital, on the other hand, are very well documented. William Browne was the most prominent figure in fifteenth-century Stamford.[163] A wool merchant and member of the Staple of Calais, he was still remembered in Leland's time as 'a marchant of a very wonderful richenesse'.[164] He also owned substantial property in Stamford and surrounding counties. He was Alderman (that is, mayor) of Stamford perhaps already in 1435 and in five subsequent years between 1444 and 1470. He and his wife founded their hospital, for two priests and twelve paupers, in what is now Broad Street in the northern part of the town, adjoining their own home, in 1475.[165] It was refounded (after a drawn-out process) and endowed in perpetuity in 1494, after William and Margaret Browne had both died in 1489, and building was complete by 1497. It still stands, and architecturally is reckoned 'one of the best medieval hospitals in England'.[166]

William Browne's spirituality seems to have been of an energetic, practical kind.[167] In addition to founding his hospital, he rebuilt his parish church of All Saints Stamford, and was active in the town's gilds of Corpus Christi and St Mary, All Saints, Holy Trinity, and St Katherine, becoming alderman of each of them. He also joined the prestigious gild of Corpus Christi at Boston, serving as its alderman in 1481. He seems to have had little time for (and he bequeathed no money to) either the friars or the monastic orders, though both had a significant presence in Stamford. His will contains only one bequest hinting at a more rarefied spirituality, but it is one that should engage our attention. He left a substantial gift of 20s 'to the ancresse in Staunford', and a further 20s every year for ten years following his death, 'if eny be there closid'.[168]

---

noted above, the donation notice is in Taillour's hand. If Trus and Taillour are the same person, the date of donation could be as late as 1524. My thanks to Alan Rogers for sharing his unpublished note on Trus/Taillour with me.
[163] See the entry by Alan Rogers in *ODNB*, and more fully his *Noble Merchant: William Browne (c1410–1489) and Stamford in the Fifteenth Century* (Bury St Edmunds, 2012).
[164] *The Itinerary of John Leland in or about the Years 1535–1543*, ed. Lucy Toulmin Smith, 5 vols (London, 1906–10), iv.89.
[165] The following account is based on Rogers, *Noble Merchant*, pp. 242–53; and Nick Hill and Alan Rogers, *Gild, Hospital and Alderman: New Light on the Founding of Browne's Hospital, Stamford 1475 to 1509* (Bury St Edmunds, 2013).
[166] Nikolaus Pevsner, *Lincolnshire*, rev. John Harris and Nicholas Antram (New Haven CT, 2002), p. 697. See further *The Town of Stamford*, Royal Commission on the Historical Monuments of England (London, 1977), pp. 37–42.
[167] Compare Rogers, *Noble Merchant*, pp. 225–8.
[168] C. W. Foster, 'Lincolnshire Wills Proved in the Prerogative Court of Canterbury 1471–1490', *Associated Architectural Societies' Reports* 41 (1932–3), pp. 61–114 and 179–218, at p. 206.

lxxii *Speculum Inclusorum / A Mirror for Recluses*

There had been an anchoress in Stamford since at least the 1380s. The cell was attached to the church of St Paul, which stood just within the walls in the north-east corner of the town. In 1382 the anchorite at the church of St Paul was one of five to receive a bequest from Geoffrey le Scrope, Canon of Lincoln Cathedral.[169] In 1398 Elena Empingham was enclosed 'in a chamber in the north part of the church of St Paul'.[170] In 1435 she was succeeded by Emmota Tong of Bourne.[171] We have no record of the enclosure of the anchorite remembered by Browne in his will. She does appear, however, in the records of the gild of St Katherine whose operations were based at St Paul's.[172] The gild had been refounded by Browne in 1480 and he proceeded to reinvigorate it, recruiting new members and organising the building of a new gildhall. An inventory of the 'stock and jewels' of the gild taken in 1480 included 'a grete maser of Sylver and gilt with a coveryng of the gift of the Ancoryce'.[173] She was probably the Margaret Jeralde who appears in the list of existing members that year, and was doubtless kin to the William Jerald who had been rector of St Paul's 1458–64.[174] In subsequent years the anchoress is unnamed, appearing only as 'Domina anachorita'. She paid her annual subscription of 2d each year from 1482 (the first year for which a list is provided) until 1491, but she is absent from the list for 1492.

A plausible conjecture might be that Trus acted as confessor to the anchoress until her death in 1491–2, whereupon he gave the copy of the *Mirror for Recluses* that they had used together to the hospital founded by their common patron, William Browne.

Much more than the Sheen recluse for whom the *Speculum* was written, therefore, this probable reader of the *Mirror* conforms to the typical late-medieval anchorite: a woman, attached to a parish church in an urban location, and enmeshed in the social networks of the local community. Further evidence for such relationships are forthcoming for the Stamford anchorites of succeeding years, for Margaret Jeralde was not the last anchoress in the town.

---

[169] C. W. Foster, ed., *Lincoln Wills Registered in the District Probate Registry at Lincoln, Volume I: 1271–1526*, Lincoln Record Society 5 (1914), p. 17.
[170] Lincolnshire Archives Office, Episcopal Register XIII (Register of Henry Beaufort), fol. 5v. She was also granted a licence to choose a confessor in 1405. See *Register of Bishop Philip Repingdon, 1405–1419*, vol. 1, ed. M. Archer, Lincolnshire Record Society 57 (1963), p. 51.
[171] Lincolnshire Archives Office, Episcopal Register XVII (Register of William Gray), fol. 187v.
[172] See *The Act Book of St Katherine's Gild, Stamford, 1480–1534*, ed. Alan Rogers (Bury St Edmunds, 2011).
[173] Rogers, *Act Book*, pp. 32–3. A *mazer* is a bowl or goblet.
[174] See the discussion by Rogers, *Act Book*, p. 11.

Introduction lxxiii

In 1496, Agnes Leche, anchorite, was admitted into the gild of St Katherine. A member of a prominent family in Stamford and Grantham, she had evidently succeeded Margaret Jeralde as the anchorite at St Paul's. She received several bequests during the 1520s and '30s and was still paying her annual contribution to the gild in 1534 when the extant accounts run out: an enclosure of at least thirty-eight years.[175] She also came to the attention of Margaret Beaufort, the mother of King Henry VII who, following her vow of chastity in 1499, had taken up residence at her palace of Collyweston, some three miles south-west of Stamford.[176] Beaufort became a member of the gild in 1502. In 1505 she paid 'for makyng of a newe dore through þe towne wall in Stauneford at þe bake sid of þe […] ancresse adioynyng to þe church of seynt Poule'.[177] This was probably to allow her to make private visits to the anchorite, just as she had papal dispensation to enter the houses of enclosed monastic orders and to converse and dine with the religious there, a right she exercised most notably at Syon Abbey.[178] It may have been the anchorite of St Paul's that she visited later that year bearing gifts of apples and wine.[179] By this date, however, she was also involved with a second Stamford anchoress, Margaret White, who was enclosed at the priory of St Michael in Stamford Baron (the part of the town south of the River Welland). White was another member of the Katherine gild, having joined in 1504.[180] Though already described as 'anchorita' in the accounts, she must have been serving a probationary year, because it was not until 1505 that Beaufort oversaw the building of her reclusory, and made money gifts at her profession on 7 December. In her will of 1508 she assigned lands to provide an endowment for life for White and 'an honest womann to attend vpon hir during hir life'.[181] Margaret White was still living in 1527 (after which a lacuna in the accounts of the Katherine gild begins), but dead by 1531 (when they resume).

Had the dates fitted, it would have been tempting to construct a hypothetical narrative in which Margaret Beaufort – with her record of anchoritic friendships, associations with Syon and Sheen, and active involvement in the circulation

---

[175] Rogers, *Act Book*, pp. 11, 103. This paragraph is based on 'New Look', pp. 143–4.
[176] Michael K. Jones and Malcolm G. Underwood, *The King's Mother* (Cambridge, 1992), p. 153.
[177] Cambridge, St John's College Archives D 91.13, p. 105 (also at p. 98 in the same account).
[178] *The King's Mother*, p. 180.
[179] Cambridge, St John's College Archives D 91.20, p. 156.
[180] Rogers, *Act Book*, p. 144.
[181] Anon., *Collegium Divi Johannis Evangelistae, 1511–1911* (Cambridge, 1911), p. 116. She also made a bequest of 10s to each anchoress.

of devotional books – became the conduit by which the *Speculum* migrated from Latin to English, and from Sheen to Stamford. But as things stand, the route by which the *Mirror* (or, if the translation was done there, a copy of the original *Speculum*) ended up in Stamford is not known.

A Mirror for Recluses as translation

The *Mirror* is a very close translation of the *Speculum*, and usually an accurate one.[182] Mistakes and misconstructions are few (see notes to I.iv.74–5, I.v.15–19, I.v.33–35, III.ii.58–9), but so are the kind of alterations and expansions that might reflect a translator's reinterpretation of his source text for a new audience or a new purpose. A few such examples will, however, be discussed below.

Perhaps the most marked feature of the translator's practice is his use of doublets. Thus a quick scan of the thirty lines of the first chapter of Part I reveals ten examples where he has rendered a single Latin word with a pair of English terms. Often these have a glossing function, where a Latinism is coupled with a more accessible synonym. Into this category fall 'be [...] expedyent or speedful' for 'expediat' (10), 'motif and sterynge' for 'motiua' (20), 'ys conuenient and fittynge' for 'conuenit' (27), and perhaps 'caytifes & wrecches' for 'captiuorum' (12). In a few other cases, the doublet seems to be used where the translator is trying to capture the full range of meaning for a Latin word that has no ready English equivalent: thus 'ordeigne and purueye' for 'prepara' (14), 'drawen and gadrid' for 'colligitur' (19), 'cause and entencion' for 'facultas' (21). But in others the doublet is composed of simple synonyms, and its use seems to be no more than a matter of habit: 'defautes or blames' for 'culpis' (23), 'worschip and preysynge' for 'laudibus' (25), and probably 'hyld and pour out' for 'effunde' (15).[183] The best example of this tendency comes in the *Mirror*'s characteristic rendition of the work's *thema*, 'Videte uocacionem vestram', which becomes 'Seeth now ȝoure callynge and clepynge' (I.ii.82) or 'Byholdeþ & seeþ ȝoure callynge' (I.iv.76–7).

Related to the doublets are some periphrastic expansions that also have a glossarial function. Thus a reference to 'primis parentibus' (II.ii.153) is provided in the *Mirror* with an addition that identifies those parents as Adam and Eve, and 'Oracio Dominica' (II.i.47) becomes 'þe Dominical preiere, þat is to seyn þe *Pater Noster*'. In II.i the scholastic terms 'actualis deuocio' (16) and 'habitualis deuocio' (17) are glossed, whilst in the succeeding chapter

---

[182] Harley has a discussion of the *Mirror* as translation, broadly in agreement with the present analysis, pp. xiii–xvi.
[183] It is possible that 'pour out' glosses 'hyld', but the latter is not (as in the cases listed above) a Latinism.

'insensibiles creature' (II.ii.96) are explained as 'þat is to seyn the creatures þat hadde no felynge ne lyf'. Other terms given similar glossarial attention are 'superfluum' (III.i.89), 'prudencia' (III.ii.28) and 'communio' (III.ii.84). At II.i.71 'ineffabilem glorie beatitudinem' becomes 'blisful glorie endelees, which ys so excellent and so passynge þat no tonge can telle or expresse yt', and the derived adverb 'ineffabiliter' is similarly glossed at II.ii.142. In one case, the translator glosses his own translation, 'ualitudine corporis redeunte' (I.iii.106) becoming 'whan it is revigured – þat is to seyn, þat it haþ cauȝt agayn his strengþe and is restored to helþe'.

The Middle English text is less careful than the Latin in giving scriptural references, usually omitting any precise citations altogether (see I.ii.80–1, I.iii.4, and passim). This would fit with a female reader who is not expected to have access to the text of scripture itself. It may have been with such a relatively unsophisticated reader in mind that the translator felt it necessary to provide the correct answers ('Yis forsoþe' and 'ȝys') for the rhetorical questions at II.ii.44–51 and III.ii.95–7. And anti-feminist assumptions no doubt lie behind the addition, to the list of risks that arise from having visitors, of the possibility that they might 'schewen gay & neyce aparail and cloþis in her syȝt' (ME I.ii.57–8).

Perhaps also connected with the change to a female audience is a group of additions and alterations that, though minor in themselves, have the effect of raising the devotional temperature of the treatise. Thus in I.ii a reference to 'Dei nostri' (61) becomes 'oure Lord Iesu'; Christ is personalised and humanised with an additional 'Iesu' at II.ii.124, and 'gloriosissime passionis' at II.ii.69 becomes 'þe glorious passion of oure Lord Iesu'. Earlier in the same chapter, Latin 'Creatorem' (44) becomes 'her Lord and hir Creatour and Maker', and a catalogue of the great deeds done by God for humankind's benefit is prefaced with the impassioned addition of 'Lo þou man, lo' (cf. 16).

There are only two significant passages that add anything of substance to the text as it appears in the *Speculum*, rather than seeking to render it as clearly and accurately as possible. One of these similarly reflects the change in the gender of the intended reader: the passage in I.iv identifying her specifically as an anchoress that has been discussed above. The other passage comes in I.ii where, in the middle of a list of the things that are not appropriate for recluses to get involved with, the *Speculum* includes 'iuuenes educare' (line 64). The *Mirror*, however, tempers this: its reader should not 'bringe forth ȝoong folk *custummably as in multitude or for hyre*' (emphasis added). One or two students might occasionally be permissible, therefore. Next, recluses are forbidden to concern themselves 'de exhibicione consanguineorum uel amicorum sollicitudinem gerere'. The *Mirror* translates this faithfully, but then immediately qualifies it:

> But ȝif yt happe þat a vertuos persone, be yt cosyn or ellis, þoruȝ infortune of þe world be driuen to scharp meschief or pouert and hath but smal or no confort of socour or relief, thanne ys yt good and meritorie to releue suych a person. And ȝet ȝe be more hoolden to releue ȝour blood – ȝif he be vertuous – þan anoþer strange persone, þouȝ it be vertuous & meritorie to releue hem bothe. (ME I.ii.73–9)

On both counts, one wonders whether the translator had a particular recluse and her circumstances in mind. But of her identity and those particular circumstances we remain ignorant.

This edition

The Latin *Speculum* and Middle English *Mirror* are printed in parallel. Each chapter begins a new page and, to facilitate comparison further, paragraphing is co-ordinated across the two texts. It is in the nature of prose texts, and translation from Latin into English, however, that any line-by-line correspondence will be coincidental.

As already noted, the extant copy of the *Mirror* lacks material corresponding to the *Speculum*'s Prologue and the opening of I.i, II.iii and part of III.i, and from III.iii to the end of the treatise. For this material I have provided a modern English translation of the Latin, printed in italic. The translation aims to be close to the Latin (as the Middle English is), though I have allowed myself some freedom in the translation of Latin idioms such as absolutes, participial and adjectival phrases, impersonal constructions, and so on. For passages of scripture I have normally reproduced the Douai translation.

The edition of the Latin *Speculum* is based on **R**, with variants from **J**; the English *Mirror* is edited from **H**, its unique manuscript. Capitalisation, word-division, punctuation and paragraphing are editorial and follow modern practice. Nouns, but not pronouns, unambiguously designating the Deity have been capitalised. The orthography is that of the manuscripts, except that initial *ff* is transcribed as *F* or *f* following modern usage; long and short *i* are both transcribed as *i*; in the Middle English, ȝ and *z* are distinguished though in H the same symbol is used for both.

Abbreviations are expanded silently, except that abbreviated references to books of the Bible are left in their abbreviated form. Ampersands and numerals are left as such. In cases of ambiguity, the expansion of an abbreviation is made with reference to unabbreviated forms elsewhere in the text, or prevailing usage in analogous forms. Thus in the Latin *sed* is preferred to *set*, for example, *uel* to *vel*, and *tanquam* to *tamquam*. In the English, w^t is expanded as *with*, and $þ^u$ as *þou*. The common mark of abbreviation for *-is* or *-es* is expanded as *-es*, which is found more frequently in unabbreviated forms than either *-is* or *-ys*, though both alternatives also occur. A couple of arbitrary decisions have had to be made. With no unabbreviated forms to guide the expansion of the suspension in Latin *-cu(m)que/-cu(n)que*, I have preferred the latter; and in both texts, *Ihu* (which is never spelt out in full) is expanded as *Iesu*. The common mark of abbreviation for *-er* is handled differently in the two texts. In the *Speculum*, it is expanded as *-er*, *-ar* or *-or* following usual Latin orthography. In the *Mirror*, since Middle English orthography is less settled, the mark is always *-er*: so for example *temp(er)el*, *m(er)ueyllously*. Finally, in the Middle English, flourishes and hairlines on letters in word-final position are treated as otiose, except for a recurved final *-r* which is interpreted as *-re*.

The texts are emended sparingly. R appears to be a better witness to the Latin than H to the Middle English, and so the latter tends to be emended more heavily than the former. Emendations are enclosed in square brackets and the original reading of the manuscript is given in the apparatus, which appears at the end of the texts. Letters and words omitted in the manuscript are likewise supplied between square brackets, but in such cases the manuscript reading is not normally included in the apparatus. Errors of this kind occur more frequently in the *Mirror* than the *Speculum*. I have also occasionally emended viable readings in H where a palaeographically plausible alternative makes for a better rendition of the Latin.

In addition to providing information on emendations, the apparatus to the *Speculum* gives substantive variants from J. It excludes transpositions, dittographies and the fairly frequent 'false starts' where the scribe has copied the first few letters of a (typically longer) word, then aborted it without cancelling what he has written, before copying the complete word. Most morphological variants are also excluded. As noted above, the majority of these are clear errors and the resultant reading of J is ungrammatical. They are, however, included if they are grammatically viable and have a bearing on the sense of a passage (for example, the use of a different tense). Readings of J which appear to be merely corruptions of R's reading (for example by the omission of several letters), and are not themselves recorded Latin words, are likewise excluded. The apparatus also gives brief details of corrections to the base texts (**R** and **H**), but diplomatic details of J are not recorded unless they are material textually. The following abbreviations are used: '*om.*' means 'word(s) not present in specified manuscript'; '*add.*' means 'word(s) additionally present in specified manuscript, following the lemma'; '*ins.*' means 'word(s) added (typically above the line or on the margin) subsequent to the copying of the main text, though in the main text hand unless specified otherwise'. Marginalia and other annotations to the base texts are given not in the apparatus but in the Notes to the Texts. For H, these do not normally include references to the marginal *notae* that are relatively frequent throughout the text; these are, however, recorded in tabular form in an appendix.

The Middle English *Mirror* is provided with glosses on the page. Glossing is selective, and designed for the reader who already has some proficiency in Middle English. The meanings given are specific to the word in its present context, and do not necessarily represent the full range of a word's possible meanings as they would appear in a dictionary. Because (as noted above) the translator of the *Mirror* uses many doublets, it is often the case that a more obscure word is paired with a familiar one, so that in a sense the work of

Introduction lxxix

glossing has already been done by the translator. I have, however, glossed these notwithstanding, so that the nature of the doublet is made fully transparent; but I have not gone to great lengths to find synonyms for the glossed terms, preferring to put clarity first. Thus in 'deffendyd or forboden' (MEI.iv.28–9), for example, 'deffendyd' is glossed simply as 'forbidden'; and later in the same chapter the pair of doublets in 'as wiel naturel or kyndely as vnnaturel or vnkyndely' (I.iv.54–5) is treated similarly. Once a word has been glossed, further occurrences of it or closely-related forms within the same chapter are not glossed again.

Where the interpretation of a particular word or phrase requires more extended comment, a parenthetical (N) after the gloss directs the reader to the Notes to the Texts, where a discussion will be found. Such items of lexical interest in the *Mirror* include 'hyld' (ME I.i.16), 'wheþre' (ME I.i.21), 'entendynge' (ME I.v.5), 'nurce' (I.ii.66), 'wyttirly' (ME I.v.26), 'edificatyf' (II.i.5), 'nedes' (ME II.i.10), 'fect' (ME II.i.70), 'vndirstonde' (as a noun) (ME II.ii.30), 'stremees' (ME II.ii.104, and cf. II.ii.129 and III.i.45), 'diffyed' (ME III.ii.113). Finally, a small number of Latin words have also attracted lexical comment in the Notes to the Texts: 'simplex' (I.i.29), 'alumpni' (I.ii.60) and 'idem' (IV.i.48).

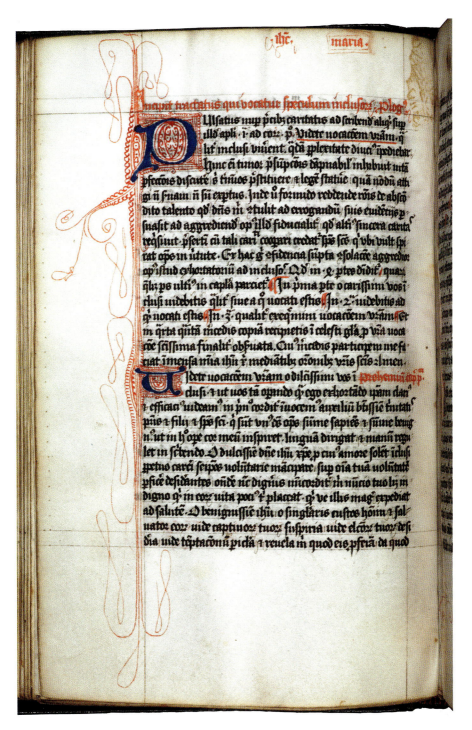

PLATE I   British Library, MS Royal 5 A v, fol. 40v. © British Library Board.

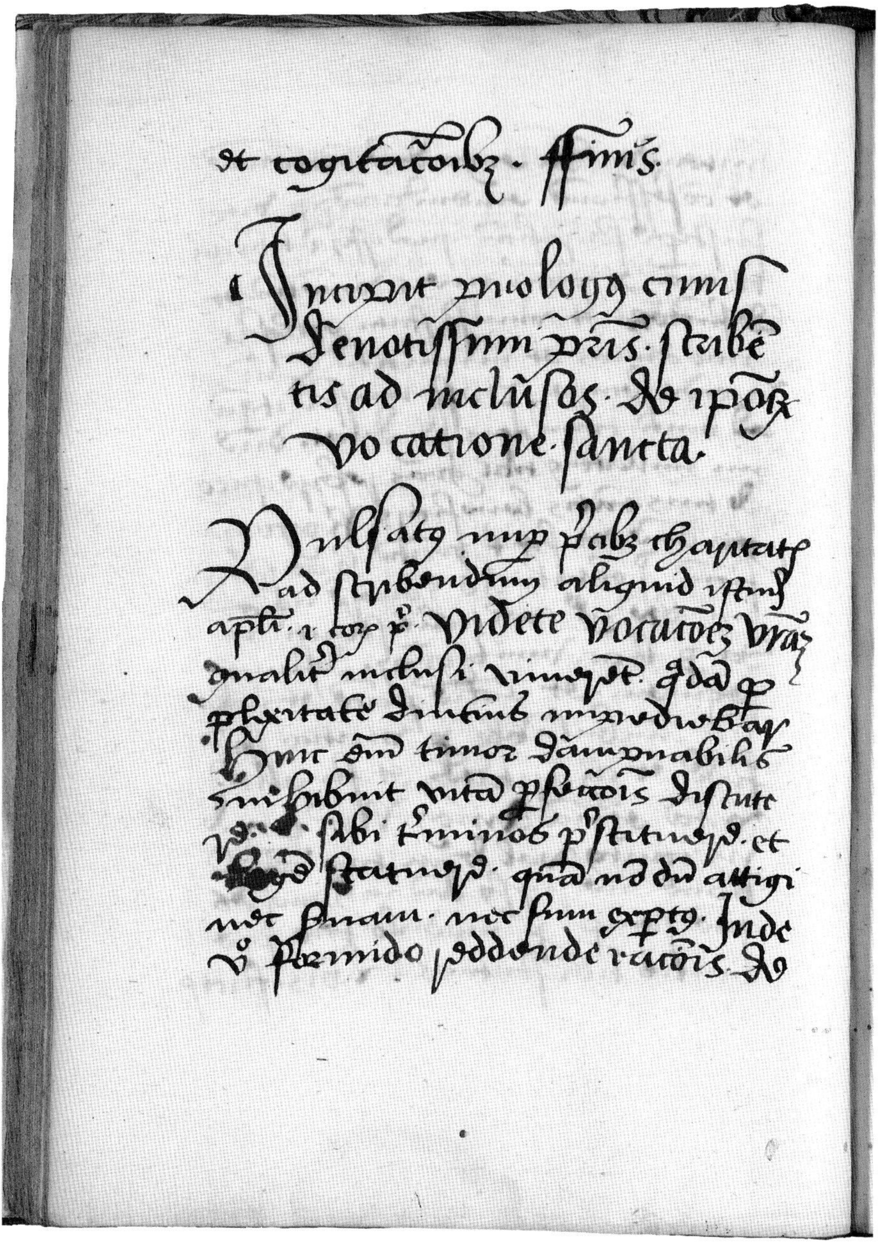

PLATE 2   St John's College, Oxford, MS 177, fol. 36v.
Reproduced by permission of the President and Fellows
of St John's College, Oxford.

to ȝou biholdeþ & seeþ ȝouȝ callynge
Capitulum primum. Siþe prius.

Soundely ȝe recluses schul biholde and seey in þis caas and
haue good consideracioun wher-
to ȝe ben principaly callyd & clept / for ȝe
ben callyd to þe exercise or vsage to toforn
platyf lyf which standyþ namly in þre
thinges / þ is to seyn in feruent preyere
in deuout meditacion / and in Cristyys
spekynge. Þ is to sey in speche streccþinge
in to vtu. A feruent preyere after þe
sentence of seyntes. ys an astendynge
or reysynge vp þ herte in to god / askynge
of hym mekly sum þyng þ is necessarie
to hefþe / wher of yt semyth by euydence
or tokne þ nedes at þe leest wey in þ bygynnynge of preyere required & askyd ȝe
lyftynge vp of þ herte in to god / may en-
tencioun & wil to performe hertly his preyere
to þ worschip of god. & vm to þe relees &
socor of þe nede of man / and þis firste entent procedynge of charite makeþ al þe

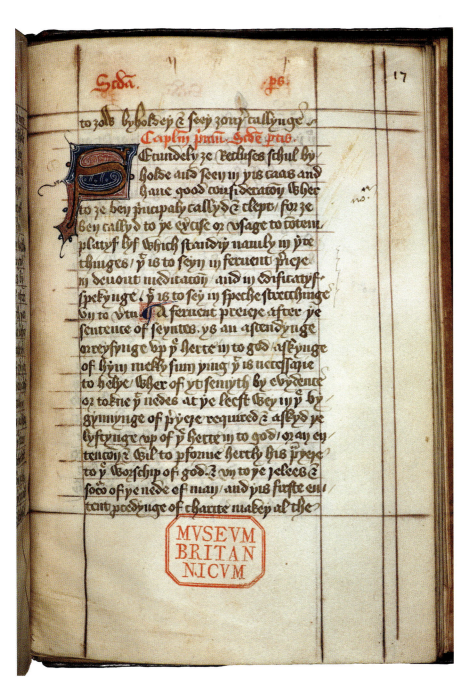

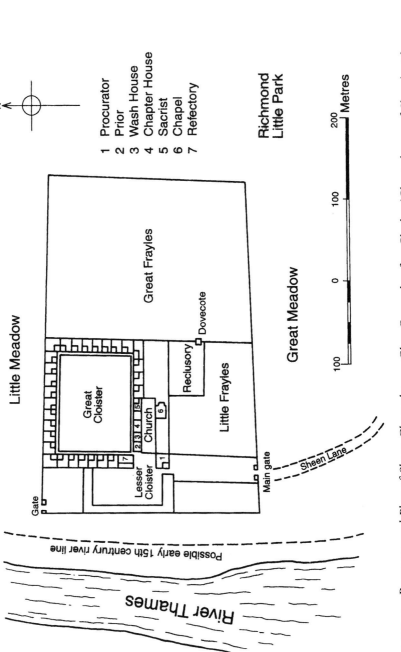

PLATE 4   Reconstructed Plan of Sheen Charterhouse. Glyn Coppack, after Cloake, 'Charterhouse of Sheen' with revisions, from Glyn Coppack and Mick Aston, *Christ's Poor Men: The Carthusians in England* (Stroud, 2002). p. 45.

The Texts

Incipit tractatus qui vocatur *Speculum Inclusorum*

Prologus

Pulsatus nuper precibus caritatis ad scribendum aliquid super illud Apostoli (I^a Ad Cor. primo), *Videte uocacionem vestram*, qualiter inclusi viuerent, quadam perplexitate diucius impediebar. Hinc enim timor presumpcionis dampnabilis inhibuit uitam perfeccionis discutere, sibi
5 terminos prestituere & legem statuere, quam nondum attigi nec seruaui nec sum expertus. Inde uero formido reddende racionis de abscondito talento quod Dominus mihi contulit ad errogandum, suis euidenciis persuasit ad aggrediendum opus illud fiducialiter, quod alterius sincera caritas requisiuit – presertim cum tali caritati cooperari creatur
10 Spiritus Sanctus, qui vbi vult spirat omnipotens in uirtute. Ex hac igitur confidencia sumpta consolacione aggredior opus istud exhortatorium ad inclusos. Quod in 4 partes diuiditur quarum qualibet pars ulterius in capitula parcietur. In prima parte, o carissimi vos inclusi, uidebitis qualiter siue a quo uocati estis; in 2^a uidebitis ad
15 quid uocati estis; in 3^a qualiter exequemini uocacionem vestram, et in quarta quantam mercedis copiam recipietis in celesti gloria pro vestra uocacione sanctissima finaliter obseruata. Cuius mercedis participem me faciat immensa misericordia Iesu Christi mediantibus oracionibus vestris sanctis. Amen.

Title Incipit ... *Inclusorum*] Incipit prologus cuius deuotissimi patris scribentis ad inclusos de ipsorum vocatione sancta J   Heading *Prologus*] *om.* J   1 super illud] istius J
2 Ad] *om.* J   4 presumpcionis] *om.* J   7 mihi] Dominus *add.* J   14 2^a] parte *add.* J
15 3^a] parte videbitis *add.* J • et] *om.* J   16 quarta] parte videbitis *add.* J

Here begins the treatise which is called A Mirror for Recluses.

Prologue

When I was pressed recently with loving prayers to write something on the Apostle's text (1 Cor. 1), 'Look to your vocation', concerning how recluses should live, I was hindered for a long time by a certain perplexity. On the one hand, the fear of damnable presumption kept me from discussing a life of perfection which I have not yet attained, prescribing boundaries which I have not observed, and laying down a law which I know nothing about. On the other, the fear of accounting for the hidden talent which God gave me to invest, eloquently persuaded me to begin faithfully that work which someone else had sought out of pure charity, especially since I believed the Holy Spirit – who is all-powerful in virtue and blows where he wills – to be working in tandem with that charity. And so, having taken encouragement from this confidence, I began this work of exhortation to recluses, which is divided into four parts, of which each part is further divided into chapters. In the first part, oh most beloved recluses, you will see how or by whom you are called; in the second you will see what you are called to; in the third, how you are to follow your vocation, and in the fourth, how greatly abundant a reward you will receive in heavenly glory for keeping to your most holy vocation to the end. Of which reward, through your holy prayers, may the immeasurable mercy of Jesus Christ give me a share. Amen.

Prohemium, capitulum primum

Uidete uocacionem vestram o dilectissimi vos inclusi, & ut uos tam operando quam ego exhortando ipsam clarius et efficacius uideamus, in principio corditer inuocemus auxilium beatissime Trinitatis, Patris & Filii & Spiritus Sancti, qui sunt vnus Deus omnipotens, summe sapiens & summe benignus, ut in hoc opere cor meum inspiret, linguam dirigat & manum regulet in scribendo. O dulcissime Domine Iesu Christe, per cuius amore solent inclusi perpetuo carceri seipsos uoluntarie mancipare, super omnia tuam uoluntatem perficere desiderantes, ostendere nunc digneris misericorditer mihi nuncio tuo, licet indigno, quid in eorum uita pocius tibi placeat, quidve illis magis expediat ad salutem. O benignissime Iesu, o singularis custos hominum & saluator eorum, uide captiuorum tuorum suspiria, uide electorum tuorum desideria, uide temptacionum pericula, & reuela mihi quod eis proferam, da quod [41r] dicam & prepara quod scribam ad tui ipsius laudem, gloriam & honorem. Effunde iam super nos Sancte Spiritus oleum misericordie tue, aperi fontem tue pietatis & gracie. Infunde lumen ueritatis & sciencie ad cognoscendum qualiter & a quo uocati sunt nostri temporis inclusi ad uitam solitariam in qua viuunt.

Numquid sicut ex uitis sanctorum & historiis colligitur patrum ut hanc uitam eligentibus quadruplex poterit esse causa motiua, seu intencio principalis? Una videlicet que est facultas uiuendi iuxta libitum sine graui labore; 2^a est uoluntas penitendi de commissis cum magno feruore; 3^a est propositum uitande oportunitatis peccandi in culpis communibus, et 4^a est uacandi liberius Dei contemplacioni & eius laudibus. Prima causa siue intencio conuenit iracundis & accidiosis sicut patet in quibusdam qui in hoc modo uiuendi minime profecerunt. 2^a causa seu intencio conuenit contritis & conscienciosis, sicut patet de Tayse quondam meretrice, Maria Egipciaca & eis consimilibus. 3^a causa seu intencio conuenit timidis & simplicibus quales fuerunt in principio Paulus Primus Heremita & Hillarion. Et 4^a causa seu intencio conuenit deuotis & perfectis spiritibus, qualis fuit in heremo

---

Heading *Prohemium capitulum primum*] *om.* J   1 dilectissimi] dulcissimum J   13 quod²] quid J   24 et] *om.* J   25 intencio conuenit] *om.* J   29–30 fuerunt in principio] *om.* J   31 spiritibus] *om.* J • in heremo] *om.* J

Proem, Chapter 1

'Look to your vocation', oh you most beloved recluses – and so that we (you in your actions and I in my exhortations) should see it more clearly and to better effect, let us at the beginning sincerely invoke the aid of the most blessed Trinity, the Father and the Son and the Holy Spirit, who are one God omnipotent, supremely wise and supremely kind, that in this work he might inspire my heart, direct my tongue and rule my hand as I write. Oh most sweet Lord Jesus Christ, for whose love recluses, desiring above all things to fulfil your will, are wont to give themselves up voluntarily to a perpetual prison, may you now deign mercifully to show to me, your mes-[1r]-sager, þou3 I vnworthi be, what is moost plesaunt to the in her lyf, or what may be moost expedyent or speedful vnto her helthe. O benigne Iesu, o singuler and only wardeyn and keper of men & her saueour, se the syghinges of thi caytifes & wrecches; se the desires of thi chosen folk; se the periles of temptacions. And schew vnto me what I schal telle onto hem, & ordeigne and purveye þat that I schal wryte, vnto þe preisynge, glorie and honour of þiself. Now, Holy Goost, hyld and pour out on vs thin oyle of thi mercy, opne the welle of thi pite and of thi grace, and put in vs ly3t of trouþe & science to knowe how & of whom bien the recluses of oure tyme callid vnto þe solitarie lyf in which they lyuen.

Now wheþre, as it ys drawen and gadrid out of the lyues and stories of seyntes, of hem that chesen this lyf of reclus fourfold may be þe causes motif and sterynge or entencion principal? The firste mai be cause and entencion of lyuynge at her [1v] owen wyl withoute labour; the secunde ys wil of gret and feruent repentaunce; the thride ys purpos to eschewe the oportunite of synnynge in comune defautes or blames, and the ferthe ys desyr of ontendynge the more frely to dyuyn contemplacion and only to the worschip and preysynge of oure Lord God. The firste cause or entencion longith to wrathful and sleuthi folk, as yt schewyth in some þat nat han profityd in this manere of lyuynge. The secunde cause and entencion ys conuenient to folk contryt and wel consciencyd, as yt schevvyth of Tayse þat was vnhonest of hir

---

11 speedful: profitable   **13** caytifes: wretches   **15** purveye: prepare   **16** hyld: pour out (N)   **18** science: knowledge   **21** wheþre: is it not the case that (N)   **23** motif: motivating • sterynge: stirring, prompting   **29** sleuthi: slothful   **31** conuenient: appropriate, applicable   **32** vnhonest: unchaste

post ascensionem domini Maria Magdalena, que 'optimam partem elegit'. Secundum igitur predictas quatuor causas seu intenciones ut estimo discerni possit cuiuslibet inclusi uita seu uocacio qualiter & a
35 quo spiritu sit incepta. De singulis ergo horum quatuor est ulterius singulariter pertractandum.

34 qualiter] *om.* J

body, Marie Egypcian, and oþir mo. The þridde cause or entencion acordiþ to dredful folk and simple as were in þe bygynnynge Paule
35 the Firste Heremyte and Hyllarion. And the ferthe cause or entencion ys conuenient and fittynge to deuout and spiritual folk as was in wyldirnesse, aftir þe Ascencion [2r] of oure Lord, Marie Maudeleyne, which 'chees þe beste paart'. Therfor aftir the forseid foure causes or entencions þe lyf & clepynge of euery reclus as I trowe may be
40 dece[rn]yd: how and of what spiryt it is bygonne. And therfor of ech of þ[e]s foure schal singulerly be tretyd.

33 mo: more, in addition   34 dredful: fearful • simple: naive (N)   39 clepynge: calling, vocation • trowe: believe   41 singulerly: individually

40 decernyd] deceyuyd (N)   41 þes] þis.

Capitulum secundum

Quosdam contingit, ut pretactum est, duci per spiritum erroris ad uiuendum solitarie ut ex deuocione christianorum fidelium abundancius habeant vnde uiuere & expendere quam in alio genere uiuendi uerisimiliter habuissent; & ut in uigiliis, ieiuniis, oracionibus, & aliis occupacionibus pro sue uoluntatis arbitrio se disponant, iugum obediencie & laboros corporales atque angustias huius uite, ex quadam uoluptuosa accidia, quantum est possibile fugientes. Sicut facere nituntur quidam moderni temporis religiosi qui – dum restringuntur aliqualiter iuxta sue religionis sacras obseruancias a suis uoluptatibus in uictu, uestitu, occupacionibus sibi disconuenientibus, & solaciis excessiuis – omnibus uiis & modis sibi possibilibus recalcitrant, murmurant & resistunt, iudicantes suos superiores maliuolos seu indiscretos set, [41v] nisi uiuere permittantur quodammodo iuxta sue uoluntatis arbitrium, fugiunt ab ordine suo tanquam perdicionis filii, uel aliquam exempcionem non sine consciencie scrupulo procurant, utputa quod sint 'capellani pape', uel 'episcopi nullatenses', & sic libere uacare valeant suis illecebris & per consequens laqueis inuolui diabolicis, nemine prepediente.

Numquid his conformes sunt qui uitam solitariam desiderant, non primo & principaliter propter amorem Dei, sed propter uitam ducendam iuxta sue uoluntatis arbitrium? Veraciter estimo quod sit ita. Sed de facili cognosci non poterit certitudinaliter qui sunt tales. Propria, tamen, consciencia cuiuslibet discuciat sine ficcione qua de causa potissime solitariam uitam elegit, & qua fuit mouens intencio principalis. Si primum & maximum motiuum fuit quies uel solacium aliquo temporale, libertas habende uoluntatis proprie, sustentacio consanguineorum & amicorum, uel subtilis acquisicio temporalium

---

Heading *Capitulum secundum*] *om.* J 2 fidelium] *om.* J 4 ieiuniis] et *add.* J
8 temporis] *om.* J 11 reclacitrant] reluctant J 12 seu] et J * set] et J, *corr. from* et R
21 ita] prima J 24 motiuum] *om.* J 25 aliquo] *om.* J 26 &] vel J

[Chapter 2]

To some it happyth, as I seide aboue, to be led by spirit of errour to lyue solitarily, þat of deuoc[i]on and almesse of trewe cristen peple þei may þe more ple[n]teuously haue temporal goodes wherof to lyue & dyspende þan thei were likly to haue in any other maner of lyuynge.
5 And þat in vigiliis, fastinges, orisons and oþir occupacions þei may ordeigne & dispose hem aftir her wil, fleynge (in as mochil as thei may) of hir voluptuus sleuthe or sleuthi fleschly lust þe ȝoke of obedience and bodili laboures and anguysches of þis lyf, as some religiouses now þese dayes enforce[n] hem to do. For the whiles þei be sumwhat restreynyd of
10 her lustes aftir her holi obseruaunces of her religioun – as in foode [2v] cloþinge, occupac[i]ons disconuenient & excessyf solaces – þei wyncen, grucchen & wiþstonden in alle þe weyes & maneres þat þei can & may, demynge her souereynes froward, euyl-willid or vndiscreet. And but þei be suffrid sumwhat to lyue aftir þe arbitrement and doom of her owen
15 wil þei fleen f[ro] her ordre as children of perdicion, & procuren and suen an exempcion or sum oþer liberte and þat nat withouten scripule or wem of conscience – as to be 'þe Popes chapleyns' or 'byscopes *nullatenses*' – þat þei mowe in þat wyse frely & wilfully entende to her unliefful lustys, and so be consequence be lappyd & inuoluyd in þe
20 feendes snares withoute lettynge or inpediment of any whyght.

Now wheþir þei ben nat conformynge to þese þat desiren a solitarie lif þat taken it nat fyrst ne principaly for þe loue of God, but for to leede her lyf aftir her lust? Treuly I trowe ȝis. But lyȝtly ne certeynly may it nat be knowyn which þo bien. [3r] Natheles lat euery mannes
25 conscience deeme wiþoute feynynge for what cause rathest he hath chosen a solitarie lyf and what was his meuynge or stirynge entent

---

1 happyth: befalls 2 almesse: alms, charitable gifts 4 dyspende: distribute, spend
5 orisons: prayers 7 sleuthe: sloth • sleuthi: slothful 8 anguysches: difficulties
9 enforce[n]: strive 11 disconuenient: inappropriate • solaces: comforts • wyncen: rebel
12 grucchen: grumble • wiþstonden: resist 13 souereynes: superiors • froward: perverse
• vndiscreet: lacking in judgement 14 arbitrement: judgement • doom: judgement
16 suen: seek, petition for • liberte: licence, legal freedom • scripule: scruple 17 wem: stain, blemish 19 unliefful: unlawful • lustys: desires • lappyd: wrapped • inuoluyd: enfolded 20 lettynge: hindrance 21 wheþir: is it not the case that 23 ȝis: yes
25 deeme: judge • rathest: above all 26 meuynge: motivating

---

9 enforcen] enforcein 15 fro] for

rerum: timeat, peniteat, & finale propositum suum amodo constituat principaliter in amore Dei & eius seruicio, postpositis inordinatis affectionibus quibuscunque.

30 Hoc modo uocacionem suam commutare poterit, Dei gracia mediante, de malo in bonum, de sinistra in dexteram, & de uiciis ad uirtutes, dicens Domino fiducialiter cum sancto Job: 'Uocabis me & ego respondebo tibi; operi manuum tuarum porriges dexteram' – ac si diceret manifeste, 'Quia iam de preteritis culpis & erroribus
35 penitere cupio, tu Deus, summe misericors, uocabis me per graciam & ego respondebo tibi, per tue uoluntatis obseruanciam. Sed ut ad hoc bonum perficiendum sufficiam, tu mihi, qui opus sum manuum tuarum, porriges dexteram celestis auxilii & conseruacionis, ut auferas a me malam consuetudinem nimium delectandi in curiosis & delicatis
40 uestibus, cibis & potibus, aliisque humanis usibus neccesariis; atque in diuiciis, amicis carnalibus, & consanguineis; in vanis, immundis & illicitis cogitacionibus, et confabulacionibus de inhonestis, inutilibus & ociosis.'

Contingit enim inclusos minus bene dispositos & incircumspectos,
45 ex abundancia rerum temporalium & frequencia diuerse condicionis homini eos uisitancium, multipliciter contaminari & in moribus peiorari. Ista patent in quibusdam nostri temporis inclusis, non in heremo sed in urbe, ut ibidem largas elemosinas recipiant vnde magnam familiam retineant; consanguineos & amicos – amplius
50 quam in alio statu poterant – iuuent & promoueant, et fere in omnibus victu delicaciori [42r] gaudeant quam in statu seculari uerisimiliter potuissent. Hos frequenter uisitat utriusque sexus, condicio diuersa, tam auribus instillans quam oculis representans uoluptuosa & turpiloquia, curiosa & inutilia, necnon & qualescunque rumores
55 seu euentus in patria contingentes, ex quibus in memoria reliquie

---

28 principaliter] *om.* J   31 &] *om.* J   32 dicens] dic ergo J   40 aliisque] aliis J

principal. ȝif þat [þe] first & þe moost motif were reste or any othir temperel solace – as fredam to haue his owen wil, sustentacion and beryng up of cosyns and frendes, or sotil adquisicion or purchasynge of temperel thinges – euery swych oon lat hym dreede, rewe & forþinke yt. And fram hennysforþ leet hym sytte and change his purpoos, sette his final entent principaly in the loue and seruise of God, and caste abak al inordinat affeccions.

In this manere by þe grace of God may thei chaunge her clepynge from evyl into good, from þe wrong into ryȝt, and fro vices into vertues, seyinge vnto God faithfully wiþ Seynt Iob: 'Thow schalt calle me & I schal ansuere þe. Thow schalt putte forth thi ryȝt hand vnto þin handwerk' – as þouȝ he scholde sey openly: 'For þat I now coueyte to repente me of my synnes [3v] and erroures þat bien passid, thow God al mercyful schalt calle me by grace and I schal ansuere þe be þe obseruaunce and kepynge of þi wil. But to þe entent þat I may suffice to performe þat good deede, þou schalt putte forþ þe ryȝt hand of þi spiritual help & conseruacion to me þat am þe werk of þin handes to voide fro me the wykkyd custom of superflu delectacion in gay and precious cloþingis, in delycat metys and drynkes and in oþer maner vses necessarie to man, and also in rychesses, flesly freendes & cosyns, in veyn and vnclene and vnliefful þouȝtes & of unhonest, vnprofitable and ydil talkynges.'

It hath happid recluses nat wel disposid ne wis, of þe abundaunce of temperel þinges and þoruȝ hauntynge of men of diuerse condicion visitynge hem, be ofte-sythes defoulyd & apeyred in her condic[i]ons and maneres. This schewyth of some recluses in þese dayes nat in wildernesses but in þe citees, þat þei may þere receyue large almes wherof þei may holde greet meynee, [4r] and helpe and promote more largely her kyn and her freendes þan þei myȝte in her oþir estat, and lyue more delicatly þan þei were likly haue doon in seculer plyt. Tho recluses bien ofte vesitid wiþ men and women þat schewen gay & neyce aparail and cloþi[s] in her syȝt, & tellen hem þing of worldly lust (as vnclene wordes and vncouenable), & tellen hem tydyng &

---

28 sustentacion: maintenance, providing for   29 cosyns: relatives • sotil: cunning
30 rewe: rue, regret • forþinke: repent   33 inordinat: disordered, uncontrolled
34 clepynge: calling, vocation   44 superflu: excessive   47 vnclene: impure •
vnliefful: unlawful • unhonest: unseemly   50 hauntynge: frequent association
51 apeyred: injured   54 meynee: household   55 estat: social status   56 plyt: situation
59 vncouenable: unsuitable • tydyng: tale[s], news

---

27 þe¹] þei   58 cloþis] cloþid

remanentes, quamuis |non| ad actus extrincecos peccati mortalis impellunt, mirabiliter tamen interius mentem uexant & distrahunt in uarias fantasias, ut reddatur leccio insipida, oracio indeuota, & tota meditacio uiciosa.

60 O generosi milites Iesu Christi, o perfeccionis alumpni, o secreti camerarii Dei nostri, iuxta consilium Johannes (prima canonica sua, capitulo unico): 'Videte uosmetipsos, ne perdatis quod estis operati.' Non enim ad statum vestrum pertinet delicate uiuere; hospites, pauperes uel peregrinos suscipere; familiam retinere; iuuenes educare; de exhibicione
65 consanguineorum uel amicorum sollicitudinem gerere, nec inhonestis seu uanis confabulacionibus occupari. Sed, habentes uictum & quibus tegamini, pro tempore his contenti eritis, iuxta consilium Apostoli, uacantes totaliter his que ad salutem pertinent animarum; neque a talibus operibus uirtuosis continuandis ira uos impediat, neque accidia
70 uos retardet, que supra modum temptare solet corporaliter ociosos. In remedium quidem accidie considerare debetis singulas creaturas. Nonne spere celestes cum suis planetis & stellis omnibus, aer cum auibus, aqua cum piscibus, & cetera irracionabilia super terram, continue mouentur & operantur iuxta legem sibi traditam a Natura ut suo
75 complaceant creatori, quamuis spem non habeant future beatitudinis

---

56 non] *ins. above line* R   60 Iesu] *om.* J, *but space left*   63 uel] aut J   70 supra modum] sine modo J   71 quidem] *om.* J   72 spere] superne J   74 sibi traditam a Natura] suam naturalem J   75 spem] *om.* J

60 auentures þat fallen in diuerse contrees. Of þe whiche þinges, þo þat
remaynen & duellyn in her mynde – þouȝ þei seme [nat] outward
mortel and deedly synnes – ȝet naþeles inward þei vexen & troublen
merueyllously her þouȝtes and dryuen hem into diuerse fantasies so
þat her redynge is þe more vnsauoury, her preier lasse deuout and al
65 her meditac[i]on vicious.
    O gentil knyȝtes of Iesu Crist! O ȝe nurces of perfecc[i]on! O secret
and priue chamberleyns of oure Lord Iesu! Dooþ aftir þe conseil of
Seynt Iohan which seith in this wyse: 'Seeth and beholdiþ ȝoure owen
self lest ȝe lese þat þat ȝe haan [4v] doon and wrouȝt.' Forsothe yt
70 appertenyth nat to ȝoure estat to lyue delicatly – as to receyue poure
folk & pilgrymes wiþ, holde meyne passynge to seruauntz, bringe forth
ȝoong folk custummably as in multitude or for hyre, or to bere the
charge of helpynge of ȝoure cosyns and frendes. (But ȝif yt happe þat
a vertuos persone, be yt cosyn or ellis, þoruȝ infortune of þe world be
75 driuen to scharp meschief or pouert and hath but smal or no confort
of socour or relief, thanne ys yt good and meritorie to releue suych a
person. And ȝet ȝe be more hoolden to releue ȝour blood – ȝif he be
vertuous – þan anoþer strange persone, þouȝ it be vertuous & meritorie
to releue hem bothe.) Also ȝe scholde nat be ocupyed wiþ vnhonest or
80 veyn wordes or talkynges. B[ut] ȝe scholde ȝow content wyth mene
foode and sustenaunce & symple cloþinge for ȝoure body, aftir þe
conseyl of þe Apostil, ente[n]dynge hooly to þo þinges þat apertienen
and longen to þe helþe of ȝoure soules. Let ne[uer] ire disturble or lette
[5r] ȝow fro the contynuance of vertuous werkes, ne slouþe tarie ȝow
85 þat vnmesurably ys accus[tu]med and wont to tempte ydyl folk. As for
þe remedie of sleuthe ȝe may concidre sondri creatures. Byhoold now
and se how þat þe heuenly speeres with alle her planetes and sterres,
the eyr with foules and briddes, the watir wiþ fyssch, and oþir þinges
vnresonable ovir þe [erthe], be meuyd & werken aftir þe lawe ȝeuen
90 and taken vnto hem of Nature to do plesaunce vnto her creatour. For
þouȝ þei han noon hope to haue eternel blisse, ȝet do they alwei her

---

60 auentures: happenings • fallen: occur   64 vnsauoury: disagreeable, unappetising
66 nurces: nurses, carers (N)   62 priue: privy, secret • chamberleyns: personal
attendant   71 passynge to: exceeding two   72 custummably: as a matter of routine
76 socour: aid • meritorie: meritorious   79 vnhonest: impure, unsuitable   80 mene:
moderate   82 apertienen: pertain   83 longen: relate • disturble: disturb, trouble • lette:
hinder   87 speeres: spheres   89 vnresonable: irrational • meuyd: moved

---

80 But] be   83 neuer] ney   85 accustumed] accus/med *over line-break*

consequende? Et hec operantur semper humanis usibus seruiendo ut, modis sibi possibilibus, homini suadeant perseueranciam in bonis operibus secundum beneplacitum Dei sui.

Numquid igitur uos qui uitam perfectissimam professi estis, bonum
80 exercicium libentissime continuabitis propter Deum, iuxta illud (Prima ad Cor. 7º): 'Vnusquisque, in ea uocacione qua vocatus est, maneat apud Deum'? Sicque, per bonam perseueranciam, *Videte uocacionem vestram.*

76 hec] *om.* J   80 illud] *om.* J   81 Vnusquisque] Vnusque J

operacion and werk, mynistrynge euyr her seruise vnto þe behoue of mankynde, ȝeuynge ensample in al þat þei may to perseuere in good werkes to plesaunce and lykynge of her God.

95 Now Lord, þan, whether ȝe þat been professid in þe lyf of moost perfeccioun schul continue good exercise wiþ glad herte for þe loue of God, aftir þe scripture þat seiþ, 'Lat euery man duelle toward God in þe same callynge þat he ys clepyd'? And þus, by good [5v] perseueraunce, *Seeth now ȝoure callynge and clepynge.*

---

92 behoue: benefit   97 duelle: remain   98 clepyd: called

Capitulum tercium

Secunda causa seu intencio principaliter inclusorum esse poterit uoluntas feruida penitendi de peccatis per totum terminum huius uite. Et tales si in suo proposito perseuerent, a Sancto Spiritu uocari creduntur, iuxta sentenciam Iesu Christi (Luc. 5°) dicentis: 'Non ueni uocare iustos, sed
5 peccatores ad penitenciam.' Sed tamen in eligentibus uitam huiusmodi solitariam est necessaria valde prudencia circumspecta ne, ex leuitate animi subito siue ex improuiso, talis uite austeritas eligatur, proposito [42v] firmetur, uel quasi uoto simplici promittatur, angelo Sathane mediante – qui se in angelum lucis sepius transfigurat, ut prius sub
10 specie sanctitatis instabilem animum alicuius alcius eleuans postea deterius atque periculosius cadere faciat in profundum; prout noui quibusdam euenisse ad desolacionem perpetuam eorumdem.

Hec enim uita perfectissima atque sanctissima est in illis qui, per abundanciam diuine gracie contra temptaciones pugnantes diucius,
15 omnes passiones perfeccione uincerunt; & omnes inordinatas affecciones, prout uiatoribus est possibile, totaliter extinxerunt; iamque contra singulas temptaciones soli pugnare sufficiunt & habent ac graciose acquirunt tantam diuine dileccionis et contemplacionis dulcedinem quod eis terrena non sapiant, sed solum in celestibus iocundentur.
20 Tales humana doctrina non indigent, nec talibus ego scribo, sed tamen imperfectis qui ad gradum maximum perfeccionis anhelant; quia talibus est uita solitaria ualde periculosa. [Nec uero mirum] quis solus proponitur ad pugnandum continue usque ad mortem contra omnes temptaciones possibiles & horribilem exercitum malignorum spirituum.

Heading *Capitulum tercium*] om. J   5 huiusmodi] om. J   8 uoto] modo J
15 perfeccione] perfecte J   16 extinxerunt] subiecerint J   17 ac] atque J   20 tamen] ad add. J   22 Nec uero mirum] ubi nimirum RJ (N)

[Chapter 3]

The secunde cause and entencion principal of recluses may be feruent wil of repentaunce and forþenkynge al þe terme of þis lyf of þe offences & synnes þat þei haan doon. And þei þat so contynue & perseuere in her purpoos, yt is to hope and to leue þat thei be callyd of þe Holy Goost, aftir þe sentence of Iesu Crist þat seyth: 'I cam nat to penaunce to calle ryȝtwys folk, but synneres.' But netheles, to hem þat chesen þis manere of lyf solitarie ful needful ys a prudent circumspeccion, þat is to sey to take good avis and deliberacion in this caas, lest of lyȝt and sodeyn assent of þe herte withoute wys purueyaunce or forsyȝt þei chese the hardnesse of þat lyf, & knytte or bynde hem þerto or make as ho seyth a promesse or byheste þerto be symple avow, by þe stirynge of þe angel Sathenas, þat ofte-tymes transfigureth hym into þe aungel of lyȝt, and sleyȝli vnder þe colour of holynesse areiseth þe herte of sum vnstable persone, excitynge [6r] hym to entre into þat heyg charge, & aftirward makeþ h[y]m falle adoun more perilously – as I haue knowen yt hath [befallen] to some, into her perpetuel desolacion.

This profyt and holy lyf ys in hem þat, by þe abundance and plente of Goddys grace, by long stryf and fyȝtynge agayn temptacions han perfitly ouyrcome alle her passions, and han quenchid alle inordinat affeccions as fer as it is possible to any pylgrym of þis lyf present, and now thei alone suffisen to fiȝte ageyn alle temptacions, & han goten & purchased hem graciously so mochel swetnesse of þe love of God & of contemplacion þat thei sauoure nat in erþely thinges, but delyten hem & reioycen hem in heuenely þinges. Suych folk han no nede to þe doctrine or techynge of man. I write to noon suyche, but al only to imperfit folk þat desiren to ascende and clymbe to þe heyest degre of perfeccion, for vnto suiche is a solitarie lif ful perilous. And it is no wonder whan a mannys soule ys put to [6v] fyȝt continuely vnto the deeth agayn al possible temptacions & agayn þe horrible oost of wykkyd spiritis. And þerfore this maner of lyf askyth and requireth a

---

2 forþenkynge: repenting   4 hope: believe, think • leue: believe   5 sentence: saying, declaration   8 avis: reflection   9 purueyaunce: preparation, foresight   10 knytte: join, tie   10–11 as ho seyth: as it were   11 byheste: undertaking   13 sleyȝli: slily, cunningly • colour: semblance • areiseth: exalts   16 desolacion: grief   19 inordinat: disordered, ungouerned   21 suffisen: are competent, able   25 doctrine: instruction   29 oost: host

---

12 ofte-tymes] that *add*   15 hym] hem

25 Et ideo hec uita requirit & exigit virum perfectum, de quo dicit Sapiens: 'Virum ex mille vnum repperi.'
Si quis igitur uitam solitariam desiderat animo penitendi, neque tale propositum sibi simpliciter dissuadeo, neque suadebo; quia nescio quis spiritus eum mouet, sed consulo per hunc modum consilii: videlicet
30 quod sanctum propositum reuelet simul duobus aut tribus discretis uiris & uite laudabilis, qui suam intencionem cum omnibus pertinentibus examinent diligenter. Deinde cum eorum consilio & assensu per annum integrum probet continue semetipsum, viuens per omnia uel consimiliter uel arcius quam inclusus facere tenetur. Non tamen medio
35 tempore uoluntatem suam ad hoc determinet siue uotum emittat. Hoc anno integraliter elapso, cum cotidianis precibus ad Patrem misericordie ut sibi inspirare dignetur de suo proposito: quod melius est ad anime sue salutem & quomodo finaliter magis Deo placebit. Tunc primo, si predictum desiderium maneat sicut prius, & discretorum consilium
40 (matura deliberacione prehabita super hoc) concurrat, stabiliat animam in hac parte, confirmet propositum, & uitam illam assumat siue uotum emittat, confidens de gracia & misericordia Dei sui. Nec aliter quam sic [uel] equiualenter alicui consulerem uitam inclusorum eligere uel uouere.

45 Postquam tamen uotum simplex emissum est seu uita talis assumpta cum deliberacione, [43r] necessario usque in finem seruabitur sub pena dampnacionis eterne. Unde singulis hanc uitam profitentibus caritatiue proponenda est exhortacio Apostoli (Ad Eph. 4), qua dicit: 'Obsecro ut digne ambuletis uocacione qua uocati estis.' Varia est
50 enim diuersorum uocacio secundum uaria dona Dei, siue talia sint bona corporis, siue bona anime, siue bona temporalia; siue horum contraria que per accidens contingunt bona esse. Hec reddunt homines

---

25 ideo] *om.* J   33 uel] *om.* J   35 determinet] detineret J (N)   38 primo] post J
40 animam] animum J   43 uel¹] J, *om.* R (Oliger) • consulerem] consulem J
45 simplex] simpliciter J   48 qua dicit] *om.* J   49 ambuletis] in ea *add.* J   52 per accidens] accidentaliter seu per ac [*gap follows*] J

perfyt man, wherof seith þe Wise Man ryȝt thus: 'I foond,' he seyth, 'o man among a M.'

And therfor, whoso desireth a solitarie lyf willinge to repente and rewe his offenses & giltes, nouþer wole I conseile hym to take it on
35 hym, ne stire ne rede hym to leue it. For I woot nat by what spirit he is led, ne what meuyth ne steryth hym. But I conseile and rede in this manere. First let hym schewe his purpos to to or þre persones togidere þat bien discret and good lyuers, þat mowe diligently and bisily examyne his entent wiþ alle pertinent circumstaunces. And þoruȝ her
40 assent & conseil lat preue hymself continuely al an hool ȝeer, lyuynge in alle þinges lik or moore streytly þan a reclus is holde to doo. But ȝet natheles lat hym nat in þe meen tyme determyne his wyl [7r] in that ne make noon avow. And whan this ȝeer is al fully passid, þanne prey euery day the Fadir of mercy þat he vouchesauf to enspire hym what
45 ys best unto the helthe of his soule, and finali what schal moost plese G[o]d. And ȝif he duelle and contynue in his desir as he dide byforn, & þat þe conseil of discreet men conforme & assente vnto hym by good and ripe avys an deliberacion, þane lat hym stablissche his wil in this caas, & knytte vp his purpoos, & take þat lyf or make his avow þerto,
50 trustynge in þe grace & mercy of his God. Oþirwyse þan þus or lik to þis wolde I nat conseile [any man] þe lyf of recluses to chese or avow.

Natheles aftir a symple avow is maad or suych lyf admittid & taken with necessarie deliberacion & avys it schal be kept vnto þe endes o[n] peyne of eternel and euerelastinge dampnacion. Therfore,
55 to alle þo þat ben professyd in þat lyf is it charitable to putte forth or schewe þe exortacion of þe [7v] Apostel wher he seyth: 'I bysechе ȝow þat ȝe walke & go worthili in þe callinge in which ȝe ben cleept.' Diuers is þe callynge of sondry folk aftir diuerse ȝeftes of God, wheþir suich be goodes of þe body, or goodes of þe soule, or
60 goodes temperel; or contrarie of hem which happyth to be goodes by accidence. Þo maken folk in diuerse kyndes stroong or feeble, symple or prudent, poore or myȝti. For some arn callyd to Goddys seruise wiþ helþe and strengþe, some wiþ febilnesse & syknesse; some wiþ good & natural complexion, some with euyl complexion; some with

---

32 M: 1000   34 rewe: rue, regret   35 rede: advise   36 meuyth: moves, impels
38 discret: discerning   40 preue: test   41 streytly: strictly   42 determyne: finalise
46 duelle: remain   47 conforme: are in agreement   48 ripe: mature • stablissche: confirm   49 knytte vp: conclude   51 chese: choose   58 cleept: called • sondry: various   60–1 by accidence: in the circumstances   64 complexion: constitution (N)

46 God] good   53 with] owt *add. above line*   54 on] of

in diuersis gradibus fortes uel debiles, simplices uel prudentes, pauperes uel potentes. Nam quidam uocantur ad Dei seruicium & honorem cum sanitate & fortitudine, quidam cum debilitate & egritudine; quidam cum naturali complexione bona, quidam cum mala; quidam cum uirtutibus multis, quidam cum paucis; quidam cum diuiciis, quidam cum paupertate; quidam cum miseriis & infortuniis, & quidam cum omnimodo prosperitate. Hec autem singula sine dubio (quatinus a Deo proueniunt & non ab humano uicio) magis expedient finaliter suis possessoribus quam facerent contraria eorum, si bene utantur eisdem.

'O altitudo sapiencie & sciencie Dei!' O graciosissima prouidencia Creatoris! O immensa misericordia Dei nostri que, cuncta futura necnon possibilia clarissime preuidens, sic singulos ad salutem uocat, quoad statum, condicionem & alias circumstancias (si non ponant obstaculum) sic ut sufficienter saluari poterunt & dampnacionis periculum euitare, intantum quod electis Dei mala quecunque contingencia perfici est ad salutem eternam, iuxta illud (Ad Ro.): 'Diligentibus Deum omnia cooperantur in bonum his qui secundum propositum uocati sunt sancti.' 'Secundum propositum' enim 'uocantur sancti' qui a Deo predestinati sunt ad uitam eternam. Tales enim non solum uocantur exterius per exemplum, per sacram scripturam, siue per predicacionem; uerum |eciam| per inspiracionem et per graciam perseruancie finaliter in caritate. Taliter pauci sunt electi in comparacione tocius multitudinis que uocantur, teste Christo (Mt. 20): 'Multi sunt uocati, pauci uero electi.' Reuera quos Deus predestinauit, hos sic uocauit; et quos sic uocauit, hos a peccato (si contigerit) per graciam penitencie iustificauit. Quos autem sic iustificantur, hos & magnificauit per abundanciam gracie & uirtutis, iuxta sentenciam Apostoli (Ad Ro. 8). Quotcunque igitur uocati estis ad penitenciam peragendam in statu perfeccionis inclusorum gaudete & exultate in Domino, firmiter confidentes de Dei gracia & eius misericordia, quod nomina uestra scripta sunt in celis.

Vnde semper omnium culparum [43v] uestrarum fasciculum ante mentis oculos constituentes, vna cum immensa misericordia Dei & multiplici gracia uobis facta, ac etiam imperpetuum penitentibus gratis oblata, simul pro Dei offensa & eius ineffabili misericordia, misceatis dolorem cum gaudio, atque leticiam cum merore. Sic sepius perfecte

---

64 sic] set J   66 sic] set J   67 quecunque] queque J • contingencia perfici est] contingentur proficient J   68 Ad²] *om.* J • Deum] *om.* J   70 enim] *om.* J   71 non solum] *om.* J   72 siue] *om.* J   73 eciam] *ins. above line* R, *om.* J   78 Quos autem sic iustificantur, hos & magnificauit] *om.* J   79 Ad] *om.* J   80 igitur] ergo J   86 simul] similiter J   87 atque] ac J

65 many vertues, some wiþ fewe; some wiþ riches, some with pouert; some wiþ wrecchidnesses and infortunes, and some with al manere of prosperite. Alle þese withouten doute (ȝif they come from God and nat of mannys vice) schullen more profite finaly to her possessoures þan scholde her contraries, ȝif thei vse hem wiel.

70 'O þe heyȝnesse of þe wysdom and science of God!' O þe gracious puruey[a]nce of oure [8r] Creatour! O þe excellent mercy of oure Lord God, þat clerly seeþ byforn alle þinges þat schullen folwen and been possible to falle, & calleþ euery wyght so to helthe as to estat, condicion & oþir circumstaunces (ȝif þat thei hemself putte noon obstacle ne
75 lettynge) þat þei may sufficiently be sauyd & eschewe þe peril of dampnacion, in so mochel þat alle maner harmes þat fallen to Goddes chosen peple schullen profite to ay-lastyng helþe: 'To hem þat loven God alle þinges werkyn into good, or werkyn wiel, and taken good effect to hem þat aftir hir purpos bien callid seyntes.' Forsoþe 'aftir her purpos
80 þei ben callyd seyntes' þat ben predestinat to God to euerlastynge lyf. Suich folk ben nat only callyd outward by ensample by holy scripture or by predicacion, but also by enspirynge & grace of perseuerance fynaly in charite. In suich wyse ben [fewe] folk chosen in comparison of al a multitude which is clepid. Hereof beryth Crist wytnes: he seith,
85 'Many ben callyd & fewe ben chosen.' [8v] Forsoþe, tho that God hath predestyned he hath callyd hem so, and wham he clepte in þat manere (ȝif þat þa[i] fall) he iustifieth bi grace of penaunce. And wham þat he iustifieþ so, hem he magnifieþ be habundaunce and plente of grace and vertu, aftir þe sentence of þe Apostel, þat seith þus. As many as ȝe been
90 þat ben clepid to do penaunce in t'estat of perfeccioun of recluses, beth ioyful and gladiþ in God, trustynge stedefastly on his grace and mercy þat ȝoure names bien wretyn in heuene.

Wherfor ordeigneth and purueyeth ȝow euyrmore a faget of alle ȝoure offences and giltes byforn ȝoure eyen of ȝoure wil & of ȝoure
95 herte, remembrynge of þe greet mercy of God & his manyfold grace doon & schewed vnto ȝow and profred frely to hem þat been penytent & repentaunt withouten ende. And for þe offense of God, & for his excellent mercy, medlith togidre sorwe with ioye, & gladnesse with heuynesse. Thus ofte þe deuocion of a perfyt [9r] contricion tolliþ out &

---

70 science: knowledge   71 puruey[a]nce: foresight   73 falle: occur • estat: status • condicion: state of being   75 lettynge: hindrance   82 predicacion: preaching
83 fynaly: to the end   93 ordeigneth: arrange • purueyeth: provide • faget: bundle
95 manyfold: multifarious   98 medlith: mix   99 tolliþ out: draws forth

---

86 manere] hem *add*.

contricionis deuocio letas producit lacrimas & leticiam lacrimantem, dum magni desiderii finis adueniens, dulces per oculos stillat guttas. Nec hunc preciosissimum liquorem peccatricis anime sanatiuum commutaret libenter quicunque habuerit pro thesauro maximo regis magni. Nam post amaras huius contricionis lacrimas diucius frequentatas, sepius infunditur inestimabilis amoris diuini dulcedo. O quis participem me constituet talium sanctarum lacrimarum? Quis sordes meas abluet cum aquis Syloe que uadunt cum silencio, cum totus sim aridus & exsiccatus? Adiuro uos igitur, qui feliciter hauritis aquas in gaudio de fontibus saluatoris, per uiscera misericordie Dei nostri: mementote mei cum bene uobis fuerit, ut de uestra felici abundancia lacrimarum uel guttas minimas caritatis intuitu detis mihi.

Ulterius contra diaboli temptamenta desidero uos sollicite uigilare, ut nichil sub specie false necessitatis austeritatem uite uestre nimis remittat, nec aliquid ipsam augeat ultra uires, sed iuxta discrecionis arbitrium sic corpus castigetur alterius uicibus & alatur, ut & imperio spiritus sit subditum & sufficiens perficere laborem iniunctum. Et ideo in magna debilitate seu infirmitate recreacionem corpori necessariam procuretis &, ualitudine corporis redeunte, forcius resumatis arma milicie spiritualis, cogitantes quod non solum pro uobismet opera meritoria continuabitis; uerum etiam pro singulis animabus Purgatorium pacientibus, atque omnibus christianis quibus per legem obligamini caritatis. O quam inestimabiliter dure plurime anime in Purgatorio puniuntur, cuius pena grauior est quam aliqua pena possibilis in hac uita! Unde Beatus Gregorius maluit eligere febrem continuam dum hic uixit, quam pati penam Purgatorii per tres dies. O quam ineffabilis tunc

---

103 &²] *om.* J   106 corporis] corporali J   107 uobismet] vobismetipsis J

100 bringiþ out gladsum teres and wepynge gladnesse, whil þat þe ende &
entent of þe greet desir comeþ out & fallith out be þe een swete dropes
of deuocion. And whosoeuyr haþ þis precious licour, which is helþe
of þe synful soule, he wolde nat gladly chaunge yt for a gret kynges
tresour. For aftir þe bittir teres of suych contricion longe exercysed &
105 vsyd entriþ þe suetnesse of þe loue of God, which loue ys more þan
man can deeme or gesse. O, who schal make me partyner of suych holy
teres? Who schal wassche my felþes wiþ þe watres of Syloe, þat goon
wiþ silence & stilnesse, syn I am al drye? I preie & biseche ȝow, þerfore,
þat þoruȝ grace drawen watres in ioye of þe welles of oure Saueour: for
110 þe hy mercy of oure Lord God, whan it is wiel with ȝow remembrith
& þenketh on me, & departiþ with me charitably of þe leeste droopes
þat fallen fro ȝow of þe abundaunce of ȝoure blysful teres.

 Moreovir, I desire þat ȝe wacche [9v] bisili agayn þe temptacions of
þe feend þat noþing sleuthe or lache ouyr-mochil þe stiburn hardnesse
115 of ȝoure lyf vndir colour of fals necessite, ne noþing augmente or
ecche it ouyr ȝour force or myȝt. But, aftir þe doom & arbitrement of
discrecion, chastise & nursche ȝoure body in diuerse tymes þat it be
soget on þat o side to þe commaundement of ȝoure spirites, & suffisaunt
on þat oþir part to performe & fulfille þe labour enioyned to þe body.
120 & þerfor, in ȝour greet febilnesse or infirmite, ordeynyth or purueyth
ȝow wysly necessarie recreacion & refresschinge to þe body; & whan it
is revigured – þat is to seyn, þat it haþ cauȝt agayn his strengþe and is
restored to helþe – þanne myȝtyly resumeþ and takeþ agayn þe armes of
spiritual knyȝthode, þenkynge þat ȝe schullen nat only continue ȝoure
125 meritorie & medful werkes for ȝoureself, but also for othre soules þat
suffren in Purgatorie, & for alle cristen peple – to [10r] þe which ȝe ben
obliged and holden be þe lawe of charite. O who can deeme or gesse
what turment þo soules suffren þat ben in Purgatorie, whos peyne ys
mochel moore greuous þan any peyne þat is in this lyf? Seynt Gregori
130 hadde leuer chose þe contynuel feueres while he lyued here þan suffre
þre dayes þe peyne of Purgatorie. O ther nys tonge þat can expresse the

---

100 gladsum: joyful 104 exercysed: practised 106 partyner: a sharer, participant
107 felþes: impurities 111 departiþ: share 114 sleuthe: allows to slip through
sloth • lache: causes neglect 116 ecche: increase • force: strength • myȝt: power •
doom: judgement • arbitrement: judgement 117 nursche: nourish 118 soget: subject
121 recreacion: nourishment • refresschinge: refreshment 122 revigured: revived
123 resumeþ: reassumes 125 meritorie: meritorious • medful: worthy of reward
127 deeme: judge 130 leuer: rather

---

130 hadde] *written twice*

est & intolerabilis – quia & interminabilis – qualibet pena infernalis! Sancta ergo et salubris est cogitacio pro defunctis exorare, ut a peccatis soluantur; necnon pro uiuis peccatoribus, ut a penis infernalibus preseruentur.

Hec & his similia memoriis vestris impressa, mo[u]endo inhereant & inherendo mo[u]eant ad continuandam uitam perfeccionis assumptam, in oracionibus, uigiliis, [44r] ieiuniis, & aliis sanctis obseruanciis quibuscunque. Sicque per Dei graciam 'in uocacione qua uocati estis, perseuerabitis' usque in finem.

Et hoc modo, per penitenciam congruam, *Uidete uocacionem vestram.*

---

116 soluantur] exsoluantur J   118 mouendo] J, monendo R (N)   119 moueant] J, moneant R

smert of þe peynes of Helle, which ben insuffrable for þei han noon ende! Therfor yt is ful holy and hoosum to preye for hem þat ben deede, þat þey may ben dissoluyd and vnknet of her synnes; and also forto
135 preie for þe synful men þat lyuen here, þat þey may [be] preseruyd and kept fro þe peynes of Helle.

These and oþir þinges lik to þes impressith and receyuyth into 3oure myndes, & lat hem styre and meeue 3ow to contynue the lyf of perfeccion which 3e haue taken, labourynge & travaylynge in orisons,
140 wakynges, fastynges, and alle oþer obseruaunces. And thus, by þe grace of almy3ty [10v] God, 3e schul perseuere and contynue vnto þe ende in þe clepynge which 3e ben clept vnto. And in þis wyse, by couenable penaunce, *Seeþ 3our clepynge and callynge.*

---

132 smert: sharp pain • insuffrable: intolerable   133 hoosum: beneficial   134 dissoluyd: released • vnknet: untied   137 impressith: imprint   139 travaylynge: working • orisons: prayers   140 wakynges: vigils   142 clepynge: calling, vocation • couenable: appropriate

---

133 hoosum] *followed by a blank space*

Capitulum quartum

Tercia causa seu intencio principalis inclusorum poterit esse propositum uitande oportunitatis seu occasionis que solet inducere mortale peccatum. Solent enim quinque sensus corporis, tanquam minus prudentes nuncii cordis humani, semper & ubique sibi referre
5 quecunque perceperint, quantumcunque uana fuerint uel inutilia, seu nociua & inclinata ad peccatum. Hinc aliquociens [est] quod simplices & timidi ad labendum in mortale peccatum, cum suam fragilitatem considerant & innumera imminencia peccatorum pericula que trahunt originem ex quinque sensibus uagantibus in seculo sine obstaculo,
10 sine freno, pro securiore uacacione omnium huius periculorum includi cupiunt, ex quodam prudenti feruore seu feruenti prudencia stimulati, iuxta consilium Salomonis (Prou. 7) sic dicentis: 'Prudenciam uoca amicam tuam' – hoc est animi tui custodem.

O qualis & quanta prudencia requiritur ad custodiam sensus uisus,
15 qui menti protinus imprimit quicquid uidet in creaturarum pulcritudine, preciositate, forma & figura, gestu & actu, semper concupiscenciam pro uiribus generans & uoluptatem nutriens, que frequencius impellit hominem incurrere in iniquitatem. Nonne uisio Dalide fuit Sampsoni fortissimo causa ruine? Nonne uisio alienigenarum mulierum cor
20 subuertit sapientissimi Salamonis? Nonne uisio uxoris Vrie balneantis se Dauid sanctissimum cadere fecit in adulterium & homicidium detestandum? Quid in Achor furtum siue cupiditatem illicitam generauit, nisi uisio rerum preciosarum? Quid matrem nostram Euam perficere fecit peccatum, nisi curiosa uisio ligni uetiti? & quid denique
25 filios Israel proniores fecit ad idolatrium quam uisio ritus gentilis &

Heading *Capitulum quartum*] *om.* J   4 referre] refrenare J   5 perceperint] preceperint J   6 est] J, *om.* R (N)   12 sic dicentis] *om.* J   13 hoc est] id est J   14 custodiam] custodiendum J   18 in] *om.* J

[Chapter 4]

The þridde cause or entencion principal of recluses may be þe purpos to eschewe [þe] oportunite or þe occasioun & cause which is wont to induce [or] leede a man into deedly synne. The fyve wyttis of þe body, as vnwys messageres of mannes herte, ben accustumed and wont alwey
5 & ouyral to recorde in hemself al þat þei han take and receyuyd, be yt veyn þinges or vnprofitable, anoyinge, greuynge or enclynynge vnto synne. Therof happith oftensithe þat þei þat ben symple and feerful to falle & to slyppe into deedly synne, whan þey byholde & considere her freelte & þe perilys of synnes þat þei ben likly to fallen ine, which
10 take her begynnynge of þe fyve wyttys þat sterten here & þere in þe world wiþouten obstacle or bridel, for þe moore syker eschewynge of alle þese [11r] periles, of a prudent ferue|ne|se or of a feruent prudence, thei werkyn aftir þe conseyl of Salomon, seyinge in this manere: 'I callyd prudence þi love or þi freend' – þat ys to seyn þe wardeyn &
15 kepere of þi wyl.

O which and how greet prudence ys askyd and requyred to þe kepynge of þe wyt of þe syȝte, þat inpressith & enpryntyth in þe herte of a person what þat he byholdeþ & seeþ – as beaute of creatures, preciosite of cloþinge, schap, port and werkynge – which engendryn
20 concupiscence of þe flesch & nurschen lustes of þe body þat causen ofte a man to do wykkydly. Wheþir þat þe syȝte of Daly[da] were nat þe cause of þe ruyne or fallynge of Sampson, þat excedyd and passyd alle men in strength? Wheþer þe syȝte of straunge wommen turnyd nat and chaungyd þe herte of Salomon þe wyse? Wheþir þe syȝte of Vries
25 wyf baþinge her maade Dauyd þe holy prophete to falle into cursyd avoutrie & manslauȝter? What þing engendred þefte & stelþe or [11v] vnlyefful coueytise in Achor but þe syȝte of precious þinges? What maade oure modyr Eve to synne but þe lycourous look of þe deffendyd or forboden tree? And what maade þe children of Israel more prest

---

3 wyttis: senses 5 ouyral: everywhere • recorde: retain, register 7 symple: naive (N)
10 sterten: leap, dart 11 syker: certain 12 feruenese: fervour (N) 14 wardeyn: guardian 17 inpressith: imprints 19 preciosite: preciousness • port: bearing
20 nurschen: nourish, nurture 21 Wheþir: is it [not] the case that 26 avoutrie: adultery 27 vnlyefful: unlawful 28 lycourous: lecherous • deffendyd: forbidden
29 prest: ready, prepared

---

3 or] to 12 feruenese] -ne- *ins. above line* 21 Dalyda] dalyaunce (N)

communicacio cum talibus qui demones coluerunt? Propterea signanter Dominum rogat propheta Dauid cum dicit, 'Auerte oculos meos, ne uideant uanitatem.'

Ulterius adhuc auditus suggerit de spurciciis peccati & illecebris quicquid audit – qualia sunt cantica amatoria & turpiloquia, litigia, vituperia; uerba detraccionis & inuidie, superbie & auaricie, adulacionis & mendacii, & quecunque talia sunt que hominem quasi exemplariter trahere poterunt ad peccandum, ut dicit propheta Dauid: 'Factus sum,' inquit, 'tanquam uas perditum quoniam audiui uituperacionem [44v] multorum commorancium in circuitu.' O felix auris hominis que sic prudenter disponitur quod contra uoces illicitas non aperitur, contra uoluptuosas seculi melodias clauditur, & contra sonos temptacionis singulos obturatur, imo (quantum est possibile viuentibus in hac ualle miserie) a cunctis mundi uanitatibus elongatur, prout patet euidencius de inclusis viuentibus sicut debent.

Tales enim securius conseruantur a periculis sensus tactus, in quo contingit uoluptas uenerea multiplex tam naturalis quam contra naturam que indisponit hominem ad omne bonum, reddit eum angelis abhominabilem, Deo odibilem, & gracie cuiuslibet alienum. Ab omnibus huiusmodi luxurie speciebus longe subtrahitur inclusus, nisi forsan a uoluptuosa delectacione mentis in illicita cogitacione que, si morosa fuerit & consensum generans ad sic delectandum, sine dubio peccatum mortale inducit. Et si uigilando talem delectacionem continuet quousque

---

27 cum dicit] dicens J 28 uanitatem] *om.* J 29 spurciciis] spurciis J 30 &] *om.* J
31 &²] *om.* J 42 uenerea] venena J (N) 46 mentis in illicita cogitacione] *om.* J

30 or redy to doon ydolatrie þan þe sy3te of þe rytes and þe lawes of þe hethen peple, and communycacion or spekynge wyth suych folk þat honureden and worschipeden feendes? Therfor þe prophete Dauyd preieþ oure Lord God & seyth þus: 'Torne awey myn eyen lest þei seen or byholde vanyte.'

35 Mooreovyr þe ere souketh and receyuyth al þat euyre he heryth of þe slym & felþe of synne – as songes & karoles of love, foul & vnclene speches, streyve, accusacions, blamynges; wordes of detracc[i]on or bacbytynge; wordes of envye, pride, auarice, glosynges and lesynges. Loo alle suych þinges þorugh her wykkyd ensample mowe ly3tly drawe
40 and sture a man to synne, as seyth þe prophete Dauyd, 'I am maad,' he seyth, [12r] 'as a vessel þat ys loost, for I haue herd þe accusacion or blamynge of many folk þat duellyn in þe circuyt o[r] compas' – þat is to seyn, of hem þat duellen aboute me. O blessyd is þe ere þat ys so prudently disposid þat he openeþ nat þe 3ates agayn suych vnleefful noyses, & ys
45 schyt & spered agayn þe voluptuous or lusty melodyes of the world & ys stoppyd agayn alle þe sounes of temptacyons, but (inasmochel as ys possible to hym þat lyueth in þis valeye of wrecchidnesse) kepith h[y]m afeer from alle worldly vanytes, as yt schewith by euydence & tokne of recluses – & naamly of anchoresses – þat bien more streytly closed þan
50 oþer religious men & wommen enclosed, enclosyd in her houses be leue of he[r] souereyns, and in alle tymes at her souereyns wyl.

Swych ancres & ankeresses ben more sekyrly conseruyd & kept from þe peryls of þe bodyly wyt of touchynge, by þe which entriþ þe lust of lecherie in sondry wyse, as wiel naturel or kyndely as vnnaturel or
55 [12v] vnkyndely, which wiþdraweþ a man fro vertu & maketh hym abhomynable to angeles, hatful to God, & alieneth hym or maketh hym straunge from al grace. Alle suych spices of lecherie ben fer from an ancresse, but 3if it happe percaas þat, of a voluptuous or lusty delectacion or delyt of þe herte in vnliefful þou3tes loonge abydynge,
60 ben engendringe a consent to delyte in þat same: þan wiþouten doute yt induceþ a man into deedly synne. & 3if he contynue suych delyt, wakynge, vnto þe tyme þat þe voluptuous pollucion of þe body folwe,

---

35 souketh: sucks   36 slym: slime   37 streyve: strife, discord   38 bacbytynge: slander
• glosynges: flattering words • lesynges: lies   39 mowe: may   42 compas: [area] round about   45 schyt: shut • spered: fastened   48 afeer: far away   49 naamly: especially
• streytly: strictly • closed: enclosed   51 souereyns: superiors   52 sekyrly: securely
54 kyndely: natural   55 vnkyndely: unnatural   57 spices: species, kinds   58 percaas: perhaps • lusty: lecherous   61 induceþ: leads

---

42 or] of (N)   47 wrecchidnesse] & *add.* • hym²] hem   60 engendringe] with *add.*

corporis uoluptuosa pollucio subsequentur, perficitur quidem luxurie species contra naturam que 'mollicies' ab Apostolo nuncupatur, vbi dicit quod 'Neque molles, neque masculorum concubitores regnum Dei possidebunt'. Nec hic alicui displiceat quod tam inhonesta refero scribendo mundis hominibus & perfectis, quia ubi temptacionis est possibilitas ibi est necessaria prudens informacio resistendi. Nam uera testatur historia quod quidam heremita, sanctissimus reputatus, dum molliciei uicio laborabat nec hoc tanquam peccatum ponderans penitebat, subito raptus a demonibus, nusquam comparuit. Quod factum sine dubio diuinitus ostensum est aliis ad doctrinam, ut semper huius uoluptuose delectacioni totis viribus resistant & nunquam consenciant. Et si (quod absit) vnquam ceciderint, digne peniteant, sicque per grauissimi spiritualis belli uictoria coronabuntur.

Consimilem coronam mereri poterit miles Christi subtrahendo se ab excessiuis uoluptatibus olfactus & gustus, que generari solent ex saporibus & odoribus delicatis, in cibis & potibus, in speciebus aromaticis, in florum & fructuum redolencia, & in omnium talium nutribilium sociali frequencia, que singulas gule species prouocare solebant, & consequenter miserum hominem ad desidiam trahere uel carnales immundicias excitare. Tales peccatorum occasiones continuas in uita seculari ex quinque sensibus prouenientes plures sanctorum patrum uitare solebant, & ideo cupiebant in angusto loco recludi [45r] vbi solum necessarium & exilem uictum & uestitum sentire ualerent. Hi omnes pie creduntur ad hoc propositum per Sanctum Spiritum inspirati & quasi diuinitus esse uocati. Quibus ueraciter congruit illud Apostoli (Prima Tessal. 4): 'Non enim uocauit nos Deus in immundiciam sed in sanctificacionem.'

Sic igitur uos inclusi, ad euitacionem continuam peccatorum, *Videte uocacionem vestram.*

---

53 quia] qui J   73 diuinitus] *om.* J.

þan ys þer doon a manere o[r] spice of lecherie agayn kynde which is
callyd (in Latyn of þe Apostyl) *molicies*. Now be yt no displesaunce to
65 ȝow þat I expresse þus vnhonest þinges in my wrytynge to folk of clene
& perfyt lyf: for where is possibilite of temptacion, þer ys a prudent
enformynge of resistence or wiþstondynge ful necessarie & meedful.
For þe trewe storie seyth þat þer was [13r] an hermyte, hoolden a ful
holy man, which custummably vsyd þis sinne & was vexid with þis
70 synne of *molicies*, and chargid yt nat in his conscience as for synne and
repentyd hym nat be contricion ne confession, wherfor he was sodeynly
ra|v|yssched & taken wiþ a feend and neuyr apperyd aftyr. Which dede,
as I suppose, was schewyd of God in ensample & to þe doctryne of
oþer folk, to make hem euyr wiþstonde in al her myȝtes suych manere
75 of voluptuous delyt, & neuere ȝeue her assent þerto; and ȝif þei falle
at any tyme in suych caas (as God kepe hem þerfro) to be sory and
repentaunt þerof, and so for þe victorie of a scharp & greuous spirituel
bataylle þei may aftir þis lyf be coroned in ioye.

Suych a corone may Cristes knyth deserue, wiþdrawynge hym from
80 excessyf & outrageous lustes of smellynge & tastynge þat be engendryd
of sauoures & odoures delicates in metys & drinkes, & in spices
aromatik, in sote sauour of floures & fruytes, [13v] & in vsynge of all
suych nurschynge þinges þat prouoken diuerse spices of glotonye, and
by processe drawen þe wrecchid man into dulnesse & sleuthe, or excite
85 & styre hym vnto fleschly vnclennesse. Suich contynuel occasions of
synnes þat comen of þe fyve wyttes in a seculer lyf many of oure olde
fadres were wont to fle & eschewe. Þerfor þei desired & coueytid to be
closyd in a streyt place whereas they myȝten haue oon necessarie foode
and cloþinge. Alle suych folk, as yt is deemyd & leeuyd, ben enspiryd
90 with þe Holy Goost & (as who seyth) been callyd of God. To whom
acordith verraily þe word of þe Apostel þat seith in this manere: 'God
callyd vs nat into [vn]clennesse but into satisfaccion.'

And therfore, ȝe recluses, *Seeþ so ȝoure clepynge* into continuel
eschewynge of synes.

---

64 displesaunce: matter of displeasure   65 vnhonest: unchaste   67 meedful: worthy
of reward   70 chargid: reckoned   72 ra'v'yssched: rapt, seized   78 coroned: crowned
79 knyth: knight   80 outrageous: excessive   81 sauoures: tastes, or scents   82 sote:
sweet   83 nurschynge: nourishing   84 sleuthe: sloth   88 oon: only (N)   89 deemyd:
judged, believed • leeuyd: believed   90 as who seyth: as it were   91 verraily: truly
92 satisfaccion: recompense for sin (N)

---

63 or] of   68 storie] þat *add*   69 with] þerwith   72 ravyssched] -v- *ins. above line*
89 deemyd] deem|myd *over line-break*.

Capitulum quintum

Quarta causa seu intencio principalis inclusorum poterit esse desiderium liberius uacandi Dei contemplacioni & eius laudibus, iuxta consilium prophete Dauid ubi dicit: 'Uacate & uidete quoniam suauis est Dominus.' Hanc uacacionem desiderant illi qui tantam Dei graciam in seipsis experimentaliter senciunt quod, dum uacant a secularibus negociis, plene feruenter & deuote Deum contemplari poterunt, & de omnibus eius donis sibi referre gracias cordiales. Et ideo, non mirum si summe cupiunt mundi sollicitudines declinare. Quia hec uacacio bona, hec ociositas sancta, hec quies proficua, solet communiter impediri per sollicitudinem mentalem, per occupacionem sensualem, & per laborem corporalem in negociis huius mundi. Nam quod sollicitudo mentis circa temporalia fructum impediat uite contemplatiue, docet experiencia in tribus partibus eiusdem uite: videlicet in oracione, meditacione & leccione.

Primo quoad oracionem: quantum distrahitur animus ab hiis que lingua loquitur, dum de aliis uanis uoluptuosis uel impertinentibus cogitat, studet, siue curiosius ymaginatur, credo quod nullus dubitat uel ignorat. Quis non afficitur erga ea que intimius cogitat amore uel odio, dolore uel gaudio? & horum quodlibet tam uehementer pro tempore mentem mouet quod non compatitur secum esse diuini seruicii memoriam cordialem. De taliter seruientibus Deo detestabiliter loquitur Propheta in persona Dei, sic inquiens: 'Populus iste labiis me honorat; cor autem eorum longe est a me.' Quoad deuotam meditacionem: patet ex euidenciis consimilibus quod minuitur, impeditur, siue penitus tollitur, per studium uehemens in prouidencia terrenorum. Et quoad sacram leccionem: patet similiter quod mentalis sollicitudo temporalium aufert ab homine frequencius tam uelle quam posse studendi, intantum quod, curis seculari mentaliter intentus, aliquociens dum sacras litteras legit uel audit, ad quod signant non aduertit.

Heading *Capitulum quintum*] *om.* J   3 ubi dicit] dicentis J   4 uacacionem] *corr. from* uocacionem R, vocacionem J   8 uacacio] vocacio J   17–18 dubitat uel] *om.* J   20 compatitur] patitur J

[Chapter 5]

The ferþe cause or entencion principal of recluses may be desyr to entende moore frely to þe conte[m]plac[i]on of God and [14r] to hys honour and plesynge, aftir þe conseil of þe prophete Dauyd where he seith þus: 'Taak heede & seeth for oure Lord ys softe and esy.' That
5 entendynge desyren þei þat felen in hemself, be experience or by preef, so mochel mercy of God þat, while þei entenden nat ne medlen wiþ worldly needes, þei may fully, feruently & deuoutly byholde God, & ȝeue & ȝeelde hym hertly þonkynges of alle hys ȝeeftes. And þerfore yt is no meruayl þouȝ þei desire & coveyte g[r]eetly to flee & eschewe þe
10 worldly besynesses, for þis entendaunce or besynesse, þis holy ydilnesse, þis profitable reste, ys wont comunely to be let be þouȝtful besynesse of þe herte, by occupacion of þe wyt, and by bodyly labour in needes of þe world. For experyence techith in þre parties of þe same contemplatif lyuynge þat þe besynesse which þat þe herte haaþ aboute temperal
15 occupacion lettiþ þe fruyt of contemplatyf lyf. And þat ys to seyn in preyere, meditacion & redynge.

First as [14v] to prayere. In as mochil as þe herte ys wiþdrawen fro þo þinges þat þe tonge spekyth, þenkynge or musynge of oþir veyn and inpertynent þinges, Y doute it nat. Euery man woot wiel þat þe þouȝt
20 which a man hath inforth – be yt love or hate, ioye or sorwe – steriþ so gretly þe herte as for þe tyme, þat yt suffreth no hertly mynde of Goddys seruise to duelle or abyde wyth hym. Of þo þat seruen God in þat wyse þe Prophete spekyth scharply in þe persone of God and seith þus: 'This peple worschepyth me wiþ her tonges but her herte ys fer fro
25 me.' As touching deuout meditacion: yt schewyth of lyk euydences þat it is abreggyd & lettyd & wyttirly wiþdrawen in besy studie & musynge of purveyaunce of erþely þinges. And as touchinge holy redynge: yt schewyth also þat hertly besynes aboute temperal þinges oftensithe byreueþ a man as wel wyl as myȝt of study[i]nge, in so mochel þat he
30 þat greetly settith his herte in þe besynesse of þe world, often-[15r]-sithe in redynge or herynge of holy scriptures hys mynde is al afeer fro þe wordes and þenkeþ nat on hem.

---

5 preef: experiment   6 entenden: pay attention to • medlen: busy themselves
8 ȝeelde: render, yield • hertly: sincere   11 let: hindered   19 inpertynent: irrelevant
20 inforth: inwardly • steriþ: stirs up   22 duelle: remain   25 euydences: proofs
26 abreggyd: curtailed • lettyd: hindered • wyttirly: utterly (N)   27 purveyaunce: provision   29 byreueþ: deprives   31 afeer: far away

30   Praeterea, quod occupacio sensualis operi contemplacionis impediat, testatur scriptura, que dicit: 'Corpus, quod corrumpitur, aggrauat animam & deprimit terrena inhabitacio sensum multa cogitantem.' Ac si diceretur: sensus [45v] terrenis multum intentus, sic ab eis deprimitur & tenetur quod affecciones anime, corpori colligate, secum
35   attrahit & retinet in terrenis. Huiusmodi ueritas clarius patet ex hoc: quod sensus naturaliter representat anime quicquid sentit, mouens ut intendat tali sensibili, & per consequens ut se diuertat ab his que cogitat precedentibus. Et inde est quod in strepitu, in societate, & in lumine, in quibus apparent multa sensibilia, distrahitur mens ab
40   oracione, meditacione, similiter & a leccione, que tamen libere suam contemplacionem in silencio, in secretis, & in tenebris, continuat & accendit. Quanto igitur minus occupatur mens in rebus corporalibus, tanto melius ad cognoscenda spiritualia preparatur. Unde nec sancti recipere solebant uisiones, seu reuelaciones de rebus occultis, de Deo,
45   de celestibus, uel de futuris, nisi uel in sompnis (quando usus sensuum est ligatus) uel quasi in raptu (quando mens non considerat res sensibiles circumstantes, sicut beatus Paulus, raptus usque ad tercium celum, utrum in corpore uel extra corpus fuerat ignorauit).

       Restat iam ulterius ostendere quod labor corporalis multociens
50   hominem impedit ab opere spirituali. Quamuis enim labor corporalis, assumptus locis & temporibus oportunis, pro caritate, pro obedencia, pro acquisicione necessarii uictus seu uestitus, uel pro exclusione accidie & ocii, sit necessarius, meritorius & expediens; nichilominus tamen cum has metas excesserit, profectum minuit uel impedit
55   operis spiritualis. Sicut patet in illis qui laborant causa cupiditatis seu curiositatis, uel qui mentem nimis sollicitant in tali labore – qualis est maior pars hominum, que circa proprios labores afficitur & ipsis apponit cordis diligenciam operosam, que communiter impedit seu

---

34 colligate] alligate J   45 usus] uisus RJ   48 ignorauit] ignouit J   54 minuit uel impedit] impedit et minuit J   57 &] in add. J

Moreovir, þat þe occupacion of þe wyt lettiþ þe werkes of contemplacion wytnessyth Holy Wryt, þat seith þus: 'The body, þat is corrupt,
greuyt þe soule, and an erthely inhabitacion þrestith dovn þe wyt
þenkynge many þinges' – as who seyth, 'The wyt þat is bysily occupyed
aboute erþely þinges ys so vexed & troubled with hem þat [yt] drawith
to erþely þinges þe affeccions of þe soule which ys knyt and bounden
to þe bodi.' The trouthe of þis may ly3tly be schewy[d] þus. Lo:
naturaly þe wyt representiþ to þe soule to entende to þat þat þe wyt
ys excityd or steryd vnto, and to wiþdrawe hym fro þe goode þou3tes
þat he hade byforn. & þerof is it þat i[n] noyse or in companye, or in
ope[n] sy3t or in open place in which many sensible þinges apperen,
þe herte ys withdrawen fro prayere and meditacion & redynge, [15v]
which frely wolde entende to contemplacion & continue þereine in
silence, in secret, and derk places. Therfore, þe lasse þat þe þou3t ys
occupied in bodyly goodes, in so mochel is it more apt or redy to knowe
spy[ri]tuel þinges. The seyntes weryn nat woont to receyue of God
vysyons or reuelacions of hyd þinges of God, or of heuenly þinges,
or of þinges þat scholden come or falle, but it were ouþer in slepynge
(whan þat the vsage of þe wyttis ys wiþdrawen for a tyme) or as þat yt
were in a rauischynge (whan þe herte or þe þou3t considereth nat þe
sensible þinges standinge or beynge aboute – as Seynt Pouel, þat was
rauysschid into þe þrydde heuene: he wyste nat wheþir he was withine
his body or withoute his body).

It is also to schewe forþermore þat þe labour of þe body lettiþ ofte a
man fro goostly werkes. Albeit þat þe bodyly labour which ys taken in
places & tymes couenable, for charite, for obedyence, or getynge |of|
necessarie lyf-[16r]-lode, or for cloþinge, or dre[u]ynge away of sleuþe
or ydylnesse, be necessarie, meritorye & byhouely; 3et natheles what yt
excedith or passeþ the boundes, it abeteþ & lettiþ þe profit of spiritual
werkynge; as yt schewiþ in hem þat labouren & trauaylen bycause of
coueytise, or setten hertes ouyrmochel in suych labour & besynesse – as
dooþ þe moost partie of folk, þat occupyen hem bysily in suych cas,
and herto putten al her diligence, which comunely lettiþ & sleutheeþ þe

---

33 wyt: faculty of sense-perception   35 greuyt: weighs down • þrestith: presses   36 as who seyth: as it were   38 knyt: fastened   40 representiþ: makes representation
47 **apt**: prepared   50 ouþer: either   52 rauischynge: ecstasy   53 sensible: perceptible
54 rauysschid: rapt, caught up   58 couenable: suitable   59 lyflode: sustenance •
dreuynge: driving • sleuþe: sloth   60 meritorye: meritorious • byhouely: beneficial
61 abeteþ: decreases, abates • lettiþ: hinders   65 sleutheeþ: causes the neglect of

---

38 to¹] hey or *add*   42 open] opey   58 of] *ins. above line*   59 dreuynge] dremynge

remittit opera contemplacionis. Et ideo frequenter admirabilis misericordia Domini nostri debiles, infirmos, & operibus siue negociis secularibus minus aptos, ad uitam contemplatiuam inspirat, & in eis per abundanciam sue gracie mirabilius operatur, iuxta id quod dicit Apostolus quod Deus 'uocat ea que non sunt tanquam ea que sunt'; & 'infirma mundi elegit Deus ut forcia queque confundat.' Hoc est ut potentes, sapientes & nobiles humiliet, ne nimis presumant de uiribus propriis sed de gracia Dei solum, dum viderint minus sapientes siue sollicitos seculariter magis Deo placere & per uberiorem graciam uirtutibus abundare. Vnde, secundum sententiam Apostoli (Ad Ro. 9), predestinacio hominis ad uitam eternam non est ex humanis meritis seu operibus, sed ex Deo uocante.

Ideo quicunque uitam solitariam eligens [46r] perceperit in se Spiritum Sanctum, per graciam & misericordiam, feruorem deuocionis accendere & conseruare, firmiter credere debet quod ad statum illum a Sancto Spiritu sit uocatus. Sicque, uos inclusi, per Dei graciam & eius misericordiam in uobis factam, *Videte uocacionem vestram.*

---

68 Ad] *om.* J   70 uocante] voluntate J   71 perceperit] parcerit (?) J   75 vestram] *om.* J

werkes & deedes of contemplacion. & þerfore, oftensiþes þe merveylous mercy of oure Lord God enspirith feble and symple syke folk þat bien nat apt ne disposyd to worldly werkes to take hem vnto lyf of contemplacion, & wondirly werkiþ in hem by þe abundaunce or plente of his
70 myȝty grace, as þe Apostel seyth: 'God calleþ þo þinges þat ben nat as tho þinges þat ben; and þe seke & þe feeble þinges of þe world haþ God chosen for to confunde & scheende alle stronge þinges' [16v] – that is to say, to make vmble & meke þe myȝti men, & wyse & greete men, lest þat þei scholde ouyrmochel presume or take vpon hem, trustynge [in]
75 her owene strengþes and myȝtes, but þat þey receyve yt meekly as ȝeuen to hem of þe grace of God only, while þei seen þat þei þat ben nat so wyse as þei, ne so besy in worldly occupacion, do moore plesaunce to God þan þey doon, & abounde in vertues by a more plenteuous grace. Wherof, aftir þe sentence of þe Apostel, he seyth þat 'þe predestinacion
80 of a man to euerelastynge lyf ys nat of þe meryt or meede of a man or of his werkes, but of God þat calliþ hym.'

And þerfore whosoeuere þat chesiþ a solitarie lyf & receyuyth into hym þe Holy Goost by grace and mercy, and schappyth hym to conserue & kepe þe feruent heete of deuocion, it ys to leeve stedefastly
85 þat he ys callyd to þat estat by þe Holy Goost. And so, ȝe recluses, by þe grace and mercy of oure Lord God ȝeuen & schewyd [17r] to ȝow, *Byholdeþ & seeþ ȝoure callynge.*

---

67 symple: naive   72 scheende: put to shame   73 vmble: humble   80 meede: reward
83 schappyth hym: sets out   84 leeve: believe

---

66 merveylous] þe *add.*   74 in] or   75 þat] *written twice*

Capitulum primum secunde partis

Secundo principaliter uos inclusi in hoc opere ad quid uocati estis consideracionis oculo uidere debetis. Nam uocati estis ad exercicium uite contemplatiue, que in tribus precipue consistit, videlicet in oracione feruida, in meditacione deuota, & in edificatoria leccione.

5 Oracio quidem feruida, iuxta sanctorum sentenciam, est ascensus mentis in Deum petens aliquid humiliter necessarium ad salutem. Unde patet euidenter quod ad minus in oracionis principio requiritur eleuacio mentis in Deum, siue intencio perficiendi talem oracionem corditer ad honorem Dei & ad indigencie humane succursum. Et hec
10 intencio prima procedens ex caritate, totam oracionem subsequentem reddit meritoriam, quamuis mens posterius preter propositum euagetur circa temporalia, rapiatur ad cogitandum illicita, uel distrahatur per uana & inutilia, sicut communiter accidit in imperfectis, qui non grauiter in hoc peccant, neque fructu oracionis carent, nisi quando sic
15 scienter & uoluntarie a proposito distrahuntur. Quia licet in distractis preter suum propositum in orando non sit actualis deuocio que est excellenter meritoria, est tamen in eis habitualis deuocio, que sufficit ad salutem, propter primariam intencionem in bono prefixam. Sed longe graciosius (ut estimo) contingit perfectis litteratis & inclusis, qui suis

---

Heading *Capitulum primum secunde partis*] *om.* J   1 in hoc opere] *om.* J   4 in¹] *om.* J

Capitulum primum secunde partis

Secundely, 3e recluses schul byholde and seen in þis caas, and haue good consideracion, wherto 3e ben principaly callyd & clept. For 3e ben callyd to þe exercise or vsage [of] contemplatyf lyf which standiþ namly in þre thinges, þat is to seyn in feruent preiere, in deuout
5 meditacion, and in edificatyf spekynge, þat is to sey in speche strecchinge vnto vertu.

A feruent preiere, after þe sentence of seyntes, ys an ascendynge or reysynge vp þe herte into God, askynge of hym mekly sumþing þat is necessarie to helþe. Wherof yt semyth by evydence or tokne þat
10 nedes (at þe leest wey in þe bygynnynge of preyere) [is] required & askyd þe lyftynge vp of þe herte into God, or an entencion & wil to performe hertly his prayere to þe worschip of God & vnto þe relees & socour of þe nede of man. And þis firste entent procedynge of charite makeþ al the [17v] prayere folwynge meedful, albeyt þat þe
15 þou3t aftyrward be stiryd or set on temperal þinges, or be rauyssched to þenke vnliefful þinges, or be drawen apart be veyn & vnprofitabyl þinges, as yt falleþ contynuely to þo þat ben inperfit, which synnyn [nat] greuously in þat, ne lakken nat ne wanten nat þe fruyt of praiere or of orison, but 3if it so be þat wetyngely & wyllyngly þei ben
20 wythdrawen from her purpos. For þou3 þat actuel deuocion w[hich is] passynge meritorie – þat is to seye, þou3 deuocion sadly set in God, nat þenkynge on worldly þinges – be nat in hem þat ben distract of her purpos in preyinge, 3et neþelees þer is in hem an habituel deuocion – þat is to seyn, as I seyde above, an old-rotid deuocion
25 willynge to contynue þ[er]in [þou3] distractynge folwe – which suffiseþ to þe helþe of soule bycause of þe firste entent groundyd and ficchid in goodnesse. But I trowe þat it falleþ mochel more graciously to þo þat ben recluses perfit and lettryd, [18r] which ben wont to 3eue þre

---

2 clept: called   4 namly: especially   5 edificatyf: edifying   7 sentence: authoritative saying   9 helþe: salvation   10 nedes: necessarily (N)   12 relees: deliverance (N)
13 socour: aid   15 rauyssched: dragged away   16 vnliefful: unlawful   17 falleþ: happens   19 wetyngely: knowingly   20 actuel: active (N)   21 passynge: exceptionally • meritorie: meritorious • sadly: soberly   23 habituel: latent (N)
24 old-rotid: well-established   26 ficchid: fixed   28 lettryd: literate

---

3 of] to   14 the] *written twice over page break*   20 which is] wiþ his   25 þerin] þᵉ in
• þou3] þou3t

Speculum Inclusorum • II.i

20 oracionibus triplicem attencionem adhibere soleant: primam videlicet ad oracionis uerba, ne in eis errent; secundam ad sensum uerborum, ut in eis sapiant; et terciam ad Deum et ad graciam siue misericordiam quam petunt pro tempore, ut impetrent. Et hec attencio tercia est oranti magis necessaria, & possibilis cuilibet illiterato. Si uero tres attenciones
25 predicte, post primam oracionis intencionem fixam in bono, tollantur per mentis distraccionem preter propositum, remanet nichilominus habitualis deuocio sufficiens ad salutem. Sed extinguitur feruor actualis deuocionis & excellencia oracionis meritorie, que inclusis maxime conuenit & perfectis. Propterea, uos inclusi karissimi, iuxta doctrinam
30 Domini nostri Iesu Christi (Marc. 13), 'Videte, uigilate & orate.' *Uidete*, inquam, ad quantum perfeccionis gradum professi estis. *Vigilate* per adhibitam diligenciam, ne in Dei seruicio distracti sitis. & *orate* cum actuali deuocione, ut diuine magestatis oculis complacencius seruiatis & vestrum meritum multiplicius aug-[46v]-mentetur.
35 Deuocionem quidem uarie solet augere modus orandi, secundum uariam hominis disposicionem. Nam aliquociens deuocionem magis excitat oracio uocalis, aliquociens oracio mentalis, aliquociens oracio publica, aliquociens oracio secreta, aliquociens oracio breuis cum honestis operibus aliis intermixta, aliquociens oracio diuterna, aliquociens oracio
40 diuinitus instituta (utputa Oracio Dominica), & aliquociens alia oracio humanitus adinuenta. Unde hec generalis regula de his omnibus est tenenda: videlicet oraciones ad quas homo tenetur ex ordinacione ecclesie uel superiorum suorum uocaliter reddat atque totaliter, iuxta modum & consuetudinem sui ordinis siue status; in oracionibus autem uoluntariis,

---

20 triplicem attencionem] *om.* J   22 ad²] *om.* J • siue] et J   30 Iesu] *om.* J, *but space left* • Marc.] Math. J   42 videlicet] quod J   44 siue] seu J

manere of entendaunces to her preyeres. The firste is þat þei taken
heede to þe wordes of her prayere, leest þei erre or defayle in hem. The
secunde ys þat þei entenden to þe vndirstondynge of þe wordes, þat
þei mowe sauoure in hem. The þridde entendaunce is to God, for to
purchace and gete þe grace and þe mercy which þat þei askyd in þe
tyme of her prayere. And þis laste & þe þridde entendaunce ys mosst
necessarie to hym þat preyeth, and yt may be had of euery vnlettrid
man. ȝyf þese þre entendaunces, aftir þe firste entencion of prayere
set & ficchid in goodnesse, be wiþdrawyn þoruȝ distractynge of hys
þouȝt besyde his purpoos, ȝet nat forþan þer remey[n]eth or duelliþ
an habytuel deuocion þat is suffisaunt to helþe. But quenchid ys in
þis caas þe feruence or heete of actuel deuocion, an þe excellence of
meedful preyere, which is mosst conuenient & acordynge to recluses
& to perfyt folkes. Therfore ȝe dere frendes, ȝe recluses, [18v] 'Seeth,
waketh and preyeth,' after þe doctrine of oure Lord Iesu Crist. *Seeþ* to
how greet or hy degre of perfeccion ȝe ben professed. *Wakeþ* & dooþ
ȝoure besy diligence, lest ȝe ben distract or astonyd in the seruice of
God. & *preieth* wiþ actuel deuocion þat ȝe may do þe more plesaunt
seruice before þe eyen of Goddes magestee, & þat ȝoure meryt may
be þe moore echyd or encreced.

    The maner of preyere may diuersely eche or encrece deuocion aftir
sondry disposicion of man. For oþerwhile the preiere to God in callynge
& crying more steryth deuocion; oþirwhile an orison of þe herte or
of þe þouȝt; oþerwhile an open preiere; oþerwhile a priue preiere;
oþerwhile a schort orison medlyd wiþ oþer honest werkes; oþirwhile a
long preiere; oþirwhile þe preiere þat is maad & ordeyned by God, as
is þe *Pater noster*, and oþerwhile an orison maad by man. Of alle þese
þinges a general reule is to be kept & holden: þat is to seye, þat þe
orisons & preieres to þe which a man is holden of þe ordynaunce [19r]
of Holy Cherche or of hys souereyns, þat man seye hem & speke hem
out fully & holy aftir þe custum of his ordre or his estat. In orisons þat
ben take of a mannes owen wil, lat euery man holde & vse for a tyme

45 quilibet illum modum, illam formam & illam mensuram pro tempore teneat, in quibus sentit quod sua deuocio magis accenditur & diucius perseuerat. Quia Oracio Dominica non est diuinitus sic instituta ut illis uerbis solis utamur in orando, sed ut nichil aliud petamus in oracionibus quam quod in ipsa sentencialiter continetur – et reuera 50 continet omne quod est necessarium ad anime uel corporis humani salutem. Similiter, sine dubio uerum est quod quantuscunque peccator perseueranter a Deo pecierit aliquid sibi necessarium ad salutem, sue oracionis effectum finaliter consequetur, si non uoluntarie contra Dei graciam posuerit obstaculum per peccatum. Quia licet pia peccatoris 55 oracio non sit meritoria eterne uite, est tamen quodammodo impetratiua diuine gracie – non ex sua condignitate, sed ex diuina misericordia & eius potentissima bonitate, iuxta quod promittit Christus (Marc. 11) dicens, 'Omnia quecunque orantes petitis, credite quia accipietis, & euenient uobis.' Et hoc subintellige sub premissis condicionibus que 60 notantur in Glossa (Luc. 11): videlicet, si quis pie & perseueranter petat aliquid sibi necessarium ad salutem.

O inestimabilis liberalitas omnipotentis! O immensa misericordia saluatoris! O admirabilis felicitas peccatoris qui, quantumcunque offenderit nequiter Dominum, si tamen confidenter ad eum redire 65 uoluerit & uoluntatem peccandi relinquere, per oracionem humilem & deuotam poterit, quando sibi placuerit, cum omnipotenti Domino fabulari, cum Rege regum sua tractare negocia, cum tocius mundi Saluatore miscere colloquia, optare quicquid uoluerit racionabiliter, quicquid desiderauerit postulare, de omnibus culpis preteritis impetrare 70 ueniam, de cunctis futuris periculis preseruacionis misericordiam, abundanciam gracie temporalem, & ineffabilem glorie beatitudinem sine fine.

---

57 Marc.] Math. J   60 notantur] nominantur J   68 miscere] missere J (N)

þat manere, þat forme & þat mesure þat he felyþ that his deuocion is moost aplyed or bovvyd to, & lengest perseuereþ & endureþ. For þe Dominical preiere, þat is to seyn þe *Pater noster*, ys nat so ordeyned ne maad of God þat we scholde al oonly vse þo wordes in oure preiere, but þat we schul aske non oþer þing in oure preieres þa[n] is sentencialy conteynyd in þat saame. And forsoþe it contenyth & comprehendiþ al þat is necessarie to helþe of mannes soule & of his body. Also þis is sooþ wythouten doute: þat, be he neuyr so greet and contynuel a synner, 3if he aske anyþing of God þat is necessarie to soules helþe, he schal fynaly haue þe fe[c]t of hys preiere, so þat he wyllyngly agayn þe grace of God putte noon obstacle ne lettynge by his synne. And þ[ou]3 [19v] þe good preyre of þe synful man be nat merytorie to eternel lyf, 3it purchaseth he þerby þe grace of alm3ti God – nat of hys owen worthynesse, ne of his desert, but of þe mercy of God & of his my3ty & excellent goodnesse. And as to þat, þus byhetyth Crist and seyth: 'Alle þinges þat 3e þat preien asken, byleueth þat 3e schullen haue hem, & þei schullen falle vnto 3ow.' And þa[t] schul 3e vndirstonde wiþ þe forseyd condicions þat bien notyd & expressyd in þe Glose of Luk, as þus: 'Whoso þat louly and perseueryngly or continuely askith anyþing þat is necessarie.' So ys yt vndirstonden.

O þe inestimable and vngessid liberalite & fredoom of Almy3ti God! O þe grete mercy of oure Saueour! O þe merueylously god auenture and þe grace of þe synnere þat, haue he neuere so wykkydly offendyd or greuyd oure Lord God, 3if he wole trustyly turne agayn vnto hym and forsake þe wyl to synne, he may talke with oure Lord God almy3ti whan þat [20r] hym lykyth by humble & deuout preiere. He may speke and trete hys needes w[ith] þe Kyng of alle kynges, & wiþ þe Saueour of al þys world medle his speche & his wordis. He may desire what hym lust resonably, and haue his askynge. He may gete perdon of alle his synnes passed, and þoru3 mercy be preseruyd and kept from alle periles þat ben to come; & haue here in þis present lyf abundaunce of grace, and blisful glorie endelees, which ys so excellent and so passynge þat no tonge can telle or expresse yt.

---

62 aplyed: connected • bovvyd: inclined   63 Dominical: Lord's   65 sentencialy: implicitly (N)   70 fect: effect, issue (N)   71 lettynge: hindrance   75 byhetyth: promises   78 Glose: Gloss (N)   79 louly: humbly   81 vngessid: unguessed   82 auenture: fortune   88 medle: exchange   89 perdon: pardon   92 passynge: exceptional

---

65 þan] þat   70 fect] feet   71 þou3] þoru3   77 þat] þan   87 with] which   88 þys] *corr. from* þes

O quantum igitur ualet deprecacio iusti assidua! Quis eius efficaciam, ualorem atque profectum sufficit esti-[47r]-mare, presertim si fiat cum lacrimis & compu[n]ccione cordis? Talis enim oracio ueniam impetrauit Petro ter Dominum deneganti, prophete Dauid homicidium & adulterium perpetranti, Marie Magdalene turpiter fornicanti, & publicano misericordiam postulanti. Per oracionem & penitenciam Niniuite subuersionem comminatam feliciter euaserunt, rex Dauid cessacionem promeruit pestilencie uehementis, rex Ezechias non solum mortis euasit instanciam – uerum etiam quindecim annos optinuit additos uite sue, & insuper uictoriam inimicorum, in tantum quod angelus Domini occidit vna nocte centum octoginta quinque milia de inimicis qui Dei populum infestabant, sicut patet 4 Reg. capitulis 19 & 20. Nonne per oracionem Moyses sanauit plagas Egipti, & uictoriam filiis Israel acquisiuit pugnantibus contra Amalech quamdiu in oracionibus manus erexit? Nonne per oracionem Josue dux populi solem stare fecit immobiliter unius diei spacio, ut persequeretur liberius inimicos? Nonne Eliseus propheta per oracionem excecauit exercitum Syrie & induxit in ciuitatem Samarie coram rege; et alias per eius oracionem Dominus obsidionem Samarie cum terroris sonitu mirabiliter effugauit, sicut patet 4 Reg. 6 & 7? Nonne per oracionem Helie prophete tribus annis & mensibus sex non pluit super terram, iterumque orauit ut plueret & statim celum dedit pluuiam copiose? Nonne cordialis oracio maximam sapienciam promeruit Salomoni? Insuper horum omnium mirabilissimum est, quod oracio infidelis regis Alexandri Magni, quia transgressores legis diuine punire uoluit, concurrere fecit montes Caspios, includens inter illos ydolatras & rebelles, sicut patet in *Historia* super librum Hester. Pessimus etiam rex

---

78 postulanti] post-tulanti *over line-break* R   83 occidit] in *add.* J   84 capitulis] *om.* J
85 &¹] *om.* J   92 sicut] *om.* J • &] *om.* J   93 Helie prophete] Hilie J

II.i • *A Mirror for Recluses* 45

O how mochel þerfore avayleþ þe besy preiere of þe ryȝtwys man!
95 Who can or may gesse þe effectual speed, þe value & þe profyt of
þat preiere – namly whan a man preyeth with plenteuous teres and
wyth compunccion of herte? Suych a preyere purchasyd & gat pardon
of forȝeue[ne]sse to Petyr, þat þries forsok oure Lord God; suych a
preyre gat grace to Dauyd, þat hadde wrouȝt and doon aduoutrie and
100 manslauȝtre; and [20v] suych a preiere caused forȝeue[ne]sse to Marie
Magdeleyne of hir fornicacion, and to the publican askynge mercy.
Also be prayere & penaunce-doynge þe peple of þe Cite of Nynyve
eschapid graciously þe manas and þe þretynge of her destruccion.
Kyng Dauyd also eschapyd by preiere þe pestilence of þe peple.
105 Kyng Ezechias also nat oonly eschaped þe strokes of Deeþ, but he
hadde xv ȝeer addid to his lyf, and moreovir he addyde victorie of
alle hys enemyes, in so mochil þat an angel of God slow in a nyȝt
an C.IIII^{xx}.v.M of his enemys þat anoyed & greuyd þe pople of God.
Wheþir Moyses þoruȝ his preiere helyd nat the hurtes and woundes of
110 þe Egipcienes, & gat victorie to þe children of Israel fyȝtynge agayn
Amalec while he reysed vp his hand in deuout preiere? Wheþir also
Iosue, þat ledere was of þe peple, þoruȝh his preiere maade þe sonne
to stonde vnmevable and steryd nat þe space of a day þat he myȝte þe
better & more frely pursue [21r] his enemys? Wheþer ek þat Elysee þe
115 prophete þoruȝ his preiere blynded or maade blynd þe hoost of Cyrye
and ledde hem into þe cite of Samarie byforn þe kyng? And how
at anoþer tyme by his preiere oure Lord God chaced & droof awey
merueylously þe sege of Samarie wiþ a soun and a noyse of gastnesse?
Wheþir eek by þe preyere of Helye þe prophete it reynyd nat on þe
120 erþe þre ȝeer and VI monþes; and he preyde agayn þat it scholde reyne,
& as faste heuen doun schedde reyn plenteuously? Wheþir also hertly
preyere of Salomon gat hym nat his excellent wysdoom? & moreouyr,
þe grettest merveyl of alle þese, þat þe preiere of þe hethen kyng, þe
gret Alysaundre, for he wolde punsche and chastyse þe offendoures
125 and trespasoures agayn þe lawe of God, he maade þe hylles of Casp
to renne togydres and close & schitte wiþine hem þe mavmett[r]es
& rebelles. Also þe cursyd & wykkyd kyng Achab: þoruh his herty

95 effectual: effective • speed: success 98 þries: thrice 99 aduoutrie: adultery
101 publican: tax-collector 103 manas: threat 107 slow: slew 108 C.IIII^{xx}.V.M:
185,000 113 vnmevable: immobile 115 Cyrye: Syria 118 gastnesse: terror
124 punsche: punish 126 schitte: shut • mavmettres: idolaters (N)

95 effectual] effectualy 109 þoruȝ] þoruȝt 125 God] & *add.* 126 mavmettres]
mavmettes (N)

100 Achab quia penituit humiliter & orauit pro tempore suo suspendebat Dominus vindictam eius domui comminatam, ut patet 3 Reg. 21.

Ex his oracionibus, uos inclusi, aduertite, considerate, attendite & uidete quantum proficere poteritis tam uobis quam toti populo, si perseuerauitis in oracione deuota. Sed forsitan hic aliquis cogitaret
105 quod nullus sufficit sine intermissione orare, nec oracio quelibet perseuerans effectum consequetur quem intendit. Ad hoc ueraciter poterit responderi quod, si quis horis sibi competentibus actualiter bene oret, licet intermediis temporibus comedet, dormiat, uel quicquam aliud faciat pro necessaria sustentacione seu recreacione corporis, ut
110 postea forcius seruiat Deo suo, uel [47v] pro mutua caritate fraterna, ita quod in omnibus occupacionibus propositum prefigatur finaliter ad Dei laudem, seruicium & honorem, semper tamen habitualiter orat per continuum desiderium & habitum caritatis. Similiter dici potest quod, quamuis interdum oracio continua multorum fidelium non consequatur
115 effectum ab eis intentum, semper tamen consequitur hoc quod illi pro quo oratur Dei iudicio est utilius. Quia quid infirmo sit utile melius nouit medicus quam egrotus. Taliter nunquam deficit oracionis effectus quin eueniat tempore magis congruo, si non illum impediat peccatum orantis, uel illius pro quo oratur continuacio peccati mortalis.
120 Per hec igitur, uos inclusi, & hiis similia que commendant, excitant, prouocant & mouent ad oracionem feruidam, *Videte uocacionem vestram.*

---

101 ut patet] *om.* J   107 sibi] *om.* J   117 nouit] *om.* J

repentaunce & humble [21v] preyere God putte in suspense for his tyme þe vengeaunce þat was manaced to hys hous.

130 Of alle þese þinges, ȝe recluses, beþenkeþ ȝow, considereþ, takeþ heede & seeþ how mochil ȝe may profite, as wel to ȝoureself as to al þe peple, ȝif ȝe perseuere & continue in deuout preiere. But parcaas sum man myȝte þenke þat no man suffiseþ to preie wiþoute styntynge, ne þat euery contynuel preiere scholde haue þe fect of hys entent. To
135 þat may treuly be answeryd þat, ȝif a man in tymes to hym compotent or couenable preye wel actuely his preyere, þouȝ þat aftirward he ete, slepe, or do any oþir þing for þe necessarie [suste]nance or refresschynge of þe body, þat he may þe more strongly serue his God, or for to have [with] his broþer vertuous communycacion & charytable speche, so þat
140 in alle occupacions þe purpos be set byforn & fynally fycchid in þe seruyse and honour of God, ȝet naþelees he preyeth euere habytuely by contynuel desyr and by þe abyt of charite. Also, þoruȝ þe [22r] contynuel preyere, as many goode folk take nat oþerwyse þe effect of hir entent, ȝyt alwey folwyth by þat preiere þat is moore profitable,
145 to þe iugement of God, to hym for whom yt was preied. For a leche knowyth better what is profitable to a syk man þan dooþ þe syke man hymself. And oþerwyse faileþ neuer þe effect of preiere, but þat yt schal come in a tyme more couenable, but ȝif þe synne of hym þat preyeþ lette yt, or elles þat it be let by þe contynuance of the deedly synne of
150 hym for whom yt was preyed.

And þerfore, ȝe recluses, by þese þinges and oþir lyk vnto þese, which styren and prouoken a man to feruent preyere, *Byholden and seeþ [y]oure callynge.*

---

129 manaced: threatened   132 parcaas: perhaps   133 styntynge: ceasing
135 compotent: suitable   136 couenable: appropriate • actuely: actively (N)
141 habytuely: habitually (N)   142 abyt: habit (N)   145 leche: medic   149 lette: hinder

---

153 youre] þoure

|Capitulum secundum|

Si oracionem impediat indeuocio, tedium uel distraccio, ad meditacionem deuotam sepius est utilius declinare. Que ex quatuor faciliter elicitur & continuatur: videlicet ex omnipotencia diuine maiestatis, que creauit propter hominem totum mundum; ex summa sapiencia
5 ueritatis, que regit ordinatissime suum effectum; ex immensa misericordia bonitatis, que redemit a morte perpetua genus humanum; & ex perfectissima iusticia equitatis, que premiabit finaliter quodlibet uel bene uel perperam operatum.

O insignis anima, o nobilis creatura, o ymago beatissime Trinitatis!
10 Si tocius mundi machinam sedula mente reuolluas – videlicet celum & terram & omnia que in eorum ambitu continentur – percipere poteris quod eorum creator Deus sit omnipotens, & eius uoluntas in creaturis sit immutabile firmamentum, que de nichilo produxit talium rerum species innumerabiles, tanto decore delectabiles & tanta
15 uirtute mirabiles quod longe transcendunt in suis naturalibus perfeccionibus intellectum humanum. Hec autem omnia creauit Omnipotens propter te, ut tuis necessariis usibus deseruirent; & tu ea referres ad Dei laudem, gloriam & honorem, semper sibi super omnia cor tuum tribuens per amorem. Et hinc est quod, post creacionem omnium
20 aliorum, quadam ineffabili dileccionis prerogatiua, hominem creauit Deus ad ymaginem & similitudinem sui ipsius, ipsum dominum constituens huius mundi. Vnde quasi ex tocius Trinitatis consilio – Patris, videlicet, & Filii & Spiritus Sancti, qui sunt vnus & idem Deus, ut in mundi principio dictum est: 'Faciamus hominem ad ymaginem
25 & similitudinem nostram', ac si diceret: 'Sicut in diuinitate ex Patre gignitur Filius, et ex Patre Filio[que] simul procedit Spiritus Sanctus, ita quodammodo in anima humana ex memoria sui ipsius oritur (siue oriri poterit) noticia siue intelligencia eiusdem, et ex [48r] memoria & noticia simul procedere potest amor seu bona uoluntas respectu eiusdem.' Vnde
30 cognoscere poterit homo quod, sicut in anima sua sunt tres potencie &

Heading *Capitulum secundum*] ins. marg. R, *om.* J   6 &] *om.* J   18 laudem] et *add.* J
26 Filioque] J, filio R (N)   27 anima] *om.* J

Capitulum secundum

Ȝyf lak of deuocion, heuynes or distr[act]inge lette preiere, þan full often is yt profitable to drawe ȝow to deuout meditacion, which may lyȝtly by drawen out and contynued of foure þinges: þat is to seyn of þe myȝt of G[o]ddys mageste, þat maade al the world of nauȝt for [22v] man; of
5 the hy wysdom of sothfastnesse, which gouerneþ moost ordynatly his affect; and þe greet mercy of his goodnesse, which delyuerede & bouȝte mankynde fro perpetuel deeþ, & of perfyt ryȝtwysnesse of equite, that schal fynaly rewarde or punsche euery good or wykkyd deede.

O thow worthi soule! þow o noble creature, the ymage of the blessid
10 Trinite! Ȝif [þow] byþenke the and remembre besyly in thi mynde al þe schap of heuene, erthe, and of alle þinges that bien conteynyd in her circuyt or compaas, þow mayst vndirstonde and conceyve þat God þat is hir maker is almyȝty, and his wil in his creatures ys an vnchaunchable stedefastnesse, the which wyl brouȝte forth of nauȝt
15 innumerable kyndes of suych þinges þat ben so delectable and so merveylously vertuous þat þei passen al out þe intelligence of man in hir perfyt naturel worchinges. Lo þou man, lo: almyȝti God maade alle þise thynges for þe, to serue þe in vses necessa-[23r]-rie, for þat thow scholdest honoure and worschipe hym alwey and ȝeue hym alwey
20 þin herte and ful love above al thinges. And þerfor, aftir creacion or makynge of alle oþir þinges, God by a special prerogatif of love maade man to þe ymage and lyknesse of hymself, & maade hym a lord of al þat was maad in the world. Wherfor lykly yt was þat by þe conseyl of al þe Trinite – þat is to seyn of þe Fader, Sone and Holy Goost, þat ben
25 o God and the same God – yt was seyd in þe bygynnynge of þe world, 'Make we man to þe ymage and oure liknesse,' as þouȝ he scholde sey in this wyse: 'Ryȝt as in the godhede the Sone [cometh] of the Fadir, and [þe Holy Goost cometh of] the Fader and of þe Sone togedir, ryȝt so in a maner yt is in a mannys soule. For of þe memorie or of the mynde
30 of the soule cometh or may come a knowynge or an vndirstonde of þe

---

1 heuynes: dullness, lethargy • lette: hinder   5 sothfastnesse: truthfulness • ordynatly: in a well-ordered way   6 affect: desire • bouȝte: redeemed   7 equite: justice   8 punsche: punish   10 byþenke the: reflect   14 stedefastnesse: foundation   16 passen: surpass • al out: completely   21 prerogatif: privilege   30 vndirstonde: understanding (N)

---

4 Goddys] gooddys

vnica substancia, ita quodammodo in diuinitate sunt tres persone, et hii tres sunt substancialiter vnus & idem Deus. Iste igitur Deus trinus & vnus est ab homine diligendus, iuxta primum & maximum mandatum, ex toto corde, ex tota anima, ex tota mente & ex tota uirtute – hoc est, ex tota potencia uolitiua, ex tota potencia intellectiua, ex tota potencia memoratiua (que sunt tres partes ymaginis Dei in anima) ac etiam ex tota uirtute corporea uel sensuali; ut videlicet omnis operacio anime uel corporis referatur finaliter ad Dei laudem, gloriam & honorem, ut sic omnia fiant finaliter propter amorem Dei.

Ad istud hominem exemplariter prouocant singule creature, tam sensibiles quam insensibiles, dum (iuxta Dei ordinacionem primariam) sunt in continuis motibus & laboribus, ministrantes homini nutrimentum, solacium & doctrinam, ad semper timendum, laudandum & diligendum super omnia Creatorem. Nonne motus celestis ordinatissimus sine defectu, modulacio auium in dulci concentu, delectabilitas florum & fructuum & utilitas omnium animalium, que singulis annis ad usum hominis mirabiliter innouantur, & legem sibi naturaliter inditam indefectibiliter prosecuntur, & modis quibus poterunt hominem mouent, instruunt & hortantur ut super omnia timeatur, laudetur & diligatur in illis omnipotencia Creatoris, summa sapiencia Gubernatoris, & infinita bonitas Conseruatoris? O igitur ymago Dei, libero racionis arbitrio pre omnibus aliis insignita, siquid potencie, siquid prudencie, siquid bonitatis, siquid utilitatis, siquid pulcritudinis, siquid honestatis, videris in te uel in aliqua creatura: statim hoc totum referas ad Dei laudem, gloriam & honorem, & illud non diligas propter te uel propter se solum, sed principaliter & finaliter propter Deum. Siquid autem defectus, siquid erroris, siquid vicii, siquid horroris, siquid malicie, siquid iniusticie, siquid inutile, siquid penale,

---

35 intellectiua] et *add.* J   36 partes] potentie J • ac etiam] et J   40 exemplariter prouocant] *om.* J   48 indefectibiliter] indeficrabiliter (?) J

same soule; and of þe mynde and cnowynge of þe soule togydre may come a loue or a good wyl [23v] to God out of þe same soule. Wherfore a man may knowe, as þer ben þre myȝtes and o substaunce in his soule, ryȝth so lyk in a manere þer bien thre persones in the Godhede, and
35 þo þre ben substancialy on and þe same God. Þerfore this God that ys þre and oon ys to be louyd, aftir þe firste & grettest commaundement, of al þin herte, of al þi soule, of al þi mynde and of al thi vertu – þat is to sey of al þe myȝt of thi wyl, of al þi myȝt of þi reson or of þin vndirstondynge, or of al þe myȝt of thy mynde (which bien þre partes
40 of þe ymage of God in þe soule); also þow schalt love thi God þerwiþ of al thy bodily vertu – þat is to seyn þat al þe operacion o[r] werkynge of þe soule or of þe body be referid and doon finaly for þe love of God.
    & vnto þis alle creatures, as wel sensible as insensible creatures, by hir ensample prouoken and styren a man, for as moche as þat (after þe
45 fyrste ordenance [24r] of God) þei ben in hir contynuel sterynge and trauayles mynystrynge and ȝevynge vnto man nurschynge, solace, and doctryne alwey to drede, preise and love aboven alle þinges her Lord and hir Creatour and Maker. Wher þat þe heuenly sterynge or meuynge moost ordinatly maad wiþouten defaute, the mery noyse of briddes
50 in her swete soun, þe delyt of floures and fruytes, þe auauntage and profyt of alle beestes, þat euery ȝeer ben merveylously renewyd to þe byhoue of man, and folwen withoute fayle þe lawe þat is ȝouen to hem of nature, & in al þat þei may enformen & steryn a man to dreede, preise and love abouen [al] þinges þe excellent myȝt of her Maker, þe
55 hy wysdoom of hir Conseruatour or Kepere, & þe infynyt or endles goodnesse of hir Creatour? [Y]is forsoþe. O þou, þerfor, ymage of God, endued & maad noble aboven alle oþere with a free wyle & choys of reson: ȝif þat þou se in thiself, or in [24v] any oþer creature, be yt myȝt, prudence, bountee or honeste, as blyue referre thou & putte al þat to
60 the preysynge, glorie and honour of God, and loue nat that al only for ytself but principaly and finaly for God. Ȝif þow byholde and se in thys world anyþing of defaute, errour, vice, dreede, malice, wrong, or anything vnprofitable or peynful: wyte and arrette al this þe synnes of

---

33 myȝtes: powers   35 substancialy: in substance   37 vertu: strength   42 doon: rendered • finaly: ultimately   44 styren: stir, move   45 sterynge: movement   46 trauayles: labours • nurschynge: nourishment • solace: comfort   47 doctryne: instruction   48 Wher þat: Is it not the case that   49 ordinatly: orderly • defaute: imperfection   52 byhoue: benefit   57 endued: endowed   59 bountee: goodness • as blyue: immediately   63 wyte: blame • arrette: attribute

---

37 thi] this   41 or] of   56 Yis] þis

Speculum Inclusorum • II.ii

videris in hoc mundo: totum peccatis homini imputes, & Dei iustissime
60 punicioni uel permissioni, ut peccator humilietur & timeat, puniatur
& resipiscat, corrigatur & diligat Creatorem. Et ad istum finem, ut
consulat Propheta, 'Videte opera Dei.'

Dileccio tamen Dei copiosius crescit in homine per cordialem contemplacionem operum Christi propter hominem, a prima salutacione
65 angelica Virginis usque ad Sancti Spiritus missionem. Sed inter cetera maxime stimulat peccatorem ad cordis compuncionem, prouocat deuocionis lacrimas, mouet [48v] ad paciendum aspera propter amorem Dei, fortificat & confirmat ad resistendum singulis temptacionibus, frequens memoria gloriosissime passionis. Mentaliter igitur videas,
70 o peccator, qualiter ex omnibus uiribus tam ainime quam corporis pro te uehementissime passus est filius Dei omnipotens, rex glorie, misericors Christus, qui |est| caritas ineffabilis, ut cuilibet peccato tuo possibili correspondeat medicina sufficiens & satisfaccio superabundans, si uolueris corditer misericordiam postulare. Nam anima eius
75 tristis fuit usque ad mortem, pro sananda tua illicita leticia uoluptatis. Oculi eius lacrimas amarissimas produxerunt cum clamore ualido, ut tue uisionis excessibus veniam impetrarent. Aures Regis glorie paciebantur blasphemias, falsa testimonia & improperia, ut pro tui auditus illecebris satisfecerint & tibi tribuerent paciencie documentum.
80 Os Dei omnipotentis in siti sua maxima fellis & aceti amaritudinem degustauit, ut culpas dilueret gustus tui. Nares sue speciosissime faciei olfaciebant saliue immundicias in ipsum derisorie proiectas, ut per hoc tui olfactus culpa remedium habere ualeret. Et sensus tactus in eo supra modum paciebatur, pro tui tactus usu illicito,
85 per totum corpus, quod fuit nodosis flagellis asperime cesum, alapis illusum, crucifixum, lancea clauis atque spinis vndique perforatum, & a planta pedis usque ad uerticem sanguinolentum; primitus tamen,

---

60 uel] et J   72 est] *ins.* R   74 anima] *om.* J   78–9 tui auditus] tuis J   86 atque] ac J

man, and vnto þe riȝtwys punschynge or suffraunce of God, þat doþ it
for þe synful scholde be maad hvmble and haue God in dreede, and þat
he scholde be punsched, and turne aȝen to God, & be correctid, and
loue his Creatour. And vnto þis ende, as conceylid þe prophete Dauyd
& seyde, 'Seeth þe werkes of God.'

Naþeles the love of God wexiþ more plentevously in man þoruȝ
hertly byholdynge of þe werkes of Crist for mannes profyt, f[ro] þe firste
salutacion of þe angel to þe Blessyd Virgine vnto þe sendynge doun of
the Holy Goost. But among [25r] alle oþer þinges ofte to remembre
hertly on þe glorious passion of oure Lord Iesu moost prikkeþ and
sterith þe synful man to compunccion of herte; it prouoketh a man to
teres of deuocion, it sterith a man to suffre paciently scharpe þinges for
þe loue of God, and strengtheth a man to withstonde alle temptacions.
Wherfore, þow synnere, byhoold and see wiþ þe yen of þi soule how
þat, wiþ alle þe myȝtes and strengthes as wiel of soule as of body, þe
almyȝty sone of God, þe King of glorie, mercyable Cryst, which is
hymself charitee, suych and so greet þat þer nys no tonge that may
telle yt, suffrid strongly for þe, to þat entent þat suffisaunt medicyne
and an habundaunt satisfaccion may answere to ech of þi synnes þat
thow hast do or mayst do, ȝif þow wylt hertly aske mercy. For his
soule was þersty vnto þe deeþ, forto heele þe vnleefful gladnesse of þi
fleschly lust. Hys eyen schedden out & droppyd bitter teres with a loud
& greet cry [25v] to purchace perdon of forȝeuenesse to þe excesse and
offense of þi syȝt. The eres of þe Kyng of glorie suffrid blasphemes,
disclandres and scornes, fals witnesse and blames, forto ȝeue vnto þe
þe lore and techynge of pacience to make satisfaccion for þine vnleefful
herynges. The mouth of God almyȝty in his mooste þirst tastide the
bittyrnesse of gall and eysil to wassche awey þe gyltes of þi taast. The
noseþrel of his fayr face smelden þe felþes and vnclenesses and spotil
þat scornful[y] weren þrowen on hym, þat þoruȝ þat þe trespaas of þi
smellynge myȝte have a remedie. And the wyttes of touch he suffryd
in hym by al hys body, for þe vsage of þin vnliefful touch. Which
body was scharply beeten wyth knotty scorges, buffettid, crucified, &
with a spere & nayles & þornes þolede & perside ouyral, & al forbleed

64 punschynge: punishing • suffraunce: tolerance   67 conceylid: counselled
70 hertly: earnest   73 prikkeþ: stimulates   84 vnleefful: unlawful   86 perdon:
pardon   88 disclandres: slanders   89 lore: instruction   91 eysil: vinegar
92 noseþrel: nostril • spotil: spittle   97 þolede: pierced • perside: pierced • forbleed:
covered in blood

---

70 fro] for   93 scornfuly] scornful þat

brachiis atque tibiis per cordas in longum & latum extractis, corpus sanctissimum affixum est cruci penaliter, & tam crudeliter eleuabatur in altum, & iterum ad terram corruit uiolenter quod omnes vene atque nerui corporis rumpebantur, vnde fons misericordie indeficiens effluxit peccatoribus ut lauentur a sordibus. Et si forsan tibi appareat quod sanguis non sufficit emendare delicta, de corde suo per acutam lanceam perforato exiuit aqua preciosissima, ut contritorum vulnera perfeccius collauaret. Huius uehemencie passionis condoluerent etiam insensibiles creature. Omnia Christo paciente compaciebantur: Iudei lapidibus duriores pectora percusserunt; sol suos subtraxit radios & facte sunt tenebre super vniuersam terram; velum templi scissum est in duas partes; terra tremuit; mortui surrexerunt; & petre durissime, quia oculos non habebant quibus se totas diffunderent in lacrimas & dolores, scisse sunt per medium pro signo doloris, tam [49r] dure, tam uilis, tam iniuste, & tam mirabilis passionis. Vnde signanter nobis dicit Dominus per Prophetam (Tren. primo), 'Attendite & videte si est dolor sicut dolor meus.'

O dolor amabilis! O passio plena uirtutibus! O mors summe necessaria peccatoribus, vnde indeficienter effunditur oleum misericordie, erumpit fons pietatis & gracie, propinatur liberaliter omnibus medicina salutis, in riuulis preciosisimi sanguinis Iesu Christi septempliciter effusi: ad satisfaciendum pro omissione VII operum misericoridie & commissione VII mortalium peccatorum, quo ad omnes penitere uolentes et misericordiam postulare. Videas igitur sepius, o peccator; contempleris diligencius & deuocius; adores primo riuulos sanguinis decurrentis a capite Christi pro tuis sceleribus spinis acutissimis ad obprobrium coronati, ut diluat quicquid peccasti per illicitum usum tui capitis cum quinque sensibus in eo fixis; et superbie peccatum

---

91 atque] et J   108 Iesu] *om.* J   111 igitur sepius] ergo semper J

fro þe sole of þe foot vnto þe top of his heed; and his [26r] armes and
his legges drawen out along with cordis & ropes, & þan his holy &
100 blessid body peynfully ficchid to þe croys, and cruely was he reryd on
hy and agayn þrowen adoun violently & dispitously to þe erthe, þat
alle þe veynes & synwes of hys body were broken & brosten, wherof
þe welle of mercy þat neuere schal cece ne fayle flowed out in large
stremees vnto synners to wassche and purge hem of her gyltes. And ȝif
105 percas yt semeth to þe þat his blood suffiseth nat to clense þe, þanne
remembre the of þe precious water that stremyd out from his herte
þat was þerlyd wiþ a scharp spere to wassche awey perfitly þe synnes
of contryt folkes. The insensible creatures, þat is to seyn the creatures
þat hadde no felynge ne lyf, [h]adden sorwe and heuynesse of his greet
110 and scharp passyon. The Iewes, whoos hertes ben hardere þan stones,
cnokkyd on her brestes whan Crist suffryde alle his tormentz. [26v] Þe
sonne wythdrow hys bemes & derknesses apperden on the erthe. [The
erthe] quok, the dede man roos vp, and the harde stones (for thei hadde
noon eyen wiþ whiche þe[i] myȝt caste out teres and sorwes) weren kut
115 atwo in þe myddes, in tokne of sorwe and heuynesse of so dispitous, so
vniust, and so merueylos a passion. Wherof God seith be [o]pyn tokne
to vs by the Prophete: 'Taketh hede,' he seyth, 'and seeth ȝif þer be any
sorwe lyk to my sorwe.'
 O louynge sorwe! O passion full of vertues! O necessarie & byhoueful
120 deeth vnto alle synneres, wherof wellyd out þe oyle of mercy þat
neuere schal fayle; wherof sprong also the welle of pyte & grace, and
þe medicyn of helþe spradde out largely to alle folk in þe ryueres of
the precious blood of Iesu Crist schede for vs in vii^e maner wyses: to
make satisfaccion and redresse for the omyssion and leuynge [of] þe
125 vii^e werkes of mercy, & for þe offense or trespace in þe vii^e deedly
syn-[27r]-nes, as vnto alle þo þat han wil for to repente and rewe her
wykkydnesse & aske mercy. Therfore, o þou synnere, often byhalde
and see bisili and deuoutly. First, honoure and worschipe thow þe
stremees & þe ryueres þat ron doun from þe heed of Crist þat was
130 coronyd for thi synnes wiþ scharp þornes, bysechynge hym in al
meknesse þat he do awey al þat þow hast synnyd by vnleefful vsage of
þin heed, with þe v wyttes ficchid in it; and þat þe humble & meke

---

100 reryd: raised up   101 dispitously: cruelly   102 synwes: sinews • brosten: burst,
broken   103 cece: cease   104 stremees: streams (N)   105 percas: perhaps   107 þerlyd:
pierced   111 cnokkyd: beat   113 quok: shook   115 atwo: in two • dispitous: cruel,
violent   119 byhoueful: beneficial   130 coronyd: crowned

109 hadden] ladden   116 opyn] apyn   124 of] for

tollat a te humilis inclinacio capitis Christi in cruce. 2° contempleris purissimum sanguinem cordis Christi pro te crudeliter lanceati, ut mundet quicquid peccasti per immundam cogitacionem seu illicitam uoluntatem; & a te peccatum inuidie longe propellat quia ipse cecum cor suum perforantem protinus illuminauit. 3° contempleris vndas sanguinis effluentis de Christi manibus pro te crudeliter perforatis, ut lauet quicquid peccasti per manuum tuarum illicitam operacionem; & tuam cupiditatem attenuet Christi nuditas pro te pendentis in cruce. 4° contempleris fluentem sanguinem pro te ex tocius corporis Christi durissima flagellacione, ut abluat quicquid peccasti per illicitum usum tui corporis; ut ire stimulos in te mitiget, quod ipse pro suis tortoribus exorauit. 5° contempleris guttas sanguinei sudoris Christi pro te currentis in terram, ut purget quicquid peccasti per usum illicitum temporalium superfluum; et esuries Christi, ieiunium, atque sitis per aceti & fellis amaritudinem saturatam, illecebram tue gule refrenent. 6° contempleris tenerrimum sanguinem puerilium membrorum Christi die octauo pro te circumcisi cum cultro lapides, donec temptaciones luxurie reprimat in te & euanescat omnis illicita concupiscencia carnis tue. Et 7° contempleris fluuios sanguinis distillantis de Christi pedibus conclauatis, qui pro amore tuo uersus tale tormentum non renuit crucem propriam baiulare, donec auferat a te peccatum accidie & tibi concedat in bonis actibus [49v] diligenciam operosam. Sic igitur, iuxta consilium Helisei prophete, 'Lauare sepcies in Iordane & recipiet sanitatem caro tua atque mundaberis.'

His corditer attentis, quis peccator poterit de uenia desperare, dum in Saluatore nostro nobis misericordiam promittente concurrunt [in]impedibilis omnipotencia, infallibilis ueritas, summa & ineffabiliter

---

117 cordis Christi] om. J   137 igitur] ergo J   142 inimpedibilis] J, impedibilis R • ineffabiliter] ineffabilis J

inclinacion or bowynge of Cristes heed in þe croys wiþdrawe fro the þe synn[e] of pride. Secundely, byhoold þe clene blood of Cristes herte cruely woundyd with a spere, þat he clense and purge þe of al þat euere þou hast synnyd by vnclene þouȝt and vnliefful wyl; & þat he putte awey fer fro þe þe synne of envie. The IIIe, byhoold wel þe cours of blood þat cam out of Crystes handes þat weren cruely þerlyd for þe, þat i[t] may wasshe awei al [27v] þat þow hast synned by vnliefful werkynge of þine handes; and lat þe nakkydnes of Crist hangynge in the croys make þe nakyd and baare of coueytous desire. The IIIIe, byhold thow þe flowynge blood passynge out for þe in strong stremes of scharp scourges of þe body of Iesu Crist, þat it may wassche away al þat þou haast synned by vnleefful vsage of þi body; and þat he asswage & abregge in the þe prikkynge, þe styrynges, of ire or of wratthe, inasmoche as he preyde for hem þat weren his tormentoures. The V^e, biholde þe dropes of þe blody swoot of Crist þat fil doun to þe erthe for the, þat yt may clense al þat þat þou hast synnyd by þe superflu or outrageous vsage of temperal goodes; and þat þe honger, the fastynge, & þe þirst of Crist, which weryn fillid by þe bittyrnesse of eysil and gall, mowe refreyne or withdrawe þin excessyf and vnliefful glotenye. The VI, byhoolde & see the tendre blood [28r] of þe ȝonge, childissch membres of Crist þat was circumcised for the þe VIII day with a scharp stoon, til þat al þin vnliefful concupiscence or fleschly desir dist[r]oye, or quenche in the þe temptacions of lecherye. And þe VIIe, byhoold and se þe flodes of blood distillynge & droppynge doun fro þe nayle[d] feet of Crist, which for thi love forsook nat ne lothid nat to bere his owen croys toward the same torment, that he kepe þe fro þe synne of sleuthe, and þat he graunte the continuel besynesse in good & vertuous werk. Thus, lo, after þe conseyl of Helyse the prophete, 'Wassch þe VIIe sythes in Iordan, and þi flesch schal receyve helþe, and þou schalt be clensyd.'

Now ȝif a man take hertly heede to þese þinges, what synnere may dispey[r]e or myshope of pardon or forȝe[ue]nesse, whiles in our Saueour, byhetynge vs his mercy, been concurrent or knyt togydre his hi myȝt þat may nat be let, his infallable or vndeceyuable trouthe, and

133 inclinacion: bending down   144 asswage: lessen • abregge: diminish
145 prikkynge: provoking   147 swoot: sweat   148 superflu: excessive • outrageous: excessive   150 refreyne: restrain   158 sleuthe: sloth   160 Helyse: Elisha • sythes: times
163 myshope: despair   164 byhetynge: promising • concurrent: conjoined • knyt: tied
165 vndeceyuable: certain

---

134 synne] synnd, *but some sign of attempted correction*   146 þat] he *add*   156 nayled] nayles   163 dispeyre] dispeyse

erga nos dileccio caritatis? In tante dileccionis signum caput Christi pendentis in cruce nobis inclinatur ad osculum, brachia expanduntur ad amplexum, cor aperitur ad amorem, manus & pedes crucifiguntur ad nobiscum pro perpetuo permanendum. Nam usque ad finem seculi manebit nobiscum Christus corporaliter in altaris sanctissimo sacramento, ubi cotidie sub specie panis & vini pro nobis offertur eius anima in nostre redempcionis precium, corpus in spiritualem cibum, sanguis in salutis poculum, & aqua lateris in lauacrum, totumque in nobile confortatiuum contra demonis temptamenta.

Crux enim Christi est uerissime lignum uite, cuius fructus, summe virtutis, venenum ligni uetiti a primis parentibus propagatum destruit. Quemlibet sacramentum altaris digne sumentem nutrit, roborat & confortat ipsum ueraciter, vniens capiti suo Christo tanquam eius membrum suo sanguine propria viuificatum. Unde, si Christi corporis & sanguinis generositate fueris insignitus, & sic decesseris ab hac luce, nec Infernus, nec diabolus, te retinere poterit; nulla te pena cruciabit perpetua, sed tanti sanguinis precio redemptus, celesti gloria dignus eris, & tanquam consanguineus Regis eterni ad celestem gloriam finaliter ingredieris.

Ne tamen tot & tanta diuine misericordie beneficia tibi liberaliter oblata presumpcionem, negligenciam uel accidiam generent in te, contempleris interdum diuine iusticie seueritatem, dolorose separacionis anime a corpore necessitatem, & illius temporis incertitudinem, quando maliciosi demones terribiliter apparebunt singula peccata tua pro quibus satisfactum non fuerit etiam usque ad minimum verbum ociosum uel cogitacionem illicitam proferentes. Tunc conabuntur miseram animam secum rapere ad Infernum uel ad Purgatorium ualde penale & ad

---

150 &] *om.* J   166 tua] sua J

[28v] his entier dileccion or loue of charite to vs-ward, which is so greet and so excellent þat tonge of man suffiseþ nat to telle yt? In signe or tokne of which dileccion, the heed of Cryst hanginge in þe croys ys enclyned or bowed doun to profre vs a kus, his armes ben outstrecchid
170 to enbrace or clippe vs, þe herte is opnyd wyde to love vs, his handes and feet ben ficchid to þe croys to duelle wyth vs perpetuely. For vnto the worldys ende Crist schal duelle with vs bodyly in the holy and blisful sacrament of the autier, where euery day vndir þe figure or liknesse of breed and wyn hys soule ys offred vnto vs into þe prys of
175 oure redempcion, þe bodi into spirituel mete, þe blood into drynke of helþe, and þe watir of his syde into oure lauour of clensynge, and al into a noble confortatyf agay[n] the fendes temptacions.

The croys of Crist ys þe verray [tree of] lyf, whos excellently vertuous fruyt hath destroyd þe venym þat sp[r]ang [29r] out or was
180 engendrid of þe deffendid or forboden tree þoruȝ þe offence of oure firste progenitoures, Adam & Eve. That blysful sacrament of þe auter nurscheth, strenthith and confortiþ euery man & womman þat takyth yt worthily; knyttiþ hymself verrayly to hys heed, Crist, as a membre of hys, qwykned wiþ his owen blood. Wherfore, ȝif þow be honured
185 or maad noble þoruȝ þe gentylnesse of his body, and þou passe so out of þis present lyf, nouther Helle ne the deuel may holde the, and þer schal no peyne perpetuel turmente the. But þow þat art bouȝt with the prys of so precious blood schalt be worþi to haue heuenly ioye, and þou schalt fynaly entre into þe blisse of heuene as a k[yns]man of þe
190 euerlastynge Kyng of heuene.

Ȝyt natheles, lest so manye and so large benefices of þe mercy of God freely profred to þe engendre presumpcion, negligence or slouthe, behoold euere among þe steerne ryȝtwysnesse of God, þe sorwe- [29v]-full departynge of þe soule fro þe body, & the vncerteynte of
195 tyme whan þe malicious feendes schullen feerfully appere byforn þe, tellynge and schewynge vnto þe alle þe synnes þat þow hast wrouȝt for the which þou hast [nat] maad satisfaccion. Þer schal nat so moche be forgetyn as þe leeste ydyl word or vnleefful þouȝt. Than wole þei enforce hem to take with hem þe wrecchid soule vnto Helle, or to Purgatorie

---

166 dileccion: love • to vs-ward: towards us   170 clippe: embrace   173 autier: altar
174 prys: price   175 mete: food   176 lauour: washing liquid   177 confortatyf: balm, source of comfort   178 verray: true   180 deffendid: forbidden   185 gentylnesse: nobility   191 natheles: nonetheless   193 euere among: now and then   195 feerfully: terrifyingly   198–9 enforce hem: strive

---

189 kynsman] knyfman (?)

170 terribile iudicium irati Iudicis omnipotentis, cuius summa iusticia sinere non poterit aliquid peccatum impunitum. Ad hoc iudicium uocaberis subito, nec dabuntur inducie, nec ualebit appelacio a Iudice, nec poterit vlla esse excusacio culpe, vbi tam Iudici quam singulis creaturis manifestabuntur [50r] omnia peccata etiam occultissime cordis cogita-
175 ciones, teste propria consciencia remordente. Nam ibidem strictissimus compotus exigetur a te de quolibet Dei beneficio preaccepto, ac etiam de quolibet momento temporis uite tue qualiter expensum fuerit ad Dei honorem, necnon de qualibet modica commissione mali uel omissione boni, ab annis discrecionis tue usque ad articulum mortis tue.
180 O quot oblita peccata, quot defectus, quot neglicencie, tunc inopinate prorumpent quasi ex insidiis, & miseram animam captiuabunt! Si uero (quod absit) ad hoc iudicium ueneris cum mortali peccato, superius te terrebit iratus Iudex districtissimus & omnipotens; inferius te tremere faciet patens puteus infernalis, ut te absorbeat in penis intolerabilibus;
185 interius te torquebit remordens consciencia; ante te stupefacient omnia peccata tua Deo, angelis omnibus, & omnibus hominibus manifesta; retro tibi timorem non modicum incucient tortores cum instrumentis infernalibus ut te rapiant ad tormenta. A sinistris te communiter accusabunt omnes demones & dampnati quod, non solum Deum
190 offendisti, uerum etiam ipsorum omnium penas perpetuas aggrauasti: quia quanto cicius uenerit Dies Iudicii, & plures dampnati fuerint, tanto grauius punientur. A dextris te conformiter accusabunt omnes beati ordines hominum & angelorum quod, permanens in peccato mortali usque ad dampnacionem, fugisti ab exercitu christianorum;

---

173 singulis] omnibus J   179 tue] *om.* J   187 tibi] te J   190 omnium] omnes J • perpetuas] *om.* J

II.ii • A Mirror for Recluses   61

200 which ys ry3t peynful, & vnto þe feerful doom of þe almy3ty Iuge, whos hy ry3twysnesse may suffre no synne vnpunsched. Vnto þat tremlynge or quakynge iugement schalt þow sodeynly be callyd. Þer schal no respyt been had, ne noon apeel fro þe Iuge schal þere avayle, ne noon excusacion of synne schal ben admyttid or receyued, where
205 alle synnes schullen openly be schewyd, as wel to þe Iuge as to alle creatures, in so mochil þat þe moost priue þou3tes schullen also be cnowe, wit-[3or]-nessynge a mannes owen conscience þat sore fretiþ and gnawyth wythine hymself. Þere schal ben askyd of þe a full streit acounte of alle þe 3iftes þat God hath 3ouen the and þat þow hast of
210 hym receyuyd and taken byforn, and also þou schalt acounte of euery moment of the tyme of þi lyf here, how þou hast dispendid yt to the honour of G[o]d, & of euery wykkyd deede be yt neuere so smal. Euery man schal acounte also of al þe goodnes þat he hath left vndoon, and my3te haue doon yt, fro þe 3eres of his discrecion vnto þe tyme of hys
215 deeth.

   O how ma[n]y for3eten synnes, how many defautes, how many negligences, schul þanne sodeynly breste out, as yt were in a wayt, to trouble þi wrecchid soule! 3if þow come (as God defende yt) in deedly synne to þe doom, the [h]ly Iuge aboue þe, [þe] wrat[h]ful & streyt
220 Iuge, þe almy3ti Lord, schal agaste þe full sore; and byneth-forth schal þe opyn pyt of Helle make þe to tremble [30v] and quake, to swolw the in peynnes vntollerable or vnsuffrable; wiþine-forth þin owen conscience schal sore frete and gnavve; byforn the, alle thy synnes schul fere þe, for þei schullen ben knowen openly to God, to
225 his angeles, and to alle oþere; byhynde þe schul tormentoures putte the in huge dreede wiþ her instrumentes, infernaly or hellely to take þe into torment. On the lyf[t] hand alle þe feendes and dampnyd folk schullen accuse the in comune þat þou hast nat only offendid God, but þou hast also encrecyd þe perpetuel peynes of hem alle. For þe sonner
230 þat þe day of Doom approcheþ or ney3eth, and the mo folk þat ben dampnyd, þe more greuous schal ben hir torment and punschinge. On the ry3t hand alle þe blessyd ordres of men and angeles schullen accuse the þat þou, duellynge & contynuynge in deedly synne, fleddest vnto dampnacion fro the hoost of cristen peple, & abreggedist and madist

---

200 doom: judgement   203 apeel: appeal   206 priue: secret   207 fretiþ: eats   208 streit: strict   211 dispendid: spent   217 breste: burst • wayt: ambush   220 agaste: terrify • byneth-forth: underneath   222 swolw: swallow   226 hellely: hellishly   233 duellynge: remaining

---

212 God] good   219 hy] vy   221 þe opyn] opyn þe   232 and] *written twice*

195 minuisti eorum aciem contra temptaciones; ad multorum malum exemplum, non iuuisti pacientes in Purgatorio per opera caritatis sed, per tuam uitam dampnabilem, communem resurreccionis gloriam retardasti, quando etiam celestes orbes – sol, luna, cum ceteris planetis & stellis omnibus – terra, mare, & elementa singula, mutabuntur in
200 septempliciter clariorem seu perfecciorem statum, & sic premiabuntur in eterna quiete pro seruicio quod (Deo uolente) hominibus temporaliter exhibuerint. Et ideo hec omnia in circuitu de te, qui suam felicitatem taliter retardasti, modis sibi possibilibus conquerentur. Non igitur sine causa racionabili, si ad Iudicium ueneris cum mortali peccato, singule
205 creature ad suum Iudicem contra te taliter conclamabunt: 'Vindica iustissime Iudex non solum tuam iniuriam, sed etiam dampnum illatum tuis omnibus creaturis.'

Propterea, iuxta consilium prophete Dauid, sepius mentaliter 'Videte opera Dei terribilis in [50v] consiliis super filios homini.' O
210 quam terribilis sentencia, o quam horribilis pena, o quam interminabilis dolor, post hunc clamorem sequetur igni eterno iustissime condempnatos. Nam, secundum quorumdam sanctorum sentenciam, in Die Iudicii omnes sordes, omnes venenosi serpentes, & omnes immundi fetores, ad centrum mundi subito descendent ut ibi, tanquam
215 in loco Inferno congruentissimo, sine fine peccatorem puniant. Nec mirum igitur si Infernalis pena sit horribilis & acerba, cum pena Purgatorii, secundum beatum Augustinum, sit durior quam quicquid penarum uideri uel cogitari poterit, in hac uita. Torquebunt siquidem sine fine miseros in Inferno ignis inextinguibilis, vermis immortalis,
220 sitis insaciabilis, aspectus demonum horribilis, tenebre palpabiles, fetor intolerabilis, de summo frigore in summum calorem subita mutacio, diuine uisionis & cuiuslibet gaudii carencia, summa cordis tristicia, & desperacio cuiuscunque remedii uel succursus. Quia ut in breuibus multa concludam, nichil erit ibidem delectabile, nulla consolacio, nulla
225 confortacio; sed quodlibet tale erit ibidem quod punire poterit uel nocere, & hoc irremediabiliter sine fine. O igitur anima misera, iuxta consilium Prophete (Ier. 2°), sepius 'Uide, quia malum & amarum est reliquisse te Dominum Deum tuum, & non esse timorem eius apud te.'

Sic conformiter, uos inclusi, per meditacionem tempore necessariam,
230 *Uidete uocacionem vestram.*

---

195 malum] *om.* J, *but space left*   197 communem] *om.* J   213 venenosi] venosi J
217 beatum] *om.* J   218 siquidem] *om.* J   223 uel] et J   224 erit] est J

235 lasse þe companye of hem [end of 30v] *in the fight against temptations; as a poor example to many people you did not help those suffering in Purgatory through works of charity but, by your damnable life, delayed the glory of the general resurrection, when even the celestial bodies – the sun, the moon, with the other planets and all the stars – the earth, the sea, and all*
240 *the elements, will be transformed into a state seven times brighter or more perfect, and thus will receive their reward of eternal rest for the service that (according to God's will) they have offered to people through time. And so all these whose happiness you have postponed in this way, surrounding you on all sides, will denounce you in whatever way is possible to them. And*
245 *so not without reasonable cause, if you come to the Judgement in a state of mortal sin, will every creature thus cry out against you to their Judge: 'Do not avenge only your own injury, oh Judge most just, but also the harm brought upon all your creatures.'*

Afterwards in your mind, following the advice of the prophet David,
250 *frequently 'See the works of God, who is terrible in his counsels over the sons of men.' Oh how terrible a sentence, oh how horrible a punishment, oh how unending a misery, will, once this cry has been issued, most justly accompany the condemned into the enternal fires! For on the Day of Judgement, according to the opinion of various saints, all filth, all poisonous*
255 *serpents, and all disgusting stenches, will suddenly descend to the centre of the world, so that there, as being most suited to that place, which is Hell, they might punish the sinner without end. And it is no wonder if the pains of Hell are horrible and bitter, when the pains of Purgatory, according to Saint Augustine, are harder than any of the pains that can be experienced*
260 *or conceived of in this life. For the wretched souls in Hell will be tormented endlessly with inextinguishable fire, undying serpents, insatiable thirst, the horrifying appearance of the demons, palpable darkness, an unbearable stench, sudden changes from extreme cold to extreme heat, being deprived of the sight of the divine and all his joys, the greatest sadness of heart, and*
265 *a lack of hope of any remedy or help. And so, if I might summarise many things in a few words, there will be nothing delightful there, no consolation, no comfort; but there will be all such things there that can punish or injure, and that without remedy and without end. Therefore, oh you wretched soul, according to the counsel of the prophet Jeremiah, frequently 'See that it is an*
270 *evil and a bitter thing for thee, to have left the Lord thy God, and that my fear is not with thee.'*

In a similar way, you recluses, by timely and necessary meditation, 'Look to your vocation.'

---

235 of hem] *catchwords at foot of fol. 30v. A lacuna follows*

Capitulum 3

Postquam diuini seruicii debitum completum est, quod semper hora competenti uocaliter est reddendum cum omni deuocione quam ipse Spiritus Sanctus dignabitur inspirare, residuum temporis expendetur alternatim in oracione, meditacione & edificatoria leccione, uel in opere
5 aliquo manuali. Vnde de his 4^{or} exercendis (ultra seruicium debitum) hec lex tanquam magis expediens statuatur: videlicet quod, tepescente deuocione uel attenuata uel attediata natura fragili & mutabili in vno istorum 4, statim ad aliud recurratur, ut occupacionis uariacio vitet ocium, expellat accidiam, deuocionem continuet & naturam
10 recreet fatigatam. Si igitur oracio uel meditacio minus sapiat seu delectet, aliqua leccio edificatoria protinus requiratur, cuius utilitas omnem estimacionem excedit, cum sit speculum viciorum omnium & uirtutum, mentis distraccionem euacuans, ad uirtutes singulas alliciens animam & inuitans, ac etiam a viciis omnibus separans per quandam
15 [51r] racionis uiolenciam, ac per instanciam timoris, pariter & amoris.

Hinc est quod lex Dei dabatur in scriptis, ut magis moueret mentem humanam labilem & distractam. Sic liber |legis|, lectus coram rege Iosia, compunxit tam cor eius quam populi, mores ipsorum corrigens & auferens omnes immundicias terre sue, sicut patet 4 R. 21. Sic lex,
20 lecta coram filiis Israel, deuocionem cordibus eorum infudit, laudes Dei produxit, & eorum uitam in melius commutauit, vt patet Neemie 8. Nonne benedicta uirgo Maria dum incarnacionis propheciam deuote legeret, celestem nuncium Gabrielem audire meruit, & Dei filium concepit ad tocius mundi gaudium & salutem? Nonne vir Ethiops
25 eunuchus, legens in curru suo deuocius Ysaiam, quamuis non intelligeret que legebat, cicius per nutum diuine misericordie Philippum apostolum instructorem habuit in fide Christi, & promeruit baptizari? Nonne sanctarum scripturarum leccio plenius intellecta fidelissime ponderat & describit verum & falsum, licitum & illicitum, bonum & malum,
30 uirtutes & uicia, penas & premia, cuilibet morbo spirituali remedium conferens salutare?

Propterea (si litteratus fueris) legas libencius sacras litteras, sanctorum uitas, martirum passiones, deuotorum meditaciones; &, inter hec

---

Heading *Capitulum 3*] *om*. J   4 &] *om*. J • in^2] *om*. J   5 aliquo] *om*. J   7 uel^2] seu J   14 animam] *altered to* animum J   17 legis] *ins. marg. with caret mark in text* R   19 sicut patet] *om*. J   21 vt] *om*. J   22 Maria] *om*. J, *but space left*

Chapter 3

After you have fulfilled the requirements of divine service, which should be performed out loud at the appropriate hours with all the devotion that the Holy Spirit sees fit to inspire, the rest of your time should be spent by turns in prayer, meditation and edifying reading, or in some manual work. And concerning the use of these four things (over and above the requirements of divine service) this law is laid down as being the most expedient: that is that, when your devotion cools or is lessened, or your frail and changeable nature grows weary, in one of these four, you should straight away turn to another, so that variety of occupation may put idleness to flight, drive out lethargy, prolong your devotion and refresh your weary nature. And so, if your taste for prayer or delight in meditation decreases, immediately seek out some edifying reading, the profit of which exceeds all estimation, since it offers a mirror of all vices and virtues, clearing distractions from the mind, attracting and enticing all virtues to the soul, and also sundering it from all vices, by a kind of assault on the reason, and by the urging of fear, as well as of love.

This is why the law of God was given in written form, so that it might work more effectively on the unstable and distracted human mind. In this way the book of the law, when it was read before King Josia, moved both his and the people's hearts to compunction, so that they amended their manners and ceased from all the unclean practices in his land, as it shows in 4 Kings 21. In the same way the law, when it was read before the sons of Israel, filled their hearts with devotion, stimulated them to praise of God, and changed their lives for the better, as it shows in Nehemiah 8. Wasn't it while she was devoutly reading a prophecy of the incarnation that the Blessed Virgin Mary was considered worthy to hear the heavenly messenger Gabriel, and conceived the son of God for the joy and salvation of the whole world? Wasn't it when he was very devoutly reading Isaiah in his chariot, even though he did not understand what he read, that the Egyptian eunuch suddenly, by the command of divine mercy, had the apostle Philip to teach him in the faith of Christ, and became worthy to be baptised?

Therefore (if you are literate) you should gladly read holy literature, saints' lives, the passions of the martyrs, devout meditations; and, from amongst

omnia, frequencius illud legas quod per experienciam tuam deuocionem
35 magis accendere consueuit. In leccione siquidem percipies quod semper,
a mundi principio, superbi & impenitentes abiecti fuerunt a Deo
finaliter & reprobati, contriti & humiles per penitenciam sunt saluati,
iusti & pacientes penalia propter Deum eternaliter premiabantur,
obedientes & in pugna spirituali contra temptaciones uiriliter perseu-
40 erantes ad celestis glorie coronam immarcessibilem diuinitus sunt
uocati. Ex his, quantuscunque peccator prius fueris, consolacionem
percipies & spem venie de peccatis tam propriis quam alienis pro quibus
decreueris orare in caritate. Iuxta quod dicit Apostolus, 'Quecunque
scripta sunt ad nostram doctrinam scripta sunt, ut per pacienciam &
45 consolacionem scripturarum, spem habeamus.' Ideoque in sacris litteris
inspicere debemus statum nostrum, prout hortatur Christus (Marc. 13)
dicens, 'Videte vosmetipsos.'

O nobilissimum sacre leccionis speculum! O ueritatis testimonium!
O perfeccionis forma! Tu es mestorum consolacio, temptacionis
50 frenum, & sanctarum prouocacio lacrimarum. Tu es desperantibus
anchora spei firme, superbis humilitatis regula, iracundis paciencie
occasio, incentiuum amoris [51v] cupidis, & auaris sacietas uirtuosa.
Tu es luxuriosis extinccio uoluptatis, desidiosis stimulus, gulosis
moderacio uictus, & columpna fortitudinis timorosis. Quis vnquam
55 potuit seriose legere & intelligere diuine misericordie multitudinem &
magnitudinem, & de uenia desperare, dum in Petro negacio Christi,
in Magdalena prostitucio corporis sui, & in latrone iniuriacio proximi,
veniam promeruit modica penitencia precedente? Quis in serie sacre
scripture considerans humilitatem Iesu Christi & Luciferi superbiam,
60 non ex hoc humilior reddetur? Quis cogitans Saulis iram & inuidiam,
sancti Dauid caritatem, Iob pacienciam, non fieret proximis benignior,
in aduersis paciencior, & beneuolencior vniuersis? Nemo cupiditatem
prouideret dum in sacris litteris inueniret quod multi propter eam tam
corporaliter quam spiritualiter perierunt. Nemo luxuriam diligeret sed
65 odiret, dum legeret qualiter propter peccatum luxurie destructus fuerat
totus mundus, sic quod aque diluuii per xv cubitos montes altissimos
transcendebat, & qualiter propter uicium Sodomiticum Deus pluit
sulphur & ignem super v ciuitates, ipsas subuertendo cum tota regione
propinqua, prout in historiis Gen. satis patet. Similiter, nemo gulam
70 & accidiam frequentaret, cum mente reuolueret qualiter per gulam
in primis parentibus genus humanum perdidit Paradisum, qualiter

---

46 Marc.] Math. J   55 seriose] serio J   59 Iesu] om. J, but space left   67 propter] post J   69 prout in historiis Gen. satis] in Gen. J

all these, you should read particularly frequently whichever tends in your experience most to increase your devotion. By reading you will certainly see that, ever since the beginning of the world, the proud and impenitent have been cast out by God and finally condemned, the contrite and humble are saved by penitence, the just and those who suffer hardships on God's account have been given eternal reward, the obedient and those who have persevered manfully in the spiritual battle against temptations receive the divine call to an imperishable crown of heavenly glory. From this, however great a sinner you have been before, you should derive consolation and hope of pardon for both your own sins and those of other people for whom you have decided to pray in charity. In accordance with which, the Apostle says, 'What things soever were written were written for our learning: that, through patience and the comfort of the scriptures, we might have hope.' And so we should contemplate our condition in holy literature, as Christ tells us (Mark 13), saying, 'See yourselves.'

Oh holy reading, you are the noblest of mirrors! Oh you're a witness to the truth! Oh you're a model of perfection! You are a consolation to the sorrowful, a curb to temptation, and a stimulus to holy tears. To the despairing you are a secure anchor of hope, to the proud a yardstick of humility, to the wrathful an occasion of patience, an enticement to love to the covetous, and to the greedy a source of virtuous fulfilment. To the lustful you offer the quenching of their desire, a spur to the slothful, to the gluttonous a moderation of their intake, and a tower of strength to the fearful. Who could ever seriously read and understand the range and magnitude of divine mercy, and lose hope of forgiveness, when Peter for his denying of Christ, the Magdalene for the prostitution of her body, and the thief for the harm done to his neighbours, all gained pardon after a little penitence? Who, earnestly considering in Holy Scripture the humility of Jesus Christ and the pride of Lucifer, would not by that be made more humble? Who, thinking on Saul's anger and jealousy, holy David's charity, Job's patience, would not become more generous to his neighbours, more patient in adversity, and better-disposed to all people? No-one would concern himself with avarice when he found in holy literature that many have perished both in body and in spirit on account of it. No-one would love lustfulness, but hate it, when he read how on account of the sin of lust the whole world was destroyed, so that the floodwaters exceeded the highest mountains by 15 cubits, and how on account of the vice of the Sodomites God rained sulphur and fire on 5 cities, destroying them together with the whole surrounding area, as it shows clearly enough in the story of Genesis. Similarly, no-one would practise gluttony and sloth, when he reflected on how humankind lost paradise by the gluttony of our first parents, how

Esau per gulam uisis lenticulis primogenita vendidit, & qualiter panis saturitas & ocium peccatum Sodomiticum introduxit. Sic per peccata singula discurrendo patebit quod sacras litteras frequencius legens contra temptaciones armabitur, abhorebit uicia, uirtutibus adherebit, firmam spem uenie concipiet de peccatis, & induet paciencie fortitudinem in penalitatibus huius vite.

Siquis uero Latinum non intellexerit, leccionem deuotam Anglico, uel Gallico, siue in suo ydiomate vulgari, frequentet, ut consimiliter edificetur. & audibili uoce legat, quia maxime solet corda compungere uox viua legentis. Si autem simpliciter illiteratus fuerit aliquis, in loco leccionis aliquid honestum manibus operetur, commiscens interdum operi suo Pater Noster & Aue Maria, ne distrahatur animus ad cogitaciones uanas, uoluptuosas, seu illicitas. Sed opus continuet in cordis mundicia, ut semper expellatur ociositas, que est anime (ultra quam credi poterit) inimica. Nec causetur aliquis quod non poterit oracionem miscere cum opere, quia frequenter solent artifices laborantes ad suum solacium gesta narrare forcium, [52r] seu canere delectabiliter amatorias cantilenas. Numquid igitur tu, serue Dei, tantum gaudenter perficere debes ad eius laudem, gloriam & honorem, quantum facillime faciunt seculares pro amore mundi & suo solacio corporali? Ulterius & tibi laico totus mundus liber esse poterit ad legendum Dei potenciam & bonitatem, misericordiam & veritatem, iusticiam & equitatem, malorum supplicia & bonorum premia, eternorum gaudia & temporalium vanitatem. Vbi nunc, queso, sunt Sampson fortissimus, Salomon sapientissimus, Absolon pulcherrimus, Alexander potentissimus? Vbi Cresi diuicie? Ubi cunctorum leticie precedencium antiquorum? Nonne transierunt ista omnia uelud umbra? Nec hic poterunt diucius permanere, sed a mundi Gubernatore iustissimo & omnipotentissimo transferuntur a nobis ad inuisibilia loca penarum uel premiorum eternalium, iuxta quod in hac uita uocati diuinitus uel reprobati finaliter meruerunt. Unde signanter dicit Apostolus (Ad Ro. primo) quod 'Inuisibilia Dei a creatura mundi, per ea que facta sunt intellecta, conspiciuntur.'

Sic igitur, uos inclusi, per huiusmodi leccionem edificatoriam, *Videte uocacionem vestram.*

---

73 per] *om.* J   76 paciencie] *om.* J   77 penalitatibus] penalibus J   82 manibus] *om.* J
83 &] cum J   87 miscere] misere J   90 laudem] et *add.* J   92 poterit] potest J * &]
om. J   93 &¹] *om.* J   94 &¹] *om.* J   98 hic] nichil J * permanere] manere J   102 Ad]
om. J * quod] *om.* J   104 igitur] ergo J

by gluttony Esau sold his birthright when he saw the lentils, and how an abundance of bread and idleness led the Sodomites to their sin. Thus, having run through each of the sins, it will be clear that the person who most often reads holy literature will be armed against temptations, will keep from vice, cleave to virtues, feel a sure hope of pardon for his sins, and imbue himself with the strength to withstand the trials of this life.

But if someone does not understand Latin, he should practise devout reading in English or in French, or in his vernacular language, so that he may be similarly edified. And he should read aloud, for when one reads the living voice usually has the greatest effect on the heart. If however someone is completely illiterate, instead of reading he should do some suitable work with his hands, interspersing his work with 'Our Father' and 'Hail Mary', so that his mind should not be distracted into vain, lustful, or illicit thoughts. But let him continue his work in cleanness of heart, in order constantly to drive out idleness, which is (more than you could believe) the enemy of the soul. And don't let anyone claim that he cannot mingle prayer with work, for workmen often as a diversion tell tales of heroes, or sing love-songs with delight. So shouldn't you, God's servant, gladly do for his praise, glory and honour as much as worldly people do so easily for the love of the world and the comfort of their bodies? And further, if you are a layperson, the whole world can be a book for you to read of God's power and goodness, mercy and truth, justice and equity, the punishments of the wicked and the rewards of the good, the joys of eternity and the vanity of the world. What has become now, I ask you, of Samson, the strongest man? Solomon, the wisest? Absolon, the fairest? Alexander, the most powerful? Where are the riches of Croesus? Where are the joys of all those who came before us? Have all these not passed as a shadow? Nor will they be able to remain here any longer, but will be taken from us by the most just and almighty Ruler of the world to the invisible places of eternal punishment or reward, according as they have deserved while in this life to be chosen by God, or cast out. This is exactly why the Apostle says (Romans 1) that 'The invisible things of him, from the creation of the world, are clearly seen, being understood by the things that are made'.

And so, you recluses, by edifying reading of this kind, 'Look to your vocation.'

Capitulum primum tercie partis

Tercio principaliter in hoc opere videbitis, uos inclusi, qualiter exequemini uocacionem vestram. Quia (sicut superius est ostensum) uocati estis ad iugiter orandum, meditandum, legendum, uel aliquid honestum manibus operandum. Ideo, per consideracionem vestri profectus uel
5 defectus in istis, uidere potestis qualis fuerit execucio uocacionis uestre.

Unde primo, quoad oraciones debitas uel consuetas: ad noctem cotidie, priusquam detis oculis uestris sompnum, a vobismetipsis fidelem compotum mentaliter exigatis, qualiter Dei seruicium illo die fuerit persolutum. Si plene, si deuote, si sine mentis distraccione, si cum cordis
10 compunccione uel aliquali sanctarum lacrimarum dulcedine, solitum pensum solueritis, reddatis Deo gracias cordiales, totum quod bonum est in vestris operibus sue gracie & misericordie – non vestris uirtutibus – tribuentes. Si autem diminute, tepide, cum mentis distraccione circa vana, vilia uel inutilia, uel sine deuocionis feruore uel dulcedine,
15 diuinum feceritis seruicium, quod omissum est protinus [a]bsoluatur, pro defectus reliquiis pectus tundatur, cordialia suspiria prouocentur, pro indulgencia votiuis affectibus pulsentur viscera misericordie Dei nostri, & uos tali die reputetis fuisse seruos malos, inutiles & indignos.

Hic expedit intelligere quam terribiliter sacra scriptura loquitur de
20 [52v] his qui aliquo modo deficiunt in Dei seruicio persoluendo. Nam de dicentibus diminute scribitur in Ieremia, 'Maledictus qui facit opus Dei fraudulenter.' De tepidis in dicendo – qui nec totaliter sunt frigidi per indeuocionem & manifest[um] mortale peccatum, nec ardentes seu calidi per deuocionis feruorem, sed quasi accidia & ocio torpentes –
25 dicitur in Apocal., 'Vtinam calidus esses aut frigidus. Sed quia tepidus es incipiam te euomere de ore meo.' Et de distractis per cogitaciones vanas seu illicitas in orando, dicit Dominus indignanter, 'Populus hic labiis me honorat; cor autem eorum longe est a me.'

Contra tales mentis multiplices euagaciones in orando remedium
30 poterit esse aliquando: si uiua uoce legatur oracio super librum, & interdum de precibus non debitis sed uoluntariis dum in oracione uocali distrahitur quis, statim pro querendo remedio talis oracio sit mentalis.

Heading *Capitulum primum tercie partis*] *om.* J   6 primo] *om.* J   10 aliquali] aliquantuli J   11 bonum] *om.* J   15 absoluatur] obsoluatur R, soluatur J (N)
21 Maledictus] homo *add.* J   23 manifestum] J, manifeste R (Oliger)   26 te] *om.* J
31 uocali] *om.* J

The first chapter of the third part

The third principal thing that you will see in this work, you recluses, is how you should carry out your vocation. For (as was shown above) you are called to unceasing prayer, meditation, reading, or performing some suitable manual work. And so, by reflection on your progress or failings in these, you are able to evaluate the performance of your vocation.

And so to the first of these, your required or customary prayers: each day at night time, before you give your eyes to sleep, you should require of yourself a faithful mental account of how your service to God has been rendered that day. If your usual quota has been fulfilled fully, or devoutly, or without your mind becoming distracted, or with compunction of heart or perhaps the sweetness of holy tears, give heartfelt thanks to God, attributing everything that is good in what you do to his grace and mercy, not to your abilities. But if you have performed divine service inadequately, or half-heartedly, or with your mind distracted into vain, worthless or unproductive things, or without the fervor or sweetness of devotion, then immediately complete what has been omitted, and for your failings in the remainder beat your breast, bring forth heartfelt sighs, bombard our God in the bowels of his mercy with intense prayers for forgiveness, and for that day account yourself a wicked servant, worthless and unworthy.

Here you should be aware of the terrible things that holy scripture says regarding those who are in any way deficient in their performance of God's service. For of those who recite inadequately it is written in Jeremiah, 'Cursed be he that doth the work of the Lord deceitfully.' Of those who recite in a lukewarm way – who are neither completely cold because of an absence of devotion and flagrant mortal sin, nor burning or hot with the fervor of devotion, but languishing as if in sloth or idleness – it is said in the Apocalypse, 'I would thou wert hot or cold. But because thou art lukewarm I will begin to vomit thee out of my mouth.' And of those who are distracted from their prayers by vain or unlawful thoughts, the Lord says with indignation, 'This people honoureth me with their lips; but their heart is far from me.'

Against these various wanderings of the mind during prayer, this can sometimes be a remedy. If someone is supposed to be reading his prayer aloud from a book and, while he is engaged in vocal prayer, he is distracted now and then by voluntary prayers rather than those that are required, then in order to find a remedy he should straight away switch to mental

Speculum Inclusorum • III.i

Si neque sic temptator deficiat infestare, queratur ulterius nobilissima medicina cuiuslibet temptacionis, videlicet cordialis aspectus Christi pacientis in cruce; qui, ex amoris magnitudine quo te dilexit, ut pro tuis peccatis satisfaceret, & contra singulas temptaciones tibi uirtutem tribueret resistendi, asperam coronam spineam sustinuit impressam suo capiti usque ad ipsius cerebri contaminacionem &, ex omni parte distillantes preciosissimas guttas sanguinis ad medelam, amorem etiam sui cordis tibi liberaliter offert in effluxu sanguinis & aque de suo corde crudeliter lanceato pro sanandis vulneribus peccatorum. Insuper & manus eius & pedes crucifiguntur firmiter cum duris clauis ferreis ad tecum permanendum in temptacionibus; & liquorem fundunt copiosissime, ad cuiuslibet spiritualis morbi possibilis medicinam perfectam. Ad hanc medicinam nos inuitat scriptura, que dicit: 'Videte Salomonem in diademate quo coronauit eum mater sua.' Et alibi dicit Christus, 'Quid turbati estis & cogitaciones ascendunt in corda vestra? Uidete manus meas & pedes.'

O visio salutaris! O medicina sufficiens ad salutem! O preciosa passio, per serpentem eneum figurata, que quoslibet percussos ab ignitis serpentibus temptacionis perfectissime sanas, dum te corditer aspiciunt, auxilium postulantes. Hanc passionem frequenter aspicias cum distractus fueris uel temptatus. Hic succursum quere, hic pete, hic pulsa; non discedas, non desinas, non desistas, donec aliquam receperis me-[53r]-dicinam. Dicas Domino fiducialiter cum Propheta, 'Ab occultis meis munda me Domine.' Et iterum, 'Sana me Domine & sanabor, saluum me fac & saluus ero, quoniam laus mea tu es.' Ecce ego, iam miser & mendicus, indigens & indignus, ad fontem indeficientis misericordie tue uenio, & ad tue gracie cumulum infinitum, quos ab eterno disposuisti & misericorditer promisisti distribuere liberalissime miseris

---

36 contra] uirtutes *add. but subpuncted* R   37 asperam] asperimam J
38 contaminacionem] contimationem J   45 que dicit] dicens J   54 non desinas] *om.* J

III.i • *A Mirror for Recluses* 73

prayer. If this does not bring an end to the tempter's attacks, he should go on to try the supreme [31r] medicyn for euery temptacion, and þat is þe herty biholdynge and remembraunce of Cristes passyon in the croys.
40 Which, of the excellent love þat he hadde vnto þe, to make satisfaccion and amendys for thy synnes, and to ȝeve þe myȝti vertu of resistence or wiþstondynge agayn alle temptacions, baar a crowne of þorn on his heed, which stak scharply and soore vnto þe touchynge or þirlinge of þ[e] brayn, and on euery part droppyd doun precious droopes of blood
45 vnto þe medycyn and heele of þe. Also he profreed frely to þe the love of his herte whan blood and water flowed out of yt, þat was cruely woundid wiþ a spere, to hele þe hurtes & woundes of synful folk. Moore[o]uyr, his handis and his feet were faster ficchid to þe croys wyth harde nayles of yren forto duelle and abyde wyth þe in temptacions;
50 and þei schedden out lycour in greet abundaunce or plente to þe perfyt medycyn of euery spiry-[31v]-tual hurt or syknesse þat man may have. Vnto þat medycyn clepith vs and byddiþ vs to come þe scripture þat seyth þus: 'Seeth þe kyng Salomon wyth þe dyademe wiþ þe which his modir coronyd hym.' And in anoþir place seyth Crist in þis wyse: 'Whi
55 or wherto be ȝe troublyd and whi ascenden þouȝtes into ȝoure hertes? Byholdeth myn handes and my feet.'

O a hoolsum syȝte! O a suffisaunt medycyn of helþe! O precious passion, figuryd or lyknyd by þe serpent of bras, þat perfitly heelest alle þo þat be smeten or hurt of þe fyry serpentes of temptacion whan
60 men hertly byholden þe, askynge þin help and confort. Whan þou art distract or temptyd, bihold often þis passion. Here seek þi socour, here aske, here kno[kk]e, go nat awey, stinte nat til þow have receyuyd sum medycyn, seyinge feiþfully to oure Lord wiþ [þe] prophete, 'Lord purge or clense [me] of myn hid synnes.' Also, 'Hele me Lord and I
65 [32r] schal ben helyd, make me saaf and I schal be sauyd.' Lo now Lord I, wrecche and beggere, nedy and vnworthi, come vnto the welle of þi mercy þat schal neuere fayle, and vnto þe infynyt & plenteuously heepyd grace which þou hast disposyd & ordeynyd wythouten ende, and haast mercyablely beheygh[t] to deele and departe it liberaly and
70 freely to wrecchyd synneres and to hem þat ben temptyd. Þerfore

---

39 herty: earnest   40 satisfaccion: recompense   41 vertu: strength   43 stak: pierced • þirlinge: piercing   45 heele: healing   48 ficchid: fixed   49 duelle: remain   50 lycour: fluid   52 clepith: calls, summons   54 coronyd: crowned   57 hoolsum: salutary
59 smeten: struck   61 socour: assistance   62 stinte: desist   68 disposyd: decreed • ordeynyd: ordained   69 beheygh[t]: promised • departe: share out

---

44 þe] þi   48 Mooreouyr] Moore euyr   62 knokke] knowe

peccatoribus & temptatis. Fiducialiter igitur queram, petam, pulsabo, & lamentabiliter clamabo, quousque per aliquid fuero confortatus. Scio, misericordissime Domine, quod non repelles miserum humiliter mendicantem. Credo, clementissime Custos hominum, quod non claudes totaliter sinum gracie contra misericordiam veraciter postulantem. Et si non merui, da mihi tamen, per tuam ineffabilem bonitatem, uel modicum ex tue immense pietatis abundancia, quia miserum me reficere poterit ualde paruum. Licet indignus fuero, concede nichilominus indigenti misero uel porciunculam aliquam tui preciosi sanguinis, ut hoc asperum cor meum protinus tibi vniatur indissolubiliter per amorem, & omnis contraria mentis distraccio cicius euanescat. Et si de sanguine cordis uel capitis uel manuum habere non ualeam, de beatorum pedum tuorum fluuiis sanguineis uel minimum perceptibile distribuas mendicanti. Et reuera indigenti, querenti, petenti, pulsanti, & certe recedere nolenti sine tua consolatoria benediccione percepta. Scio, Domine, scio quod quantumcunque modicum tui sanguinis preciosi mihi concedere decreueris, talis est efficacie & tante uirtutis quod non solum mihi sed & toti mundo sufficit ad salutem; & satis est ad refrenandum, ad fugandum, ad terrendum, & ad vincendum, omnem demonis potestatem. Talis oracionis instancia per Dei graciam finaliter uictoriam optinebit. & si, in pugna spirituali contra temptaciones seu cogitaciones illicitas, multum fatigatus fuerit aliquis & turbatus labore & timore, tristicia seu dolore (dum tamen non plene consenciat in aliquod mortale peccatum), totum hoc exercicium est meritorium, totum confert ad meriti cumulum, totum est occasio magni premii, totum coronas glorie preparat in futuro.

---

70 ut] uel J   83 &] om. J

schal I feythfully seeke, I schal aske, I schal kno[kk]e, and I schal crye lamentably or sorwefully tyl I be confortid in sum wyse. I woot wel, mercyable Lord, þou wylt nat putte awey þe wrecche þat beggeth mekly. I byleve, benygne Wardeyn and Kepere of men, þat þou schalt nat wyttyrly schitte the lappe or b[os]um of thi grace fro hym that verrayly & mekly askyth þi mercy. And þouȝ I haue deseruyd no mercy, ȝit naþeles, þoruȝ þi souereyn bounte, ȝif me a lytyl of þin abundance of þin hy pite, for a ful smal thing may feede & [32v] refressche me, synful wrecche. Alþouȝ I be vnworthi, ȝit graunte natheles to myn indigence sum lytyl paart or sum droope of thi precious & holy blood, þat my scharp herte may be onyd or knyt to þe by love wythoute dissolucion or disseuerance, and þat al distractynge or astonynge of þouȝt may þe sonnere vansche away fro me. And ȝif I may nat haue of the blood of þin herte or of þin heed or of þin handes, I byseche þe humblely, mercyful Lord, ȝeue & dele to me, þat preie vnto þe & begge of þe, be yt neuere so lytyl of þe blody floodes of þi blessed feet. For douteles I am ful nedy, I seke to þe, I aske of þe, I knokke at þe ȝate of þi mercy, & certeyn nat wyllynge to departe withoute receyuynge of þin confortable helpynge. I woot wel, Lord, I woot wel þat, þouȝ þou ȝeue or graunte me neuere so lytyl of þi precious blood, it is of suych force & suych vertu þat nat only suffiseth to the he[lth]e of me, but also to al þe worldes helthe; & it is inowȝ plen-[33r]-te to refreyne, to chace, to agaste, and to ouyrcome, al þe power or myȝt of þe feend. The besy instance of suych a preiere þoruȝ þe grace of almyȝti God schal opteene and haue þe victorie. And ȝif, in spiritual batayle agayn temptacions or vnleefful þouȝtes, any man be maad weery or be troublyd þoruȝ trauayle and dreede, heuynesse or sorwe (so he nat fully assente to any deedly synne), al þat exercise ys merytorie & meedful, al hepith & gadreþ meryt togidre, al is occasion or cause o[f m]eede, al purueyeth and al ordeyneth corones of glorie in tyme comynge.

---

72 woot: know   74 Wardeyn: guardian   75 wyttyrly: utterly • schitte: shut
81 onyd: united • knyt: joined   82 dissolucion: separation • disseuerance: cutting apart, separation • distractynge: confusion • astonynge: perplexity   83 vansche: vanish   92 inowȝ: enough   93 refreyne: restrain • agaste: terrify   94 besy: energetic • instance: urgency   95 opteene: obtain   96 vnleefful: unlawful   98 so: provided   99 merytorie: meritorious • meedful: worthy of reward   100 purueyeth: prepares • ordeyneth: makes ready • corones: crowns

---

71 knokke] knowe   75 bosum] bot sum   86 of³] *written twice, first crossed*   91 helthe] herte   92 inowȝ] 3 *supplied by a corrector*   99 is] his   100 of meede] or neede

Iam (Dei gracia mediante) quiete mentis habita, est sollicite considerandum quod nichil petatur in oracione diuine uoluntati contrarium, nichil superfluum, nichil nisi saluti corporis uel anime necessariam, nec aliquid repugnans caritati. Ex caritate namque procedere debet oracio & extendere se ad omnes homines – etiam inimicos, quamuis [53v] vicissim magis specialiter orare poterit aliquis pro seipso & pro his quibus fuerit magis obligatus. Vnde caritas orantis respicere debet indigencias pauperum & peregrinorum, passiones debilium & infirmorum, sollicitudines principum & prelatorum, miserias exulum & incarceratorum, graues labores operancium & itinerancium, terrores & pericula nauigancium ac militancium – & breuiter: omnium hominum temptaciones, angustias & tribulaciones. Pro his omnibus inclusus frequencius viscera misericordie Dei pulsabit gemitibus, lacrimis exorabit & suspiriis prouocabit misericordiam, graciam & succursum. Hoc est sacrificium Deo suauissimum; hec est oblacio munda; hec est elemosina Deo gratissima, proximis utilissima, & fructifera facienti.

Sic igitur, uos inclusi, per vestram oracionis examinacionem sollicitam, *Uidete uocacionem vestram.*

---

89 nichil¹] uel J 92 seipso] se J 104 igitur] ergo J * oracionis] *om.* J

Now, þoruȝ þe mediacion of Goddes grace, and by possession or hauynge of hertes quieet & reste, it is to considere þat noþing be askyd in preyere þat is contrarie to þe wyl of God, no superflu or outrageous þinges, þat is to seyn ovir-mochil or out of mesure. Aske nothing but yt be necessarie to þe helþe of body or of soule; nothing þat is contrarie to charite. Out of [33v] charite schal procede orson & preiere, and stretche as wiel to enemys as freendes, alþouȝ bytuexe-whiles a man may preie more specialy for hymself and for hem þat he ys moost bonden or holden to. The charite of hym þat preyeth schal beholde and se the needes of pore folk [&] pilgrymes, passyons and diseses of feeble & syke folk, the chargeable besynesse of princes and prelates, the myseries & wrecchidnesses of outlawed folk and of hem þat bien in prison, the greete laboures of werkmen & of hem þat trauayle[n], þe dreedes & perilles of schipmen and of laboureres – &, shortly to spek: to þe temptacions and anguissches and tribulacions of alle men. For alle þese þinges recluses schal often calle & knokke on mercyable God wiþ sorweful teres, & þoruȝ sighynges prouoke and stire God to do mercy, grace & socour. And þis is an holy þing; þis is a swete and plesaunt þing to God; & this ys a clene oblacion & offrynge; þis ys an accep-[end of 33v]-*table offering to God, the most beneficial to our neighbours, and the most rewarding for the one who makes it.*

And so, you recluses, by careful consideration of your practice in prayer, 'Look to your vocation.'

---

104 superflu: excessive • outrageous: excessive   105 out of mesure: beyond all bounds
107 orson: prayer   108 bytuexe-whiles: from time to time   110 holden: committed
112 chargeable: burdensome   114 trauaylen: labour   116 anguissches: difficulties
120 oblacion: gift, sacrifice

---

114 trauaylen] trauayle in   117 þinges] & *add.*

Capitula 2ᵐ

Secundo, de vestris deuotis meditacionibus ad noctem cotidie computetis quantum profeceritis & quantum defeceritis illo die. De quolibet profectum Deo gracias agatis, & de quolibet defectu corditer doleatis. Tunc enim proficit meditacio quando Dei timorem peccatoribus incutit, eius amorem in tepidis & in indeuotis accendit, deuocionis lacrimas prouocat, laudes Dei multiplicat, generat odium peccati, & auget desiderium honeste uite, atque in celestibus mentem figit. Vnde de uiro contemplatiuo dicit Propheta quod 'Sedebit solitarius, & tacebit, & leuabit se supra se.' In huiusmodi meditacionibus multi taliter profecerunt quod aliqualem future beatitudinis dulcedinem pregustabant, in delectacione diuine bonitatis & eius summe pulcritudinis, in futurorum reuelacione, in angelorum collocucione, ac etiam in ipsius Omnipotentis aliquali uisione & ineffabili consolacione, iuxta quod dicit propheta Dauid: 'Gustate & uidete quoniam suauis est Dominus.' O gustacio graciosa! O visio preciosa! O suauitas supra cunctas mundi delicias delectabilis! Dum enim solitario contemplanti feruens amor Dei dulcessit, omnis secularis leticia nimirum marcessit. Cui sinamomum sapit & redolet fex vilis non complacet; quem amenissimus flos & fructus delectat deformis stipula non confortat, & cui fons dulcedinis inestimabilis sapit & effluit abundanter uilescunt liquores alii qui primitus sapuerunt. Sic reuera quicunque pregustat delicias paradisi dulcedinem, videlicet ardentis amoris Dei, mundi uoluptates omnimodas paruipendit, sicut quidam qui experti sunt in scriptis reliquerunt & suis familiaribus narraue-[54r]-runt. De quibus dicit Domino propheta David: 'Memoriam abundancie suauitatis tue eructabunt.'

Heading *Capitula 2ᵐ*] *om.* J   10 aliqualem] aliqua[n]tulem J   12 etiam] *om.* J
13 aliquali] aliqua[n]tuli J   15 suauitas] sanitas J   19 flos & fructus] JR, *corr. from* & fructus flos R (N)   21 liquores] loquores J • primitus] prius J   22 videlicet] vi J • ardentis] *om.* J

Chapter 2

Secondly, every day at night time you should reckon up how much you have profited in your devout meditations for that day, and what you have lost. For the profits you have made you should give thanks to God, and for your deficits you should feel heartfelt sorrow. Now meditation
5 *is profitable when it strikes the fear of God into sinners, inflames the lukewarm and the impious with his love, provokes tears of devotion, increases God's praises, produces a hatred of sin, and increases the desire to live a virtuous life, and fixes the mind on heavenly things. Therefore the Prophet says, concerning the contemplative man, that 'He shall sit*
10 *solitary, and hold his peace, and he shall raise himself above himself'. In meditations such as these many people achieve so much profit that they experience some taste of the sweetness of the bliss to come, in the delight of the divine goodness and his supreme beauty, in the revelation of future events, in conversation with angels, and even in a kind of vision of the*
15 *Almighty himself and his ineffable comfort, according to the words of the prophet David: 'Taste and see, for the Lord is sweet.'*

Oh how full of grace that taste is! Oh what a precious vision! Oh what a delightful sweetness, exceeding all the delights of the world! For when the sweetness of the burning love of God comes to the solitary contemplative,
20 *all his joy in the things of this world loses its savour for sure. Someone who tastes and smells cinnamon will not be happy with common dregs; coarse straw will not content someone who delights in the most beautiful flowers and fruit, and to someone for whom to an unimaginable degree the source* [34r] of swetnesse sauoureþ & floweþ out habundauntly alle oþer
25 lycoures leesen hir sauour þat first hadden good taast. Ryȝt so, sooþly, whoso þat taasteþ þe delyces of Paradys – þat is to seyn þe swetnesse of þe brennynge love of God – he settiþ at nauȝt alle manere of worldly lustes, as some þat weren expert & knowynge in þis caas lefte wryten & tolde to her famylier foolk. Of suych þe prophete Dauyd seiþ vnto
30 oure Lord þus: 'Lord,' he seyth, 'þey schul telle out or expresse the abundaunce of thi swetnesse.'

---

24 sauoureþ: is delightful   25 lycoures: liquids • sauour: pleasant taste • sooþly: truly
28 lustes: desires • expert: experienced   29 famylier: of their family or household
30 telle out: enumerate

---

30 the] *written twice, second time as* þe

Sed in his omnibus dum hic viuimus, duo iugiter sunt timenda, pro quibus neccesaria est prudencia circumspecta cum remedio oportuno. Vnum est ne angelus Sathane, in lucis angelum se transfigurans, decipiat & ducat subtiliter in errorem. Contra cuius periculum, in apparicione quacunque uel reuelacione priusquam fides adhibeatur eidem, premittenda est ad Deum oracio cordialis ut ignoranciam serui sui continue custodiat a fallaciis inimici; memoriterque tenendum est quod, iuxta sanctorum sentenciam, angelus bonus hominibus apparens communiter timorem incutit in principio, et posterius consolatur, sed e contrario malignus spiritus apparens demulcet in principio, & posterius horrorem inducit. Aliud in hac materia timendum est, ne videlicet magnitudo reuelacionis, siue alterius beneficii diuini graciosi, superbiam pariat in aliquo, ut nimis reputet de seipso. Contra quod periculum, uera cordis tenenda est humilitas per memoriam omnium tam propriorum defectuum quam munerum diuinorum, ut sic se indignum quis reputans, cum Apostolo corde clamet, 'Gracia Dei sum id quod sum.' Et quia 'omne datum optimum & omne do[num] perfectum desursum est descendens a patre luminum,' pro sing[u]lis beneficiis dicat, 'Deo gracias ago. Gloria in excelsis Deo sit. Et non nobis, Domine, non nobis sed nomini tuo da gloriam de cunctis nostris operibus bonis.' Sic semper seruetur uera cordis humilitas, que (secundum beatum Augustinum) est signum euidentissimum electorum. Nec mirum, quia tantum 'humilibus dat Deus graciam,' & 'humilem spiritu suscipiet gloria,' teste scriptura.

Ulterius est sciendum quod, sicut ex omnibus creaturis, ex singulis sacris scripturis & ex cunctis Christi operibus elici poterit deuota meditacio & expediens, si quicquid bonum, quicquid utile, quicquid honestum reperitur in illis, reducatur ad nostram edificacionem, siue referatur finaliter ad Dei amorem, laudem, gloriam & honorem. Quia

But of alle þese þinges whiles we lyven here, to þinges ben gretly to dreede, for þe which a circumspect prudence (þat is to seyn a wys syȝte seynge byfore & behynde) is necessarie wiþ byhoueful or covenable remedie. On ys: lest the angel of Sathenas, transfygurynge hym into þe angel of lyȝt, sotylly deceyve & leede folk into errour. Agayn the peril of wham, in al his apperynge, ar ȝe ȝeve any credence or [34v] feyth vnto hym, maketh a deuout and hertly preyere to God þat he kepe and defende contynuely þ[e] ignoraunce & vncunnynge of his seruaunt fro þe fallaces & deceytes of þe feend. And it is good to remembre and haue in mynde þat, after þe sentence of seyntes, þe good angel þat apperyth to men comunely impresseþ dreede in a man in þe bygynnynge & confortith hym aftyrward; but al anoþer dooþ þe wykkyd spiryt, for in his apperynge he fyrst conforteþ and aftirward he induceþ or bryngyth in errour. Anoþir þyng ys also to dreede in this matere: þat ys to seyn lest þe gretnesse of reuelacion or sum oþir gracious ȝefte or schewynge of God swelle or bolne so greetly in a man þat he sete ovir-mochil by hymself. Agayn þat peryl þe verray humilite of þe herte ys to been had and holden by remembraunce of alle þinges, as wyel of his owen defautes as of þe ȝeftes of God; and þat he holde hymself vnworthi, and crye and seye wyth [þe] Apostil [35r] in this manere: 'By the grace of God I am þat I am.' And for þat 'euery good ȝefte & euery perfyt ȝefte from above ys descendynge from þe Fadir of lyȝt,' for alle benefices sey þus: 'I ȝelde þonkynges to God. Glorie & ioye be to God on hy.' And 'Lord, nat to vs, nat to vs, but ȝ[eue] þow glorie to thi naame' of alle oure good werkes. Thus lat alwey þe humylite of herte be kept, which is (after Seynt Austyn) an euydent or open signe of Goddys chosen folk. And no meruayl, for God ȝeueth al only grace to humble or meke folkes, and glorie schal exalte or ryse vp hym þat is humble of spiryt, as wytnesseth Holy Wryt.

Moreovir yt is to knowe þat, ryȝth as of alle creatures, of alle holy wrytynges and of alle þe werkes of Cryst may be drawen out a deuout meditacion and expedyent, ȝyf any good, profitable or honest þing be founde in hem, lat yt be reducyd vnto þe edificacion and profyt of vs, and lat yt finaly be referryd to the l[ou]e, preisynge, glorie & honour

---

32 to: two   34 byhoueful: appropriate • covenable: suitable   36 sotylly: cunningly
37 ar: before   38 hertly: earnest   39 vncunnynge: ignorance   40 fallaces: tricks
41 sentence: pronouncement   42 impresseþ: produces   43 anoþer: in a different manner   44 induceþ: introduces   47 bolne: swell, puff up   48 verray: true, genuine
49 defautes: failings   56 after: according to   62 expedyent: profitable   63 reducyd: referred

---

36 sotylly] to add.   39 þe] þin   55 ȝeue] ȝif   64 loue] lawe

precipue in |vero| Dei amore consistit fructus uberrimus legis nostre, iuxta illud Apostoli: 'Plenitudo legis est dilectio.' Sic contingit defectus in istis, si mens rapiatur ad uana & illicita; si affectus finem sue delectacionis ponat in aliqua creatura, uel si intellectus erret in fide catholica,
60 seu in articulis fidei ab ecclesia determinatis. De mentis distraccione, & de creatura non diligenda nisi finaliter propter Deum sufficiant prius dicta. Sed pro intellectus errore possibili prodest quod articuli fidei, qui continentur in Symbolo Apostolorum & in Symbolo Athanasii, plenius intel-[54v]-ligantur, firmiter credantur & memorie commendentur, nec
65 aliquis pertinens ad fidem disputetur uel aliter credatur quam prius, sine consilio theologi sapientis, sed credulitati sancte matris Ecclesie firmissime quilibet adhereat sine hesitacione, quamuis in quibusdam non habeat euidenciam racionis. Quia, secundum beatum Gregorium, 'Fides non habet meritum vbi humana racio prebet experimentum.'
70 Precipue namque due sunt materie legis nostre que omnem hominis intellectum longe transcendunt, videlicet quod Pater & Filius & Spiritus Sanctus sunt tres persone distincte, quarum nulla persona est alia, & tamen he tres persone sunt substancialiter vnus & idem Deus. Et similiter quod media persona, videlicet Dei filius, ab eterno,
75 per operacionem Sancti Spiritus, ex purissimis guttis sanguineis Virginis benedicte subito, quando uoluit, corpus assumpsit pro nostra salute, ut sic idem Dei filius, factus homo, in suis actibus & doctrinis formam tribueret nobis uite perfecte. Tandemque, pro satisfaccione nostri peccati, durissimam mortem paciens in assumpta natura,
80 corpus suum et sanguinem sub specie panis & vini nobis relinqueret in perpetuum nutrimentum, remedium & solacium spiritale. Hoc

---

56 vero] *ins. marg.* R, *in text* J (N)   57 illud] id J   73 est alia] *om.* J

65 of God. For the moost plente-[35v]-vous fruyt of oure lawe standiþ principaly in the love of God, aftir the wordes of þe Apostel þat seith þus: 'The foulnesse or abundaunce of lawe ys loue.' Thus happyth or falleþ a defaute in þese þinges ȝif þe þouȝt be rauysschid or ȝeuen to veyn or vnliefful þinges; ȝif þat þe wil or delectacion þat a man hath
70 in any creature finaly, or ȝif þe vndirstandynge or reson inwardly erre in the feyth of Holy Cherche, or in þe artycles of the feyth determynyd by Holy Cherche. Of dystractynge of þouȝt, and of a creture þat ys nat for to be louyd but finaly for God: to þo twey materes ben seyd above sufficiently. But for the errour þat may be of vndirstondynge, it
75 profite[t]h þat þe articles of þe feyth þat ben conteynyd in the Byleve of þe Apostles and in þe Byleve of Athanasie be fully vndirstonden, beleued stedefastly, and taken vnto memorie or mynde; and þat nothing þat longiþ to þe feyth be disputyd, ne be [36r] othirwise beleeuyd þan was byforn, withoute conseyl of a wys devyn. But euery man knytte
80 hym stedefastly & myȝtyly, wiþoute hesitacion or doute, to þ[e] byleve of oure modyr of Holy Cherche, þouȝ he haue nat in some articules euydence or tokne of reson. For, after þe wordes of Seynt Gregory, 'Feyth hath no meryt where mannes reson ȝeueth experyment or preef.'
To materes namly þer be of oure lawe þat passen ful feer the
85 intelligence or reson of euery man. Þat ys to sey þat þe Fadir & Sone and Holy Goost ben þre persones distynct, of þe wyche noon ys otheres persone, and ȝyt nathelees þo þre persones ben substancialy oon & þe same God. And also þat þe myddyl persone, which ys þe sone of God wiþouten bygynnynge or endynge, by þe operacion and werkynge of þe
90 Holy Goost, sodeynly, whan hys wyl was (or whan he wolde), took his body of the clennest blody dropes of þe blessid Virgine, for oure helþe; þat so þe same sone of God, which was [36v] maad man, in his deedes and doctrines scholde ȝeue vs a forme of perfyt lyf. And at þe laste, for the satisfaccion of oure synne, he suffrid harde deeþ in oure nature þat he
95 took; left wiþ vs hys body & hys blood vndyr lyknesse of breed & wyn into perpetuel nurschynge, remedie and solace spirituel. This blessyd

---

67 foulnesse: fullness, plenitude • happyth: happens   68 falleþ: occurs • rauysschid: taken off   69 vnliefful: unlawful   70 finaly: ultimately   73 twey: two   75 Byleve: Creed   79 devyn: divine, cleric • knytte: bind   83 experyment: experiential proof   84 namly: in particular • passen: exceed   86–7 otheres persone: the same person as the other (N)   87 nathelees: nonetheless • substancialy: in substance   91 clennest: purest • helþe: salvation   93 doctrines: teachings • forme: model   94 satisfaccion: redemption   96 nurschynge: nourishment • solace: comfort

---

78 feyth] to *add*   80 þe] þi

autem sacramentum sub talibus speciebus disposuit Omnipotens que magis conueniunt hominis nutricioni, ne horror crudi corporis uel sanguinis a communione retraheret christianos, & ut firma credulitas intellectus contra proprii sensus experienciam meritum multiplicius cumularet. Credere namque debetis firmissime quod, licet uirtute uerborum sacramentalium que Christus instituit & sacerdos vicarius eius profert sub specie panis solum sit caro Christi, & sub specie vini solum sanguis eius per consecracionem, tamen quia ex uoluntate Dei sanguis non separabitur a carne, nec anima a corpore, nec humanitas a diuinitate, ideo sub utraque specie (videlicet tam panis quam vini), facta consecracione, est caro, sanguis, corpus, anima, & ipsa diuinitas totus Christus, uerus Deus & homo.

Hanc fidem inducere quodammodo seu firmare poterunt quedam similitudines in natura. Nonne panis & vinum per modicum tempus in stomacho calore naturali digesta conuertuntur in veram carnem & verum sanguinem manducantis? Quare igitur non potest Creator omnipotens, qui solo uerbo de nichilo produxit mundum, panem & vinum etiam in corpus & sanguinem suum conuertere subito uirtute uerborum? Nec aliquem moueat a recta fide quod equaliter post consecracionem sicut ante manent accidencia – videlicet color, sapor & pondus panis & vini – quando nec est ibidem panis, nec vinum, nec ulla substancia nisi substancia corporis & sanguinis Iesu [55r] Christi cum deitate, dum naturaliter fieri possit, iuxta Philosophum in fine 4 *Metheorum* (secundum antiquam translacionem), quod vnum metallum (utputa cuprum) propriis accidentibus spolietur & induatur accidentibus argenti vel auri, ut argentum vel aurum appareat in pondere & colore. Similiter, si diuidatur hostia consecrata, non dubitet

---

91 diuinitate] deitate J   92 diuinitas] deitas J   99 &] et in J   102 ibidem] nec *add.* J
103 Iesu] *om.* J, *but space left*

sacrament vndir suych lyknesse disposyd & ordeyned almy3ty God
which ben moost conuenyent to þe nurschynge of man, leest d[r]eede or
wlatsomnesse of a raw body or blood scholde wiþdrawe cr[i]sten folk fro
þe communyon or receyuynge of þat precious body, and for þat stedefast
byleve scholde manyfoold more encrece his meryt agayn þe experience of
þe vndirstondynge of his owen syt. 3e schalle stedefastly byleve þat, þou3
be þe vertue of þe wordes sacramental þat Crist ordeynyd and þe preest
hys viker seyth, oonly vndir þe lyknesse of breed ys þe flessch of Cryst
and [37r] vndir þe lyknesse of wyn oonly ys blood, 3et be þe consecracion
naþeles – for þat of þe wyl of God the blood schal nat be deseuered ne
departid fro þe flessch, ne soule fro þe body, ne þe manhode fro þe deite
of Godhode – þerfor vndir eyther lyknesse (þat ys to seyn as wiel of
breed as wyn) whan þe consecracion is maad yt ys flessch & blood, body,
soule and þat same Godhede: al Crist, verray God and man.

Ther ben some similitudes in nature mowe as in manere induce a
man and make hym þe moore strong in the feyth. As thus. Wheþer
breed and wyn, dygest or diffyed in a litil tyme in þe stomak of man,
þorugh naturel heete been turnyd into verray flessch & verray blood of
þe etere and drynkere? 3ys. Wherefore may nat God almy3ti, maker
of al þing, þat maade al þis world of nau3t only wyth woord, turne
sodey[n]ly breed and wyn into hys flessch and blood þoru3 þe vertu of
þe wordes? Ne lat yt stire no man, ne make hym flecche or varie fro
[37v] þe ry3t byleeue, þat in euen wyse after þe consecracion duellen as
þer diden biforn accidentes – þat is to sey colour, sauour, and weyghte
– of breed and wyn, whan þer is neyþer þere breed ne wyn, ne noon
oþer substance but substance of þe body and of þe blood of Iesu Crist
wiþ the godhede. And þat is no wonder whiles, as seith þe Philesofre
(after þe oold translacion), þat o metal, as coper, may be robbyd of his
owen accidentes and be cloþed wiþ accidentes o[f] syluyr or gold, þat
it may seeme syluyr or gold in weyghte & colour. Ry3t so, 3if þe hoost
consecrat be departyd, let no man doute but þat hoolly & fully þe body

---

97 disposyd: decreed • ordeyned: ordained   98 conuenyent: suitable
99 wlatsomnesse: disgust   101 manyfoold: many times • agayn: against, contrary to
102 syt: sight   103 vertue: power   104 viker: vicar, representative   106 deseuered:
separated   107 manhode: manhood, humanity   108 Godhode: Godhead   111 mowe:
[that] may • induce: persuade   112 Wheþer: is it not the case that   113 diffyed:
digested (N)   115 3ys: Yes   118 stire: disturb • flecche: waver   119 duellen: remain
120 accidentes: 'accidents' (N) • sauour: taste   123 Philesofre: Philosopher, *sc.* Aristotle
(N)   124 o: one   125 syluyr: silver   127 departyd: divided

---

118 fro] *written twice over page-break*   125 of] or

aliquis quin totaliter corpus Christi & sanguis sub qualibet diuisionis
particula perseueret. Sicut accidit naturaliter in speculo fracto, quod in qualibet parte fracta relucet eadem ymago que prius in integro speculo relucebat. Preterea firmiter credere debet quilibet christianus quod, eodem modo tam corpus Christi quam sanguis quod assumpsit de Uirgine & quo pro nobis passus est in cruce, ueraciter est in qualibet hostia consecrata. Nec est hoc Deo dificile, qui facit quod eadem uox loquentis multiplicetur naturaliter in singulis auribus auditorum. Ulterius adhuc credendum est quod quelibet paruitas hostie corpus Christi continere poterit, quod prius exiuit de clauso Uirginis utero, & posterius, ianuis clausis, ad discipulos intrauit. Hic per fidem 'State & videte magnalia Dei', prout Moyses hortabatur populum (Exod. 14). Nam hec omnia firma fide credenda sunt potissime propter auctoritatem ineffabilis Veritatis, que dicit (Joh. 5°): 'Ego sum panis vite. ... Et siquis manducauerit ex hoc pane viuet in eternum. Et panis quem ego dabo caro mea est pro mundi uita. ... Caro mea,' inquit, 'uere est cibus, & sanguis meus uere est potus.'

O preciosissimum nutrimentum! O nobilissimum restauratiuum! O efficatissimum confortatiuum, in quo mundis animabus absconditur omne delectamentum, & omnis saporis suauitas spiritualis! Ad quid queris alibi, o anima misera, solacium, auxilium vel succursum? Alibi sunt creature; hic est Creator omnipotens. Alibi sunt sanctorum reliquie; hic est omnium sanctorum Conditor, Rex & Dominus. Nulla alia aliquid facere possunt, nisi per uirtutem istius. Alia non sunt amanda vel honoranda, nisi propter istius amorem, laudem, gloriam & honorem. Hic Deus & Dominus omnium seipsum cotidie liberaliter offert tibi, ut ostendas tuam indigenciam, queras misericordiam, petas graciam, & recipias quicquid tibi fuerit necessarium ad salutem. Ne igitur timeas defectum in necessariis, ne paueas in angustiis & tribulacionibus, nec desperes in temptacionibus quibuscunque, quia Pater misericordie semper concedet humiliter supplicanti hoc quod petit, vel quod utilius est petenti.

His omnibus firmam fidem adhibere debetis, uos inclusi, & sic, per sancte meditacionis frequenciam, *Uidete uocacionem vestram*. [55v]

---

115 Deo] modo J   126 preciosissimum] preciosum J   129 alibi] *om.* J • misera] alibi *add.* J   133 gloriam] *om.* J   138 nec] ne J

& þe blood of Crist perseuereth and duelleth vndir euery part of þe dyuysion or departynge – as yt falleth or happeth naturaly in a broken myrour, in euery broken part of þe whiche þe same ymage schyneth and schewyth as yt dide fyrst in the hool myrrour. Moreovir, euery cristen man schal stydefastly byleve þat in [þe] same manere as wel þe body of Crist as ys blood, which he took of þe blessyd Virgine, and [end of 37v] *in which he suffered for us on the cross, is truly present in every consecrated host. And this is no difficulty for God, who brings it about that when a single voice speaks it is disseminated naturally into the ears of each person listening. And again, furthermore, we should believe that the tiniest part of a host can contain the body of Christ, that once issued from the Virgin though her womb remained closed, and afterwards, though the doors were shut, came in among the disciples. Here, through faith, 'stand, and see the great wonders of the Lord,' as Moses urged the people (Exodus 14). For all these things are to be believed most strongly with a secure faith, on the authority of the ineffable Truth, which says (John 5): 'I am the bread of life. ... If any man eat of this bread, he shall live for ever; and the bread that I will give, is my flesh, for the life of the world. ... For my flesh,' he says, 'is meat indeed: and my blood is drink indeed.'*

Oh food most precious! Oh sustenance most noble! Oh nourishment most effective, in which are hidden away for pure souls all delights, and all sweetness of spiritual savour! Why, oh wretched soul, are you looking anywhere else for comfort, help and assistance? On one hand you have created things; on the other, there is the almighty Creator. On one hand, there are the relics of the saints; on the other, the Ruler of all the saints, their King and Lord. No other thing can do anything except by his power. Nothing else should be loved or honoured, except for the sake of his love, praise, glory and honour. Here God who is the Lord of all offers himself freely to you every day, in the hope that you will reveal your need, seek mercy, ask for grace, and receive whatever might be necessary for your salvation. And so do not fear that you will lack for those things that are necessary, nor be scared in times of difficulty or tribulation, nor lose hope in the face of any kind of temptation, for the Father of mercy always grants the humble suppliant what he asks for, or something that is more useful to the person asking.

You should hold onto all these things with a secure faith, you recluses, and thus, by the practice of holy meditation, 'Look to your vocation.'

---

133 ys: his

133 and] in which he appeared is in þe breed and wyn *add. at foot of page* (N)

Capitulum 3ᵐ

Tercio, diebus singulis discutere debetis profectum vestrum in sacra scriptura uel in aliqua edificatoria leccione. Si per huiusmodi leccionem fides, spes uel caritas in uobis aucta fuerit uel confirmata; si dileccio Dei & proximi magis accensa fuerit uel continuata; si timor diuine offense uel metus Purgatorii uel Gehenne uobis amplius incuciatur; si odium cuiuslibet peccati mortalis in vestris cordibus augeatur; si uoluptas carnalium, si cupiditas temporalium, repressa fuerit & refrenata; si quelibet superueniens angustia seu tribulacio propter amorem Dei & indignitatis proprie consideracionem humiliter toleretur, & gaudenti animo sit accepta: corditer Deo gracias referatis pro his beneficiis magnis. Si uero libencius aliquando legeritis curiosa quam edificatoria, aures curialiter demulcencia quam deuocionem redolencia; si tempus oracioni debitum occupaueritis in leccione; si a recto sensu scripture distracti fueritis in vana, vili, seu illicita cogitacione: pectora tundatis, veniam postuletis, & de cetero in leccione uos circumspeccius reguletis.

Mens enim nunquam Deum poterit perfecte querere, cognoscere uel amare, dum distracta fuerit & illecta per cogitaciones & affecciones uarias creature. Ideo cognitis primo propriis defectibus & indigenciis, pro eorum succursu & remedio cuilibet impertinenti cogitacioni renunciandum est, & sacre leccioni totaliter vacandum, ut cognoscatur Dei omnipotencia & eius immensa bonitas, Dei summa iusticia & eius misericordia infinita. Vnde ad hoc nos hortatur Dominus per Prophetam cum dicit, 'Uacate & videte quoniam ego sum Dominus.'

O vacacio fructuosa! O visio consolatoria! O cunctorum medicina malorum, que ministras peccantibus compunccionem, desperantibus spem, bene viuentibus deuocionis graciam & feruorem, atque desolatis omnibus consolacionis exemplum, ad laudandum Dominum pro tribulacionibus quibuscunque. Nonne, secundum Apostolum, diligentibus Deum omnia cooperantur in bonum, his qui secundum propositum uocati sunt sancti? Quid est hoc quod dictum est, 'omnia cooperantur in bonum'? Numquid cooperari alicui poterit in bonum temptacio uel mortale peccatum? Imo ueraciter ex Dei misericordia sic contigit, licet nullus peccare debeat ut inde bonum proueniat ullo modo. Nostri

---

Heading *Capitulum 3ᵐ*] *om.* J   8 superueniens] superueniet J   10 referatis] agatis J   18 propriis] *om.* J   25 peccantibus] peccatoribus J   30 dictum est] dicit J

Chapter 3

Thirdly, each day you should analyse how you have profited from your reading of holy scripture or other edifying material. If by such reading faith, hope or charity have been increased or confirmed in you; if an increased love of God and of your neighbour has been kindled or continued; if you have been inspired with a greater fear of causing divine displeasure, or a greater terror of Purgatory or Hell; if the hatred of every kind of mortal sin has been increased in your hearts; if the desire for fleshly things – if the desire for worldly things – has been checked or restrained; if you have humbly borne whatever difficulty or tribulation has come your way, due to your love of God and reflection on your own unworthiness, and you have received them with rejoicing in your soul: give heartfelt thanks to God for these great favours. But if on occasion you have read for curiosity more than edification, more concerned that your reading should soothe your ears than that it should yield devotion; if you have been distracted from the proper sense of scripture into vain, worthless or illicit thoughts: you should beat your breasts, crave pardon, and govern your reading more carefully in future.

For the mind can in no way perfectly seek, know or love God, when it is being distracted or seduced by various thoughts and desires for created things. Therefore you should first recognise your own failings and neediness, because it is to help and remedy them that you must renounce all irrelevant thoughts, and make yourself completely empty to receive your holy reading, so that you might know God's omnipotence and his immeasurable goodness, the supreme justice of God and his infinite mercy. And the Lord calls us to this through the Prophet when he says, 'Be still and see that I am the Lord.'

Oh you fruitful emptiness! Oh you consoling vision! Oh you medicine for all ills, that bring compunction to sinners, hope to those in despair, the grace and fervour of devotion to those who live well, and to all who feel abandoned examples to give them comfort, so that they praise the Lord for all their tribulations. Isn't it the case that, according to the Apostle, 'to them that love God, all things work together unto good, to such as, according to his purpose, are called to be saints'? How can it say 'all things work together unto good'? Can temptation or deadly sin really work together for someone's good? Well yes, that truly does happen, through God's mercy, though by no means should anyone commit sin just so that good might come of it. But

tamen Saluatoris ineffabilis pietas & prouidencia incomprehensibilis,
35 que timentes & humiles in temptacionibus preseruat a lapsu, ut in mundicia crescant & multis proficiant ad exemplum presumptuosos & tepidos etiam electos interdum peccare permittit, ut tandem, [56r] sui sceleris grauitate confusi, feruenciores resurgant per penitenciam, semper de se humilius sencientes, & aliis cadentibus benignius compacientes.
40 Vnde & apostolo Paulo datus est stimulus carnis sue, ne magnitudo reuelacionum ipsum in superbiam eleuaret. Nonne quia prius ecclesiam Dei persecutus est, posterius sic humiliatus est quod reputauit se indignum ut apostolus uocaretur? Nonne criminum multitudo memorie commendata Mariam peccatricem postea semper humiliorem,
45 feruenciorem et magis beniuolam reddidit in agenda penitencia, in contemplacione deuota, & in operibus caritatis? Nonne propheta Dauid propter commissum homicidium & adulterium semper fuit erga Deum & hominem humilior corde, feruencior in amore, circumspeccior in prosperis, & paciencior in aduersis? Sic sancto Tobie captiuitatis
50 tribulacio, paupertatis angustia, & cecitatis miseria, uirtutis exercicium contulit, meritum cumulauit, & ineffabile gaudium preparauit. Sic in sanctissimo Job: quia – cum infirmitate corporis grauissima, cum perdicione temporalium complete, & cum horribili morte liberorum ac familie subit[ane]a – humilitas, amor Dei & paciencia perseuerabant,
55 ideo singula temporalia sunt sibi restituta copiosius &, preter hec, est ei sine dubio in celestibus excellentis glorie corona parata.

O humana fragilitas nimium delicata, desidiosa & improuida, que contra temptaciones & angustias murmuras & torpescis, dum talia negligencias expellunt, merita cumulant, & occasionem tribuunt
60 uictorie gloriose! 'Quis coronabitur nisi prius legittime certauerit?' Quis certabit nisi pugnam habuerit? Et quis pugnam habens vincet, nisi fortis perseuerauerit usque in finem? Presertim in pugna spirituali, vbi mors ipsa vincit aduersarium, & nichil militem captiuat nisi fuga, desidia uel consensus uoluntarius inimico. O spiritualiter pugnantis consolacio
65 plenissima graciarum, vbi Deus continue, cum omnibus sanctis, angelis & animabus beatis, suos milites respicit contra temptaciones uarias dimicantes, vincentibus congratulans & eis coronam glorie preparans; fatigatis autem & eius auxilium corditer inuocantibus statim (supra quod credi potest) graciose succuret Omnipotens in uirtute. Cur igitur

---

38 sceleris] sterilis J   49 in prosperis, &] om. J   54 subitanea] J, subita R (Oliger)
56 ei] om. J

the ineffable pity and incomprehensible providence of our Saviour – which keep fearful and humble people from falling when they are tempted, so that they might grow in purity and profit greatly, as an example to those who are presumptuous and lukewarm – allow even the elect to sin from time to time, so that in the end, overcome by the enormity of their villainy, they might rise up again by penitence, more fervent than before, every time feeling themselves to be more humble, and more kindly compassionate towards other people who fall. This is why the apostle Paul was given the thorn in his flesh, so that the greatness of his revelations would not exalt him in pride. Wasn't it because he had previously persecuted the church of God that afterwards he was so humbled that he considered himself unworthy to be called an apostle? Wasn't it the multitude of sins fixed in her memory that afterwards made the sinner Mary ever more humble in performing penitence, more fervent in her devout contemplation, and better-disposed in her works of charity? Wasn't it because he had committed murder and adultery that the prophet David was always, in his relations with God and man, more humble of heart, more fervent in love, more cautious in prosperity, and more patient in adversity? Likewise the tribulation of captivity, the hardship of poverty, and the misery of blindness, brought the holy Tobias to the exercise of virtue, increased his stock of merit, and prepared him for unspeakable joy. Similarly in the most holy Job: because his humility, love of God and patience persisted alongside the most severe infirmity of his body, the total loss of his wordly things, and the horrible death without warning of his children and household, so every one of his worldly things was restored to him in greater abundance, and moreover without doubt a distinguished crown of glory is waiting for him in Heaven.

Oh human fragility! You are too delicate, idle and thoughtless, the way you grumble and respond half-heartedly against temptations and difficulties, when in fact such things drive out carelessness, build up merit, and provide an opportunity for a glorious victory. 'Who shall be crowned, except he first strive lawfully?' Who shall strive unless he joins battle? And which of those who joins battle shall have the victory, unless he remains strong until the end? And especially in spiritual battles, where death itself overcomes the adversary, and nothing can take the soldier captive except for flight, idleness or his voluntary consent to his enemy. Oh it's a comfort full of grace for those engaged in spiritual battle to see that God, together with all the saints, angels and blessed souls, continously watches over his soldiers as they struggle against various temptations, congratulating the victors and preparing for them a crown of glory; and when they get tired and make a heartfelt cry for his help, at once the Almighty in his strength comes graciously to their aid, beyond anything you would believe. So,

70 christiane in temptacione, tribulacione, uel angustia, deficis & causaris de intolerabili vexacione, cum temptacio sit uita hominis super terram, & per multas tribulaciones oportet nos intrare in regnum Dei? Si uictoriam intendis habere, cur fugis? [56v] Si gloriam inestimabilem desideras, cur laborem exiguum pro ea complere recusas? Et si ad 75 celestem patriam pertingere proponis, cur deuias a recta uia? Sane nichil hominem impedire poterit a patria celesti nisi mortale peccatum. Quia omnis temptacio, omnis tribulacio, & omnis pena uel passio corporalis, cedere potest ad augmentum meriti, si gratanter accepta fuerit propter amorem Dei. Vnde pro his omnibus laudandus est Dominus, defectus 80 proprius humiliter cognoscendus & Dominus iugiter exorandus, ut contra tempactiones uirtutem tribuat resistendi, contra tribulaciones graciam paciendi, & in bonis operibus finaliter perseuerandi.

Insuper opus manuum vicissim excludere poterit ocium & accidiam, atque proximis proficere caritatiue. Presertim autem scriptura sancte 85 & edificatorie leccionis meritoria videtur que, post mortem scribentis, forsitan usque ad diem Iudicii ipsum quodammmodo viuere faciet & mereri, in edificacione & profectu singulorum legencium uel audiencium scripta sua. Hec nimirum & omnia saluti neccesaria leccio sacra (si diligencius aduertatur) docet, monet, consulit & hortatur.

90 Propterea, uos inclusi, per edificatorie leccionis discussionem debitam, *Videte uocacionem vestram.*

---

78 gratanter] gratulanter J   85 videtur] viuitur J   90 debitam] *om.* J

you Christian, why, in times of temptation, tribulation or difficulty, do you desert the field and make excuses about intolerable distress, when temptation is the condition of human life on earth, and it is through many tribulations that we must enter the kingdom of God? If you mean to gain the victory, why take flight? If you desire glory beyond measure, why refuse to do a tiny bit of work for it? And if you aim to reach your homeland in heaven, why deviate from the proper route? It's certain that nothing can keep a person from their heavenly home except for mortal sin. For every temptation, every tribulation, and all bodily pain or suffering, can turn to the increase of your merit, if it is received with joy for the sake of the love of God. Therefore we should praise the Lord for all these things, humbly recognise our own failings, and constantly pray to the Lord that he will give us the strength to resist against temptations, the grace to be patient in the face of tribulations, and to persevere to the end in good works.

Also manual work, for its part, can keep idleness and sloth at bay, and profit your neighbours in charity. And in particular, the writing of material that is holy and edifying to read seems commendable, because, after the person that wrote it has died – and even perhaps right up until the Day of Judgement – it can make him live and gain merit in some way, by the edification and profit of each of those who read or hear what he has written. Of course this, and everything necessary for salvation, is taught, demonstrated, advised and urged by holy reading, if one pays proper attention to it.

Therefore, you recluses, by due analysis of your edifying reading, 'Look to your vocation.'

Capitulum primum quarte partis

Quarto principaliter in hoc opere videbitis, uos inclusi, quantam mercedis copiam recipietis pro vestra uocacione sanctissima finaliter obseruata. Huius mercedis copia continet in presenti temporalis gaudii & consolacionis centuplum, quod promisit Christus relinquentibus
5 temporalia propter Deum; & in futuro duplicem stolam glorie, corporis videlicet & anime, preter accidentale gaudium quod habebit quilibet in celo de singulis creaturis.

Unde primitus in hac vita fidei firmitas, consciencie serenitas, & spei stabilitas certa, consequitur centuplum spiritualis gaudii & consola-
10 cionis, in comparacione quorumlibet temporalium que relinqueret aliquis propter Christum. Istud non credunt, sensiunt, nec sapiunt, nisi qui hoc in seipsis experti sunt, vel perfectorum conuersacionibus siue dictis adhibent fidem firmam. Et tamen id ipsum racio naturalis quodammodo persuadet. Nam in mortis articulo, in huius uite termino,
15 vel in examine districtissimi Iudicis omnipotentis quem nichil latere poterit, quis careret fide firma, consciencia pura, & spe certa – que a morte perpetua liberant & ad eternam disponunt gloriam – [57r] pro quantiscunque diuiciis siue delectacionibus huius mundi? Cumque mortis hora sit incerta, mundicia uite & predicta Dei dona tam preciosa
20 sunt cotidie sicut tunc erunt, si iusto libramine ponderentur.

Sed hic forsitan aliquis cogitaret qualiter centuplum gaudii vel consolacionis habere poterunt in hac vita qui relinq[u]unt omnia propter Christum, & tamen continue uexantur per corporis infirmitates, temptaciones & tribulaciones, & varias angustias usque ad mortem. Reuera
25 dici poterit quod in pacientibus propter Christum vexacio corporalis destruere non poterit gaudium spirituale; quin per temporis interualla gaudebit paciens de omnibus que pro Christo patitur, ac etiam tempore passionis confortabitur – sicut confortari solet miles animosus de prelio propter spem uictorie seu mercedis; mercator in maris periculo propter
30 spem lucri grandis, & mulier in puerperio propter amorem pueri nascentis. Sic enim apostoli 'ibant gaudentes, quoniam digni habiti sunt pro nomine Iesu contumeliam pati.' Ne mirum, cum predixerat eis Christus (prout patet Mat. 5), 'Beati eritis cum maledixerint uobis homines & persecuti uos fuerint & dixerint omne malum adversum

---

Heading *Capitulum primum quarte partis*] om. J   2 vestra] om. J   15 in] om. J •
districtissimi] districti J   19 incerta] certa J (N)   33 prout patet] om. J

Part Four. Chapter 1

The fourth principal thing that you will see in this work, you recluses, is how abundant a reward you will receive for keeping to your most holy vocation to the end. The scale of this reward will be, in the present time, a hundredfold in worldly joy and comfort, as Christ promises to those who
5 renounce the things of this world for the sake of God; and in the future the twin robes of glory – that is, of the body and the soul – above and beyond the accidental joy that everyone in Heaven will derive from all created things.

And the first of these – strength of faith, serenity of conscience, and sure
10 stability of hope in this life – will be followed by spiritual joys and comforts that will be a hundred times any of the worldly things that someone might renounce for Christ. No-one will believe, feel or understand this unless they have experienced it for themselves, or derived a secure belief in it from the behaviour and sayings of perfect people. And yet it would be possible for
15 their natural reason to persuade them of it. For at the point of death, at the end of this life, or in the most severe examination of the almighty Judge, from whom nothing can be concealed, who would want to find himself without a strong faith, pure conscience and sure hope – which can free us from everlasting death, and set us in the way of eternal glory – for any
20 amount of this world's riches or delights? And since the hour of our death is uncertain, a pure life and the aforementioned gifts of God are as precious to us every day as they will be then, if we reckon their value correctly.

But here someone might be wondering in what way those people who renounce everything for Christ can have a hundredfold joys and comforts
25 in this life, when they are continuously afflicted by bodily infirmity, temptations and tribulations, and all sorts of deprivation right up until their death. Well, it can be said that, for those who undergo suffering for Christ's sake, bodily hardship cannot destroy their spiritual joy; indeed, during that period of time the person who is suffering will rejoice at
30 everything he undergoes for Christ's sake, and will even find comfort during the time when he is suffering – just as a courageous soldier is comforted in battle by the hope of victory or reward, the merchant in peril on the sea by the hope of vast profit, and a woman in labour by love for the child that is being born. And in the same way the apostles 'went around rejoicing that
35 they were considered worthy to suffer scorn for Jesus's name.' Little wonder, when Christ had said to them previously (as it shows in Matt. 5), 'Blessed are ye when they shall revile you, and persecute you, and speak all that is

35 uos mencientes propter me. Gaudete in illa die & exultate, quoniam merces vestra multa est in celo.' Similiter, de tribulacionibus per quas temptari solent homines, consolatur apostolus Iacobus pusillanimes ita dicens: 'Omne gaudium existimate, fratres mei, cum in temptaciones uarias incideritis, scientes quod probacio fidei vestre pacienciam
40 operatur. Paciencia autem opus perfectum habeat, ut sitis perfecti & integri, in nullo deficientes.' Hinc est quod sancti martires omnimoda tormenta, gaudenti animo, tollerabant que poterant tiranni crudelissimi cogitare. Consimiliter, uos inclusi, quecunque penalia contingencia (preter peccatum!) cum gaudio sustinebitis propter amorem Dei vt,
45 sicut Apostolus dicit, quelibet passio corporis sit uobis refeccio spiritus, & cuilibet dolori vestro corporali seu cordiali corespondeat in Deo vestro consolacio spiritualis propter spem & desiderium uite eterne, iuxta quod dicit idem propheta Domino per hunc modum: 'Fuerunt,' inquit, 'mihi lacrime mee panes die ac nocte.' Et iterum: 'Secundum,'
50 inquit, 'multitudinem dolorum meorum in corde meo consolaciones tue letificauerant animam meam.'

O mira Domine miseracionis consolacio! O cordis iocunditas admirabilis! O mentis gaudium [57v] temporale quodlibet paruipendens, dum quelibet corporalis passio per eterne salutis desiderium superatur,
55 omnis rei familiaris penuria pro certa spe celestis glorie gratanter accipitur, et qualemcunque tribulacionem mundi reddit tolerabilem Domine consolacionis leticia spiritualis! Talem leticiam parturire solet firma spes Domine promissionis ineffabilis, qua sepius in scripturis asseritur, quod vnusquisque propriam mercedem accipiet in celestibus
60 sine fine secundum suum laborem in huius uite miseriis propter amorem Dei.

Istius mercedis porciunculas pauci & deuotissimi dum hic vixerint pregustare merentur, & hoc prout expedit fidelium animabus, iuxta dispensacionem graciosissimam Dei nostri. Vnde Spiritus Sanctus, vbi
65 vult, quando vult, & quantum vult, graciam infundit realiter. Ideo dicit Dauid, 'Gustate & videte, quoniam suauis est Dominus. Beatus vir qui sperat in eo.'

Hanc suauitatem diuersi diuersimode consequuntur, sicut tam ex confessione hominis huiusmodi graciam habentis quam ex scripturis
70 autenticis plenius intellexi. Quidam enim, in deuotis precibus coram ymagine crucifixi, uel in meditacione sue gloriosissime passionis, tanta cordis dulcedine perfunduntur & tanta delectactione diuini amoris

---

48 idem] eidem J (N)   52 Domine] diuine J   57 Domine] diuine J • leticia] *om.* J • parturire] preterire J   58 Domine] diuine J   65 quando vult] *om.* J

evil against you, untruly, for my sake. Be glad on that day and rejoice for your reward is very great in heaven.' In the same way the apostle James offers comfort to fearful souls regarding those tribulations that people are tempted by, saying thus: 'Consider it pure joy, my brothers, whenever you face trials of many kinds, because you know that the testing of your faith develops perseverance. Perseverance must finish its work so that you may be mature and complete, not lacking anything.' This is why the holy martyrs were able to withstand, with joy in their souls, all the torments that the cruellest tyrants could think of. In the same way, you recluses, whatever punishments should befall you (apart from sin!) you should put up with them joyfully for God's love so that, as the Apostle says, everything you suffer in your body should be refreshment for your spirit, and for every pain you suffer in your body or your heart there will be a corresponding spiritual comfort in God, due to your hope and desire for eternal life – according to the words of the same Prophet speaking to the Lord in this manner: 'My tears,' he says, 'were as my bread both day and night.' And again, 'According to the multitude of my sorrows in my heart,' he says, 'thy comforts have given joy to my soul.'

Oh the wonderful comfort of the Lord's mercy! Oh what marvellous delight for the heart! Oh how joyful the mind when it sets no store by any worldly thing, when bodily suffering is overcome by the desire for eternal salvation, the lack of any worldly comforts is freely accepted in return for the sure hope of heavenly glory, and joy at the Lord's spiritual comforts makes every kind of worldly tribulation bearable! Such joy is born of a sure hope in the Lord's ineffable promise, which is frequently made in the scriptures, that everyone will receive his own reward in heaven without end according to the efforts he has made for the love of God whilst in the miseries of this life.

A few very devout people may deserve to experience a little taste of this reward whilst they are living, insofar as it may profit the souls of the faithful, according to the discretion of our most gracious God. For the Holy Spirit really does pour in his grace where he wants, when he wants, and as much as he wants. Thus David says, 'Taste and see that the Lord is sweet. Blessed is the man that hopeth in him.'

Various people have experienced this sweetness in various ways, as I have learnt more fully both from the testimony of people who possess such grace and from authentic writings. Some people, whilst in devout prayer before an image of the Crucified, or in meditation on his most glorious passion, have had their hearts so infused with sweetness, and have become so drunk with the delight of divine love, that they would not be without that spiritual

inebriantur, quod pro tocius mundi deliciis illo spirituali gaudio non carerent. Et hanc dulcedinem diucius interdum habere possent sine
75 corporis recreacione; quam non audent pro timore ne corpus nimis debilitetur, vel aliquod seruicium debitum negligatur, vel de talibus scandalum incurrant & iudicium proximorum. Alii sunt (vel saltem fuerunt) quibus legentibus, orantibus siue meditantibus velut inestimabilis odoris suauitas, omnium possibilium specierum fragrancia
80 exsuperans, per nares influebat, atque per os infundebatur quasi celestis manna dulcedo, omne delectamentum in se habens; que, ad interiora tam anime quam corporis profluens, utrumque homines tam interiorem quam exteriorem inenerrabili dulcore perfudit, quadamque suaui iocunditate & iocunda suauitate arras celestis glorie contulit pregust-
85 andas. Hos autem omnes non extra corpora raptos, sed in corporibus, estimo talem consolacionem diuinitus habuisse.

Fuerunt autem alii, prout narrat sanctus Alredus (*De Hominibus Babilonis*), quibus orantibus mira quedam suauitas superueniens omnes mundanas cogitaciones & carnales affectus extinxit, moxque rapti quasi
90 ad tercium celum cum beato Paulo, & incomprehensibili luce perfusi, quadam beatifica uisione Dei (licet imperfecta) vel [58r] saltem quodam excellenti ac inenerrabili gaudio perfusi, sic inebriati sunt quod, ab aliis pulsati, cum difficultate ad corporales sensus quos relinquirant redire ualebant.

95 Talis consolacio paucis concessa est, quia nec carnaliter viuentibus, nec de mundo sollicitis, nec his qui per reuelacionis magnitudinem faciliter extolli possent; sed tamen mundis corde, soli Deo uacantibus, & pro amore Dei multum laborantibus in secretis oracionibus, sanctis meditacionibus & deuocionis siue compunccionis lacrimis,
100 atque desolatis, quoniam eis multum proficere poterit ad salutem, vel ignem in eis reficere feruentis amoris Dei. Tunc quidem, modo predicto talibus dulcedinis graciam infundens, realiter dicit Spiritus Sanctus illud (Exod. 9): 'Videte magnalia Dei.' Talis celestis dulcedinis pregustacio, iuxta sanctos doctores, in hac mortali uita non perfecte
105 seu continue, sed raptati & momentanee, poterit optineri; & hanc semper comitatur ardentissimus amor Dei – quo diligitur propter se solum, qui est simpliciter summum bonum, & non solum propter aliquid beneficium nobis factum. Si autem aliquis in hac uita tercium diuine dileccionis gradum acquirere possit – videlicet quod nec seipsum
110 nec aliquid creatum diligeret nisi propter Deum – veraciter in terris

---

74 interdum habere] habere interdunt J   77 &] uel J   83 dulcore] dulcedine J
98 secretis] *om.* J   99 sanctis meditacionibus] *om.* J • siue] seu J

joy for all the delights of the world. And they might sometimes be able to keep this sweetness for longer if they went without bodily refreshment, but they dare not do that for fear that they might weaken their body too much, or neglect some of the services they are obliged to do, or for these reasons become the subject of scandal or the bad opinion of their neighbours. There are others (or at least there were) into whose noses, while they were reading, praying or in meditation, there streamed a sort of immeasurably sweet odour, surpassing all possible varieties of fragrance, and a sweetness like the manna of heaven, holding all delights within it, was poured into their mouth; and, flowing deep into the soul and the body, it filled both the inner man and the outer with an indescribable sweetness, and in sweet joy and joyful sweetness allowed them to experience a foretaste of heavenly glory. But I think that all these people had such divine comforts in their bodies, not ravished out of their bodies.

There were also others, as Saint Ailred writes in his 'Men of Babylon', to whom, while they were praying, a certain marvelous sweetness came and extinguished all their worldly thoughts and carnal desires, and presently, ravished with Saint Paul as if to the third heaven, and filled in incomprehensible light with a beatific vision of God (albeit an imperfect one) – or even, rather, filled with a superlative and indescribable joy – they were so drunk that, when they were called to other things, they were only able with difficulty to return to the bodily senses they had left behind.

Comfort like this is given to few people – that is, not to those who live carnally, nor who care for the things of the world, nor those who can get carried away by the greatness of their revelations, but rather to the pure in heart, who devote themselves to God alone, and for the love of God do great work in secret prayers, holy meditations and devotions or tears of compunction, and to the forsaken – for it can help them greatly to salvation, or revive in them the fire of the burning love of God. And then the Holy Spirit truly says, to those whom he infuses with the grace of sweetness in this way, thus (Exodus 9): 'See the mighty works of God'. Such a foretaste of heavenly sweetness, according to holy doctors, cannot be had in this mortal life perfectly or continuously, but in an ecstasy and for a moment; and this always accompanies a most burning love for God – who should be loved for himself alone, and not just for the good things he has done for us, since he is uniquely the highest good. And if someone in this life is able to reach the third degree of divine love – that is, that he does not love himself or any created thing, except for God – then truly in a way he is

quodammodo beatus esset. Unde nec compunccionis lacrimis indigeret, quia uberrimum fructum faceret adherendo Deo fortissime per amorem. Sed numquid talis gradus amoris sit uiatori possibilis Deus nouit, & ipsi viderint qui experti sunt; quia in uita futura erit communis &
115 inestimabilis amor ille. Predicte tamen dulcedinis possibilitati (ut predictam est) sentencialiter concordant multi sancti doctores, necnon & sancti patres in suis *Collacionibus* (Collacione 3^{ius} cap. 7, Collac. 4us c. 3°, Coll. 6us c. 9°, Coll. 9us c. 25 & Coll. 10us c. 5° & 7°), vbi dicitur quod intencio solitarii debet esse ut ymaginem future beatitudinis in
120 hoc corpore possidere mereatur, & quodammodo arram celestis conuersacionis & glorie incipiat degustare. Ad quod consequendum summe ualere creditur ab antiquis expertis (ut patet ibidem) frequentacio huius uersiculi: 'Deus in adiutorium meum intende. Domine ad adiuvandum me festina' – et hoc in oracione seu meditacione, semper & ubique,
125 sero & mane, tam in prosperis quam in aduersis, in spirituali gaudio & in omni temptacione & periculo, quia continet uirtualiter quicquid expedit ad salutem.

In his igitur omnibus, vos inclusi, per consolacione uobis uel aliis factam a Deo, *Videte uocacionem vestram*.

---

112 adherendo Deo fortissime] fortius inherendo Deo J   116 sentencialiter] *om.* J, *but space left*   117 Collacionibus] viz. *add.* J   118 &^{1}] *om.* J * 10] 9.10 J   119 esse] *om.* J   120 possidere] *om.* J   124 et] in *add.* J   128 uel] et J

IV.i • A Mirror for Recluses   101

blessed on earth. And then he will not be lacking in tears of compunction, for by cleaving most strongly to God by love he shall bring forth rich fruit. But God knows, and those who have experienced it have seen, that to attain such a degree of love is not possible to someone still in this life
120 *because, when we reach the life to come, that love will be available to all, and it will be beyond measure. Nonetheless, the possibility of the aforementioned sweetness (as described above) is confirmed in authoritative fashion by numerous holy doctors, and also by the holy Fathers in their Conferences (3rd conference, chapter 7; 4th conference, chapter 4;*
125 *6th conference, chapter 9; 9th conference, chapter 25; and 10th conference, chapters 5 and 7), where it is said that it should be the aim of the solitary person that he might deserve to have a facsimile of the bliss to come whilst in this body, and somehow begin to experience a foretaste of heavenly life and glory. To achieve this, those who experienced it in days gone by*
130 *(as it shows in the same place) believed that the use of this verse was the most effective: 'O God, come to my assistance; O Lord, make haste to help me' – and this in prayer or meditation, always and everywhere, early and late, both in prosperity and in adversity, in times of spiritual joy and in all temptations and dangers, for it contains by implication*
135 *everything that is required for salvation.*

And so, you recluses, in all these things done by God as a comfort for you or for others, 'Look to your vocation.'

Capitulum 2

Post hanc uitam in homine glorificato multiplex gaudium & ineffabile permanebit inseperabiliter, quando omnis pregustata suauitas, in comparacione [58v] illius glorie, erit uelut exigua aque gutta respectu pulcherrimi fontis indefectabiliter scaturientis, quia totus homo (secundum omnes vires & omnem capacitatem tam corporis quam anime) replebitur inestimabili gloria Dei sui. Tunc enim vna porcio celestis mercedis erit corporis glorificacio perfecta, que 4^{or} dotes habet. Nam 4^{or} elementa – videlicet terra, aqua, aer & ignis – in hoc statu miserie corpus humanum componencia reddunt ipsum corpus obscurum, passibile, tardum & rude, quia continue adinuicem contrariantur. Sed in statu beatitudinis erunt adeo depurata & ad equalitatem reducta quod corpus ex illis compositum reddetur clarum, impassibile, agile & subtile.

Unde prima dos glorie corporalis erit impassibilitas tanta & talis quod corpus eius qui hic pro Christo passus est labores, angustias, tribulaciones, frigus, famem, sitim, uel quecunque alia dura & aspera, erit in beatitudine tam perfectum quod vulnerari, corrumpi seu ledi non possit ab aliqua creatura, licet apponeretur eidem ignis ardentissimus infernalis. Et hanc dotem impassibilitatis ostendit quodammodo Christus in seipso dum corpus suum dedit in cibum discipulis & ex hoc nullatenus ledebatur.

2^a dos glorie corporalis erit claritas multum excellens, qua 'iusti fulgebunt sicut sol' – imo septempliciter clarius sole moderno – 'in regno patris eorum.' Corpus enim illius qui dum hic vixit pro zelo legis Christi viciorum obscuritatem uitauit, latibula peccancium odiuit, & a se culparum tenebras mortalium effugauit, in uita futura tanta luminis claritate perfundetur quantam mortalis hominis oculus diucius intueri non possit, & tali lumine totum adornabitur honestissime pro uestitu. Hanc dotem claritatis ostendit Christus in corpore suo, quando transfigurauit se in monte & facies eius resplenduit sicut sol.

3^a dos glorie corporalis erit subtilitas ualde magna. Nam corpus illius qui pro statu vie velud quadam subtili prudencia siue prudenti subtilitate resistebat viriliter carnis temptacionibus uniuersis, in statu celestis patrie tam subtile fiet quod pertransire poterit murum ligneum

---

Heading *Capitulum 2*] *om.* J 2 quando] quoniam J 8 &] *om.* J 11 adeo] a deo J 16 &] uel *corr. to* et J 20 discipulis] om J, *but space left* • ex] *om.* J 33 carnis] *om.* J

Chapter 2

After this life, many kinds of ineffable joy will remain with a glorified person forever, without the possibility of separation; and then all the sweetness that he has tasted before will be, in comparison with that glory, like a tiny drop of water compared with a beautiful fountain that gushes out inexhaustibly; for the whole person will be filled, to the full extent of his strength and the capacity of both his body and soul, by the immeasurable glory of his God. And at that time one aspect of his heavenly reward will be the perfect glorification of his body, which will have four gifts. For the four elements that make up the human body in this miserable state (that is, earth, water, air and fire) make that body dark, vulnerable, slow and coarse, because they are constantly striving against each other. But in the state of bliss they will be so purified and brought into harmony that the body that is composed of them will be made clear, impassible, agile and subtle.

The first of these gifts that the body in glory will have will be impassibility, of such a kind and such a degree that the body of someone who in this life has undergone hardships, deprivations, tribulations, cold, hunger, thirst, or anything else that is hard or harsh for Christ's sake, will in the state of bliss be so perfect that it cannot be wounded, damaged or injured by any created thing, even were it to be touched by the fiercest fire of hell. And this gift of impassibility Christ revealed in a way in himself when he gave his body as food to his disciples, and was not in the least injured by this.

The second gift that the body in glory will have will be clarity or great radiance, by which the 'just shall shine like the sun' – or rather, seven times brighter than the sun is nowadays – 'in the kingdom of their father'. And the body of that person who, while he lived here, in his zeal for the law of Christ shunned the darkness of vices, hated the hiding places of sins, and fled the shadows of mortal guilts, in the life to come will be suffused with a light of such brightness that the eye of a mortal human could not look on it for any time; and he will be entirely clothed in this light as his most suitable garment. This gift of clarity Christ revealed in his own body, when he transfigured himself on the mountain and his face shone like the sun.

The third gift that the body in glory will have will be a very great subtlety. For the body of that person who, by a subtle prudence or a prudent subtlety, has stoutly resisted all temptations of the flesh whilst in the living state, in the state of his heavenly Father will be made so subtle that it can pass through wooden or stone walls, or any other body that has not been

35 uel lapideum, uel aliud quodcunque corpus non glorificatum & simul in loco coexistere cum eodem, quemadmodum solis radius uitrum penetrare uidetur. Et hanc dotem subtilitatis preostendit Dominus in seipso, quando intrauit ad discipulos ianuis clausis, ac etiam quando natus est de sue beatissime matris utero clauso pudoris signaculo &
40 uirginitatis integritate manente.

4^a dos glorie corporalis erit agilitas, quia corpus eius qui in hac ualle miserie propter Christum grauabatur [59r] miseriis, angustiis & tribulacionibus quibuscunque perseueranter usque ad mortem, post resurrecionem reddetur tam agile & subditum anime uoluntati quod
45 ad imperium spiritus vbicunque uoluerit protinus erit corpus. Et hanc dotem agilitatis ostendit Christus in corpore suo ambulans super mare, quando putabatur a discipulis esse fantasma.

Ex his dotibus corporis glorificati resultabit tanta pulcritudo, tanta fortitudo, tanta sanitas, tanta libertas, & tam completa uoluptas
50 celestium gaudiorum, quod (secundum uenerabilem Anselmum, *De Similitudinibus*) 'Dileccio quedam ineffabilis beatos inebriabit, & inestimabilis dulcedinis exuberancia saciabit, intantum quod omnia membra cordis tam mirabili delectacionis dulcedine replebuntur ut ueraciter totus homo "torrente uoluptatis Dei potetur & ab ubertate domus
55 eius spiritualiter inebrietur."' Nec mirum, quia tanta erit inter corpus & animam vnionis colligancia quod etiam gaudium anime in corpus continue redundabit. Hec nunc non uidemus nisi per speculum in enigmate, sed tunc clare uidebimus & sencibiliter percipiemus, quando Iudex omnipotens dicet finaliter illud (Math. 20): 'Voca operarios &
60 redde illis mercedem.'

O uocacio graciosa, o beati mercenarii, o merces immensa, vbi miseri peccatores ad gloriam uocantur, uocati per graciam iustificantur, iustificati per graciam meritorie operantur, & operantes meritorie supra modum magno & indelibili gaudio premiantur! Tales dotes glorie non
65 temporales sed eternas dabit dilectis suis Sponsus speciosissimus; non terrenus sed celestis; pro castitate continua, non pro carnali copula; pro decor[e] spirituali, non pro pulcritudine corporali; pro perfecta caritate, |et| non pro carnis aliqua uoluptate. Has dotes corporis, uos inclusi, cogitate, aduertite, considerate, quia has esse desiderabiles
70 premonstrat supradicta dulcedo quam feliciter degustastis. Vos enim estis paradisicole, nos mundi miserabiles incole; vos estis in porta celi, & nos in limo profundi; vos in speculo ueritatis, & nos in tenebris falsitatis; vos denique in magna cordis iubilacione, & nos in noxie

---

67 decore] J, decori R   68 et] *ins. marg. with caret in text* R, *om*. J   73 nos] *om*. J

glorified, and co-exist in the same place as it, in the same way as a ray of sunlight may be seen to pass through glass. And this gift of subtlety the Lord first revealed in himself, when he came in to his disciples though the doors were shut, and also when he was born of his most blessed mother though her womb, closed with the seal of modesty, and her virginity remained intact.

The fourth gift that the body in glory will have will be agility. For the body of one who in this vale of tears has been weighed down with misery, anguish and tribulations of whatever kind for Christ's sake, and persevered right up until his death, after the resurrection will be made so agile and subject to the wishes of the soul that, wherever he wishes to go, at the command of his spirit that is where his body will be. And this gift of agility Christ revealed in his own body when he walked upon the sea, and his disciples thought he was an apparition.

These gifts granted to the glorified body will result in so much beauty, so much strength, so much health, so much freedom and so complete an enjoyment of heavenly joys that, according to the venerable Anselm ('De Similitudinibus'), 'A kind of ineffable love will make those in bliss drunk, and an abundance of immeasurable sweetness will fill them up, to the extent that every bit of their heart will be filled with a delightful and marvellous sweetness, so that truly the whole person "shall drink of the torrent of God's pleasure, and shall be spiritually inebriated with the plenty of his house."' And that is no wonder, for the bond of union between the body and the soul will be so great that the soul's joy will in fact continually overflow into the body. We see this now only through a glass in a dark manner, but then we will see clearly and feel in our senses, when the almighty Judge finally says thus (Matt. 20): 'Call the labourers and pay them their hire.'

Oh what a gracious calling! Oh how blessed a wage-labourer! Oh what an immeasurable payment, where wretched sinners are summoned to glory, and once summoned are justified by grace, and once justified by grace perform works of merit, and while they are performing works of merit they are rewarded beyond measure with a great and imperishable joy. It is the most beautiful bridegroom who gives his beloved such gifts of glory, not temporal but eternal, not earthly but heavenly; for chastity kept continuously, not for carnal union; for beauty of the spirit, not prettiness of the body; for perfect charity, not for any delight of the flesh. Think on these gifts of the body, you recluses, pay attention and consider them, for the aforementioned sweetness that you have been lucky enough to taste shows them to be desirable. For you will be residents of paradise, we will be wretched inhabitants of the world; you will be at the gates of heaven, and we will be deep in the mud; you in the mirror of truth, and we in the darkness of falsehood; and finally you in great jubilation

sollicitudinis tribulacione. Si dixeritis quod non est ita, laboretis igitur
75 iugiter quousque sit ita. Dum statis ad portam Patris vestri tam misericordia quam gracia plenissimi & omnipotentis, orate, petite, pulsate, donec aperiat uobis Christus. Ingressi autem ardebitis amore castissimo Dei vestri, & fiducialiter in corde cantabitis quod solum perfectis contemplatiuis congruit illu[d] (Canticum Canticorum): 'Osculetur
80 me osculo oris [59v] sui,' & tanquam spiritualiter amorosi sponso vestro Christo dicent[e]s corditer, 'quia meliora sunt ubera tua vino fragrancia vnguentis optimis. ... Trahe me post te. Curremus in odore vnguentorum tuorum.' Sic odor iste diuini amoris super omnia aromata in vestris mentibus redolebit. Quare non curritis, pugiles Christi? Hic
85 est delectabilis terminus uie vestre, hic est propositi uestri finis nobilis. Quare non curritis? Ut quid tardatis, timidi? Thesaurus preciosissimus offertus uobis liberaliter, laboris uestri fructus suauissimus uos expectat. Ut quid tardatis, timidi?

Amodo igitur propter tam admirabilem corporis glorificacionem,
90 *Uidete uocacionem vestram.*

---

77 autem] enim J   79 illud] J, illum R   81 dicentes] J, dicentis R

of heart, and we in terrible tribulation and anxiety. If you say that this is not the case, then work continuously until it is. While you stand at your Father's door – who is all-powerful and supremely full of mercy and of grace – pray, beg, knock, until Christ opens it for you. And once you are inside you will burn with the most chaste love for your God and confidently you will sing in your heart that text from the Song of Songs that is fitting only for perfect contemplatives, 'Let him kiss me with the kiss of his mouth', just as, in your impassioned state, you will say spiritually to your beloved Christ, 'for thy breasts are better than wine, smelling sweet of the best ointments ... Draw me: we will run after thee to the odour of thy ointments.' In this way this odour of divine love will fill your minds with an aroma superior to all other scents. Why aren't you running, you who fight for Christ? The delightful goal of your life is here. The noble conclusion of your purpose is here. Why aren't you running? What are you waiting for, you cowards? The most precious treasure is offered freely to you; the most sweet fruit of your labour awaits you. What are you waiting for, you cowards?

So henceforth, on account of such a marvelous glorification of your body, 'Look to your vocation.'

Capitulum 3

Secunda stola glorie consistit in tribus dotibus anime, que sunt: plena Dei cognicio, siue clara Dei uisio; perfecta eius dileccio, & secura comprehensio siue possessio huius summi boni.

Vnde prima dos anime erit clara Dei uisio in gloria sine fine. Habet enim anima 3 potencias, videlicet intellectiuam, uolitiuam & memoratiuam, que secundum omnem suum appetitum in celesti gaudio saciabuntur. Nam potencia intellectiua, que in presenti uita propter auctoritatem diuine scripture firmiter credidit articulos fidei (de Trinitate, de incarnacione, de passione, de resurreccione, de sacramento corporis Christi & de extremo iudicio), quamuis illos per racionem naturalem plene cognoscere non potuit uel probare, in beatitudine tanto lumine glorie perfundetur quod clare uidebit Deum omnipotentem, eius summam sapienciam, immensam bonitatem & pulcritudinem infinitam; & in uidendo Deum cognoscet uera esse que prius credidit, ac omnia alia que uoluerit tunc uidebit. & sic saciabitur appetitus eius.

Vlterius potencia uolitiua que hic dilexit Deum super omnia, et quemlibet suum proximum propter Deum, atque sic decessit in caritate, in futuro replebitur inenarrabili gaudio dileccionis Dei, iuxta quod dicit Apostolus: 'Oculus non vidit, nec auris audiuit, nec in cor hominis ascendit, que preparauit Deus diligentibus se.' De hoc etiam dicit beatus Bernardus sic: 'Merces sanctorum tam magna est quod non potest mensurari, tam multa quod non potest numerari, tam copiosa quod non potest finiri, & tam preciosa quod non poterit estimari.' Nec mirum, quia (teste eodem beato Bernardo) 'Minus sunt omnes delicie que sunt in mundo, & erunt usque in Diem iudicii, respectu illius suauitatis quam sit vna gutta aque respectu tocius maris'. Et hac suauitate inexplicabili saciabitur potencia uolitiua.

Adhuc potencia memoratiua que, iuxta promissa Dei stabiliter tenuit in hac uita spem uenie, gracie & glorie, secure comprehendet in futuro (misericordia [61r] & gracia mediantibus) longe maiorem gloriam quam sperauit. Nam ibidem saciabitur omnis anime appetitus in clare uidendo, diligendo & comprehendendo summam ueritatem, summam bonitatem & summam pulcritudinem, cum infallibili securitate quod

---

Heading *Capitulum 3*] *om.* J   8 auctoritatem] auctorem J   13 immensam bonitatem] *om.* J   14 uera esse] quod vera esset J   24 beato] *om.* J   30 misericordia] misericordia/lem *across lacuna* J. *Leaves out of sequence* R, J *absent from here* (N)

Chapter 3

The second robe of glory comprises three gifts of the soul, and they are: the full knowledge of God, or a clear vision of God; perfect love of him; and a secure grasp or possession of this highest good.

The first of these gifts of the soul will be a clear sight of God in glory without end. Now the soul has three powers – that is the power of the intellect, of the will, and of the memory – and in the joy of heaven they will be satisfied in all their appetites. For the power of the intellect, which in the present life firmly believes, on the authority of divine scripture, the articles of the faith (concerning the Trinity, the incarnation, the passion, the resurrection, the sacrament of Christ's body, and the Last Judgement), even though those things cannot be fully known or proved by the natural reason, in the state of bliss will be filled so completely with the light of glory that it will clearly see almighty God, his supreme wisdom, immeasurable goodness and infinite beauty; and in seeing God it will know that those things that previously it believed are true; and then it will see all other things that it wished for. And so its appetite will be satisfied.

Further, the power of the will, which whilst here has loved God above all things and every one of his neighbours for God's sake, and thus has died in a state of charity, in the future will be filled with the indescribable joy of God's love, according to what the Apostle says: 'That eye hath not seen, nor ear heard, neither hath it entered into the heart of man, what things God hath prepared for them that love him.' And on this Saint Bernard says thus: 'The reward of the saints is so great that it cannot be measured, of such great quantity that it cannot be numbered, so plentiful that it cannot be exhausted, and so precious that its value cannot be reckoned.' It is no wonder, for (as the same Saint Bernard witnesses) 'All the delights that there are in the world, and that there will be right up to the Day of Judgement, are less, in comparison with that sweetness, than is a single drop of water in comparison with the whole of the sea'. And the power of the will will be satisfied by this sweetness that is beyond explanation.

And then the power of memory, which in this life has held unshakably to the hope of pardon, grace and glory, in accordance with God's promise, in the future (if mercy and grace play their part) will securely possess glory much greater than they had hoped for. For in that place every appetite of the soul will be satisfied by its clearly seeing, loving and possessing the supreme truth, supreme goodness and supreme beauty, in the unfailing confidence

sic manebit eternaliter sine displicencia qualicunque. Quia nichil in illo statu beatitudinis amabitur quod deerit, nec aliquid desiderabitur quod non aderit. De hac beatitudine dicit notabiliter beatus Augustinus (tercio *De Libero arbitrio* in finem) ubi sic inquit: 'Tanta est iusticie pulcritudo, tanta iocunditas lucis eterne, ut etiam si amplius non liceret in ea manere quam vnius diei mora, propter hoc tamen solum innumerabiles anni huius uite pleni deliciis & affluencia temporalium bonorum recte meritoque contempnerentur.' (Hec ille.) Quanto magis igitur sequitur quod misera uoluptas carnis & peccati paruipendenda est cauenda & contempnenda per modicum tempus uite nostre pro habenda tam excellenti gloria sine fine?

In predictis tribus dotibus anime consistit substanciale siue essenciale gaudium, sine quo non posset aliquis esse beatus, & secundum cuius gradus diuersos beati diuersimode beatificantur. Et hoc gaudium a quibusdam dicitur 'aurea' uel 'corona'. Aliud est gaudium accidentale, quod includit dotes corporis & omne gaudium quod prouenit ex aliqua creatura, propter quale gaudium, si augmentetur, non erit homo simpliciter siue intensiue magis beatus, sed solum multiplicius siue accidentaliter & extensiue. Sicut exempla gracia: si quis uideret rem aliquam in lumine solis clare lucentis & apponeretur ibidem lumen candele, non clarius uideret quam prius, nec maius siue intensius, sed tamen multiplicius lumen haberet. Quoddam est insuper accidentale gaudium ualde excellens, quod 'aureola' nominatur. Tribus generibus hominum – videlicet sanctis martiribus, mundis uirginibus & perfectis predicatoribus – tribuetur. Martiribus quidem dabitur propter excellentissimum opus potencie irascibilis, quo uicerunt passiones mundi illatas; virginibus propter excellentissimum opus potencie concupiscibilis, quo uicerunt passiones carnis innatas, et predicatoribus propter excellentissimum opus potencie racionalis, quo uicerunt tam in suis quam in alienis cordibus passiones per diabolum seminatas. 'Quapropter,' sicut consulit beatus Petrus (2^a Pet. primo), 'magis satagite ut per bona opera certam vestram uocacionem & eleccionem faciatis.' Nam quicunque in bonis operibus finiunt dies suos, ad cenam eterne uite finaliter uocabuntur, quando per nupcias inter-[61v]-minabilis glorie copulabuntur agnus Dei Christus & eius serui fideles quos redemit suo sanguine. De quibus (Apoc. 19) scribitur: 'Beati qui ad cenam nupciarum agni uocati sunt.'

that it can remain there for eternity without any disturbance whatsoever. For in that state of bliss there is nothing that anyone might love that will be lacking, and there is nothing that anyone might desire that will not be forthcoming. Saint Augustine says something noteworthy concerning this bliss (in the third book of 'On Free Will', at the end), where he says thus: 'The beauty of justice is so great, and the joy of the eternal light is so great that, even if we were not permitted to remain in it for a period greater than a single day, for that one day alone we would (if our thought was right and proper) reject innumerable years full of delights in this life, or the abundance of worldly goods.' (This is what he says.) How much more does it follow, then, that we should fear and despise the miserable delights of the flesh and our disregard for sin for a little bit of time in our life so as to have such surpassing glory without end?

 The aforesaid three gifts of the soul include the substantial or essential joy without which no-one can be in bliss, and according to the degree of it that they have various of the blessed enjoy bliss in various ways. And this joy is called by some people 'golden' or 'a crown'. Accidental joy is something else. It includes the gifts of the body and all joy that comes from any created things. If this kind of joy is increased, a person will not thereby be more blessed essentially or in intensity, but just blessed in more ways, or in incidence and extent – as in this example: if one is looking at something in the light of the sun when it is shining brightly, and someone comes along with the light of a candle, that person will not see more clearly than before, nor better nor more intently; he will just have more kinds of light. There is a kind of accidental joy which far surpasses this, and is called an 'aureole', and it is given to three kinds of people – that is, to holy martyrs, pure virgins and perfect preachers. It will be given to martyrs for the supreme work of their irascible power, by which they conquered the passions brought on by the world. It will be given to virgins for the supreme work of their concupiscible power, by which they conquered the passions that are born of the flesh. And it will be given to preachers for the supreme work of their rational power, by which they conquered the passions sown by the devil in their hearts and in those of others. 'Wherefore,' as Saint Peter advises (2 Peter 1), 'labour the more, that by good works you may make sure your calling and election.' For whoever ends his days in good works will at last be called to the feast of eternal life, when Christ the Lamb of God will be joined, in the everlasting wedding-feast of glory, with his faithful servants that he redeemed by his blood. Of this it is written (in Apoc. 19): 'Blessed are they that are called to the marriage supper of the Lamb.'

O beatitudo perfecta! O cena sine fine mansura! O summe desiderabiles nupcie spirituales, in quibus deliciarum fercula semper fideles plene reficient sine fastidio, & esurire facient sine defectu; vbi per summe ueritatis cognicionem totaliter quietabitur intellectus, per
75 infinite bonitatis delectacionem saciabitur appetitus, & memoria summum desiderabile comprehendens ineffabili gaudebit securitate. Quod ymaginabile poterit nocere, offendere, uel grauare vbi sacietas fuerit uoluntatis? Quod bonum non confert sacietas uoluntatis? Quod malum non aufert sacietas uoluntatis? Denique, cui creature
80 racionabili non sufficit sacietas voluntatis? Gaudium siquidem beatorum cumulabitur ex clara uisione Dei & cuiuslibet creature. Nam beati supra se gaudebunt inenarrabiliter de beatifica Dei uisione; intra se, de corporis & anime glorificacione; iuxta se, de angelorum & hominum sociali beatitudine; extra se, de irracionabilium creaturarum perfeccione
85 & pulcritudine, & sub se, de malorum iustissima punicione atque de sua felici euasione quorumlibet tormentorum. Ad enumeracionem uero celestium gaudiorum nullius hominis intellectus sufficit, omnis lingua deficit, nec ulla mens capere poterit, quanta, quot, & qualia gloriosa premia disponit Omnipotens suis electis, & his precipue qui
90 Deum in hac uita feruencius dilexerunt. Nam secundum diuini amoris magnitudinem in presenti proporcionabitur in futuro glorie magnitudo.

Quid igitur ulterius uobis scribam, carissimi uos inclusi, nisi quod, feruentes in amore Dei continue pro finali beatitudine graciosius consequenda, iuxta vestre professionis sacras obseruancias, & beati
95 Alredi doctrina (*De Institucione reclusi*), atque aliorum deuotorum egregia documenta, perficiatis studiosius ad quod uenistis? Et hoc modo, per operosam diligenciam, *Uidete uocacionem vestram.*

Ad hunc finem per Dei graciam promoueri poterit huius libelli leccio sepius iterata, ut in eo vestrum profectum uel defectum tanquam in
100 speculo uideatis, quia nunquam perficit artifex opus suum arduum & subtile sine recta regula dirigente. Uidete, ergo, prout diffusius predictum est, qualiter & a quo uocati estis, ad quid faciendum uocati estis, qualiter uocacionem perfecistis, & quam immarcessibi-[60r]-lem glorie coronam habebitis pro finali perseuerancia sanctitatis, preter
105 spirituale gaudium in presenti.

---

103 immarcessibi/lem] R *returns to sequence,* J *resumes after lacuna* (N)

Oh what perfect bliss! Oh a feast that goes on without end! Oh this spiritual marriage supper is supremely desirable, at which the faithful are continuously fed until they are full with delightful dishes, without ever feeling disgusted, and they are given an appetite for food that never fails; where the intellect will be completely at rest in the knowledge of the supreme truth, the will will be satisfied by the enjoyment of infinite goodness, and the memory, cleaving to the supremely desirable, will rejoice in ineffable certainty. What imaginable injury, offence or annoyance could there be where the will is satisfied? What good is not supplied by the satisfaction of the will? What evil is not driven away by the satisfaction of the will? And lastly, is there a rational creature for which the satisfaction of the will is not enough? The joy of the blessed will thus be filled to the brim with the clear vision of God and of every created thing. For the blessed will rejoice indescribably at the beatific vision of God above themselves; within themselves, at the glorification of their body and soul; alongside themselves, at the angels and people who are their fellows in bliss; outside themselves, at the perfection and beauty of the creatures without reason, and beneath themselves, at the most just punishment of the wicked and their own fortunate escape from every kind of torment. And no human intellect is sufficient to enumerate the joys of heaven, every tongue fails; nor can any mind comprehend how much, how many, and what kind of glorious rewards the Almighty distributes to his chosen ones, and in particular to those who in this life have loved God especially fervently. For the quantity of glory to come will be in proportion to the quantity of love for the divine in the present.

So what more shall I write to you, you most beloved recluses, except that, remaining continuously fervent in your love of God in order to achieve (with grace) bliss at the last, you should, according to the sacred observances of your profession, and the teaching of Saint Ailred ('The Rule of Life for a Recluse'), and the excellent teachings of other devout people, conscientiously bring to completion what you have started. And in this way, by your diligent effort, 'Look to your vocation.'

The reading of this little book, often repeated, can help you reach that end (with God's grace), as you see your advances and your failings in it as in a mirror – for no craftsman brings a difficult and ingenious piece of work to successful completion without aligning it against a straight edge. And therefore, as it is said in various places above, see how and by whom you are called, what you are called to do, how you should bring your vocation to perfection, and what an unfading crown of glory you will have for persevering in holiness to the end, over and above the spiritual joy you will have in the present.

Si igitur in huius opusculi leccione profeceritis, dum uobis bene fuerit mementote mei caritatis intuitu, & suggeratis vestris precibus Omnipotenti ut educat me de carcere peccatorum, & uobiscum misericorditer uocare dignetur ad uidendam suam gloriam sine fine. Amen.

Explicit *Speculum Inclusorum*.

---

106 opusculi] *om.* J   107 vestris precibus] *om.* J   108 uobiscum] nobiscum J
111 *Speculum Inclusorum*] Speculatiuum clausorum J

So if you have profited from reading this little work, when things are well with you remember me of your charity, and raise up your prayers to the Almighty that he might release me from the prison of sin, and see fit in his mercy to call me to see, with you, his glory without end. Amen.

Here ends 'A Mirror for Recluses'.

Notes to the texts

The notes aim to provide details of all citations to biblical and other authorities made in the texts. Citations to and quotations from the Bible are from the Vulgate and/or the Douai translation. Numbering of the Psalms follows the Vulgate; likewise, for the books of Kings I follow the Vulgate tradition of division into four books (1–4 Kings, rather than the division familiar from the Authorised Version into 1–2 Samuel followed by 1–2 Kings). Citations of the synoptic gospels usually refer to Matthew alone.

In Livarius Oliger, the *Speculum* benefited from the attention of an editor as imbued in the spirit and practice of *lectio divina* as its original author must have been. He was able to find biblical echoes in many short phrases, and often single words, of the text. Other than confirming the general point that scripture infused the *Speculum*-author's vocabulary, however, it is not always clear that such parallels are of significant interpretative consequence (see the note to Prol. 16, below). Unless there seems to be a strong counter-argument in a particular case, I have not noted such scriptural echoes. Patristic sources are referred for preference to the standard texts in the *PL*.

The notes also draw attention to matters of literary, historical or theological interest, including where appropriate the citation of parallel passages in other authors. Aquinas, for example, has been found relevant in a number of places. Such parallels are not (unless stated otherwise) proposed as direct sources for the passage in the *Speculum*. In the case of Aquinas, they more likely point to the author's general intellectual background and training. For the *Summa Theologica* I have used the Leonine edition: *Sancti Thomae Aquinatis, Opera omnia iussu impensaque Leonis XIII P. M. edita, t. 4–12: Summa theologiae* (Rome, 1888–9). The translations are taken from *The Summa Theologica of St. Thomas Aquinas* (1920), rev. Kevin Knight (2008) and available online at http://www.newadvent.org/summa/. References to other sources are introduced *in situ*.

Matters of textual interest are also noted. These include problems of interpretation or translation; justification for emendations, where this does not seem to be self-evident; variants that may have a bearing on the relationships of manuscripts; significant departures from the readings of the texts' previous editors. The notes also include details of annotations to the principal manuscripts of the *Speculum* and *Mirror*, and draw attention to points of interest in the *Mirror*'s translation of the *Speculum*.

References to the text are generally to the Latin *Speculum* only, and given by part, chapter and line number. It should be straightforward for the reader to look across to the parallel passage in the Middle English *Mirror*. Notes that refer only or primarily to the *Mirror* are prefaced with 'ME', and in such cases the line numbers given are those in the edition of the Middle English text.

Prologue

Title   J's variant incipit is of interest, but there is no reason to suppose that it reflects any particular knowledge of the *Speculum*'s author.

2 *Videte uocacionem vestram*   1 Cor. 1:26. The verse is used to similar purpose in Grimlaic's *Regula solitarium*, c. 23 (*PL* 103.604), and in William of St Thierry's *Epistola ad fratres de Monte Dei*, 1.1 (*PL* 184.309). Examples from late-medieval England include Edmund of Abingdon's *Mirror*, c. 1 (noted by Oliger), for which see *Edmund of Abingdon: Speculum Religiosorum and Speculum Ecclesie*, ed. Helen P. Forshaw (Oxford, 1973); and the *Cloud*-author's *Discretion of Stirrings*, in *The Cloud of Unknowing, and Related Treatises on Contemplative Prayer*, ed. Phyllis Hodgson (Salzburg, 1982), p. 116 (lines 11–12).

5–6   The author's declared lack of experience of the anchoritic life could be a conventional *topos*, though rules known to have been written by anchorites for anchorites are few in number (among English examples, only *Walter's Rule*). I have argued in the Introduction that the author was probably a Carthusian.

6–7   The allusion is to the parable of the talents, Matthew 25:14–30.

10 *qui vbi vult spirat*   Cf. John 3:8.

16 *celesti gloria*   Oliger compares 2 Tim. 2:10: 'Ideo omnia sustineo propter electos, ut et ipsi salutem consequantur, quæ est in Christo Iesu, cum gloria cælesti' [Therefore I endure all things for the sake of the elect, that they also may obtain the salvation, which is in Christ Jesus, with heavenly glory]. This is the first example of those scriptural echoes that Oliger frequently notices in his edition (as noted above). In this as in most other cases, the verbal reminiscence does not seem significant for the meaning of the passage, and henceforward such echoes will not be noted.

I.i

7 *perpetuo carceri*   On the reclusory as prison, see Warren, *Anchorites and their Patrons*, pp. 92–5. In the order for the enclosure of anchorites according to the Sarum Rite, it is advised that 'Reputet ergo se inclusus quasi peccatis dampnatum, & celle solitarie velud carceri traditum, & propter infirmitatem propriam homini consorcio indignum' [The recluse should therefore think of himself as having been condemned for his sins, and committed to a solitary's cell as if to a prison, and that, because of his own failings, he is not fit for any human interaction]. See §002 in my edition in 'Rites of Enclosure' (p. 183).

ME 16 *hyld*   'Pour out' (*MED* HIELD), half of a doublet for 'effunde' (15). Harley emends unnecessarily to 'hyle' (*MED* HILEN, 'cover, spread over').

ME 21 *whepre*   An unfamiliar sense of 'whether' to translate 'numquid' (19), 'is it not the case that' (*OED* WHETHER 5).

23 *feruore*   Oliger reads 'favore' in error.

28–30   Thais, Mary of Egypt, Paul the First Hermit, and Hilarion were among the best-known of the desert saints, whose lives were transmitted in the *Vitae patrum*. Jerome wrote influential lives of the two men (in *PL* 23.17–28 and 29–54, respectively). The two women were the most celebrated of the 'harlots', or repentant sinners. The Greek life of Mary of Egypt was translated by Paul of Naples in the ninth century (*PL* 73.671–90), but by the time of the *Speculum* she was best known from the *Golden Legend* (*Jacobus de Voragine, The Golden Legend: Readings on the Saints*, trans. William Granger Ryan, 2 vols (Princeton, 1993), no. 56 (i.227–9)). Thais's story was translated into Latin in the sixth or seventh century (*PL* 73.661–62), and was also included in the *Golden Legend* (trans. Ryan, no. 152 (ii.234–5)).

29 *simplicibus*   'Simplex' has a range of meanings, from innocent to half-witted (not unlike ME 'sely'). The collocation here of 'simplicibus' with 'timidis', and later the antonymical pair 'simplices uel prudentes' (II.iii.45) suggest that a sense somewhere in between would be most appropriate: 'naive', perhaps, or 'guileless' (*DMLBS* SIMPLEX 15). In his lives of both men, Jerome stresses the academic accomplishments that preceded their retreat to the desert. The *Mirror* consistently translates 'simplex' as 'simple'.

31–3   By popular tradition, following Christ's ascension, Mary Magdalene came to live near Marseille as a hermit, and converted Provence to Christianity. It was normal in the Middle Ages to identify her with Mary of Bethany (sister of Martha and Lazarus), who, as Jesus told her, 'hath chosen the best part' (Luke 10:42). See her life in the *Golden Legend* (trans. Ryan, i.374–83), and Katherine Ludwig Jansen, *The Making of the Magdalen: Preaching and Popular Devotion in the Later Middle Ages* (Princeton, 2001).

120   Notes to the texts: I.i–I.ii

ME 40 *decernyd*   H's erroneous reading, 'deceyued', is easily explained as a scribal error committed in copying from an English exemplar; less so as an error of translation. This, then, as noted in the Introduction, is part of the evidence that H is not the archetype of the *Mirror*.

I.ii

ME 7 *voluptuus sleuthe or sleuthi fleschly lust*   This double-translation of *uoluptuosa accidia* (7) recalls the *Speculum*'s frequent use of this kind of paronomasia. See e.g. 'prudenti feruore seu feruenti prudencia' (I.iv.11).
7   Marginal note: 'Remissio Religiosorum quorundam'.
14–15 *non sine*   Both manuscripts here have 'non sine', and the ME text has 'nat withouten scripule' (16). This certainly seems to contradict the passage's tone, but the reading is by no means impossible and, given the unanimous testimony of all the witnesses, I have let it stand.
15–16 *'capellani pape', uel 'episcopi nullatenses'*   For papal chaplains, see the Introduction. 'Episcopi nullatenses' is a sardonic name for those clerics who were appointed to titular bishoprics (typically *in partibus infidelium*), usually in order that they could serve as suffragans of a diocesan bishop. The practice was brought to an end by the Suffragan Bishops Act of 1534. See the account by David Smith, 'Suffragan Bishops in the Medieval Diocese of Lincoln' *Lincolnshire History and Archaeology* 17 (1982), pp. 17–27. The phrase seems to have been relatively common, though in the entry in *DMLBS* the *Speculum* provides the only citation. Wyclif used it scathingly – see for example *Tractatus de Ecclesia*, c. 23 (ed. J. Loserth (London, 1886), p. 583) – and so did the more securely orthodox John Lydgate: in his 'Order of Fools', the convent of fools secures a general pardon and other benefits from 'somme vnthryffty bysshop Nullatense' (ed. H. N. MacCracken, *Minor Poems of John Lydgate, Volume II, Secular Poems*, ed. Henry Noble MacCracken, EETS, orig. ser. 192 (London, 1934), pp. 449–55, at line 170, and cf. line 143).
16–17   There is extended word-play here which an English translation cannot completely reproduce: 'dangerous pleasures' (*illecebris*), which includes the sense of 'lures' or 'bait', 'snares' (*laqueis*) and 'no-one to stop them' (*nemine prepediente*), which includes the idea of tethering, are all from the same semantic domain.
32–3 *Uocabis me*   Job 14:15.
36   Marginal note: 'spiritualia'.
ME 57–8   The reference to 'gay & neyce aparail and cloþis' is a (no doubt gendered) amplification of the Latin's reference to the unspecified 'uoluptuosa' (53) that visitors might bring before the recluses' eyes. Noted as such in the Introduction.

58–9   The triad prayer, meditation and reading (in that order, rather than the one given here) will provide the framework for Parts II and III of the *Speculum*.
60 *alumpni*   Probably here 'foster father' or 'patron' (*DMLBS* 3). ME 'nurce' looks odd in the context of knights and chamberlains, but cf. *MED* NORICE 1b: 'a man who takes care of a child, foster father; a tutor'.
62 *Videte uosmetipsos*   2 John 1:8 (not 1 John, as specified in the text).
62–3 *Non enim*   Marginal *nota*.
64 *familiam retinere*   Note the ME's more precise injunction that the household should not exceed two servants. Ailred had recommended a recluse to have two female servants, one old and sober, the other young and strong for menial work.
64 *iuuenes educare*   As noted in the Introduction, ME 'custummably as in multitude or for hyre' is an addition to the Latin.
ME 73–9   The whole of the passage in parentheses is an addition to the Latin. See the Introduction for discussion.
66–7   Cf. 1 Tim. 6:8: 'Habentes autem alimenta, et quibus tegamur, his contenti simus'.
ME 83 *neuer*   MS 'ney' requires emendation. Harley's solution, 'ne', is not grammatical. I have chosen 'neuer' as being more likely palaeographically than the obvious alternative, 'nat'.
81–2 *Vnusquisque*   1 Cor. 7:20.

I.iii

4–5 *Non ueni uocare iustos*   Luke 5:32.
8 *quasi uoto simplici*   A simple vow is a promise to God, which becomes binding when made in public as a solemn vow. See Aquinas, *Summa Theologica* 2.2, q. 88 art. 7, and also his *Contra doctrinam retrahentium a religione*, 12: 'Ubi oportet distinguere, duplex esse votum: unum quidem simplex, aliud autem solemne. Simplex quidem votum in sola promissione consistit: solemne autem votum cum promissione habet exteriorem exhibitionem; dum scilicet homo actualiter se offert Deo, vel per ordinis sacri susceptionem, vel per professionem certae religionis in manu praelati, quibus duobus modis votum solemnizatur; vel etiam per susceptionem habitus professorum, quod est quaedam interpretativa professio' [A distinction must be made between two kinds of vows: simple vows, and solemn vows. A simple vow consists in a mere promise. A solemn vow is a promise accompanied by some exterior manifestation, whereby a man actually offers himself to God. Thus the reception of Holy Order, the profession of a definite religious life made in the hands of a prelate, or the reception

of the habit of professed religious, which is considered equivalent to religious profession, all solemnize a vow] (from the online version of the Leonine edition (Rome, 1969) at http://www.corpusthomisticum.org/ocr.html); trans. John Procter (1902), rev. Joseph Kenny, at http://dhspriory.org/thomas/ContraRetrahentes.htm). J's error misses the point of this distinction. See also below, note to line 45.

8–9 For Satan transforming himself into an angel of light, see 2 Cor. 11:14. The verse is ubiquitous in discussions of discernment.

13–19 This language of single combat against temptations recalls, as Oliger notes, the first chapter of the *Rule of St Benedict*. See also the discussion of masculinity and the *miles Christi* in the Introduction.

22 *nec uero mirum* The reading shared by **R** and **J**, 'ubi nimirum' ('where nevertheless'), does not make easy sense. The abbreviated forms of 'ubi' and 'nec' (a pair of minims with a superscript letter) are easily confusible; likewise the usual abbreviation for 'uero' could easily be run together with 'mirum' to give the mistaken reading 'nimirum'. A reading like 'nec uero mirum' must lie behind the ME 'and it is no wonder' (27–8). At III.ii.49 'Nec mirum' is translated 'And no meruayl' (ME 57).

26 *Virum ex mille* Eccles. 7:29.

26 Marginal *nota*.

27–44 On the arrangements outlined here for discernment and probation prior to enclosure, and their relation to contemporary practice, see the Introduction.

35 *determinet* J's 'detineret' is a clear example of that text's inferiority.

ME 51 *any man* Supplied to translate 'alicui' (43).

43–4 Marginal *nota*.

45 *uotum simplex* See above, note to line 8. Once again, J's reading misses the technical meaning of 'simplex'. It is worth noting that, for the *Speculum*-author at least, the decision to take on the anchoritic life becomes irrevocable as soon as it has been affirmed in a *simple* vow, and the solemnisation of that vow in a formal public profession merely confirms a step that has already been taken.

49 *Obsecro* Eph. 4:1.

62 *O altitudo* Rom. 11:33.

68–70 *Diligentibus Deum* Rom. 8:28.

75–6 *Multi sunt uocati* Matt. 20:16, repeated at 22:14.

76–9 Cf. Rom. 8: 30: 'quos autem praedestinavit hos et vocavit et quos vocavit hos et iustificavit quos autem iustificavit illos et glorificavit' [And whom he predestinated, them he also called. And whom he called, them he also justified. And whom he justified, them he also glorified].

ME 89 *þat seith þus* The phrase sounds as if it is referring forward, so that

lines 89–92 will be a quotation from Paul. But in fact (as is clear from the Latin) it is the preceding sentence (ME 85–9) that derives from Romans 8.
81–2 *gaudete & exultate* [...] *scripta sunt in celis*   Oliger compares Matt. 5:12 ('gaudete et exultate quoniam merces vestra copiosa est in caelis. Sic enim persecuti sunt prophetas qui fuerunt ante vos' [Be glad and rejoice, for your reward is very great in heaven. For so they persecuted the prophets that were before you]) and Luke 10:20 ('gaudete autem quod nomina vestra scripta sunt in caelis' [but rejoice in this, that your names are written in heaven]).
83   Marginal *nota*.
95 *aquis Syloe que uadunt cum silencio*   Is. 8:6. Oliger less relevantly cites Jesus's injunction to the blind man to wash in the pool of Siloe (Siloam) at John 9:7 and 11.
96 *Adiuro uos*   As Oliger points out, this entreaty is made several times in the Song of Songs (e.g. Cant. 2:7).
96–7 *hauritis aquas* [...] *saluatoris*   Is. 12:3.
97 *per uiscera misericordie Dei nostri*   Luke 1:78.
97–8 *mementote mei cum bene uobis fuerit*   Cf. Gen. 40:14.
106–7   For the image of spiritual battle, cf. 2 Cor. 10:4.
111–12   Cf. Augustine *Enarrationes in Psalmos*, Ps. 37: 'Ita plane quamvis salvi per ignem, gravior tamen erit ille ignis, quam quidquid potest homo pati in hac vita' (*PL* 36.397). Cited by ps.-Bernard, *Instructio Sacerdotis*, c. 13, where the reference is clearly directed towards Purgatory: 'Unde Augustinus super Psalterium: *Domine, ne in furore tuo arguas me, neque in ira tua corripias me*; id est, non sim inter illos quibus dicturus es in judicio: *Ite, maledicti, in ignem aeternum. Ne in indignatione tua emendes me;* id est, non sit mihi opus igne emendatorio, qui et purgatorius dicitur: qui cum gravior sit omni eo quod pati potest homo in hac vita' [Thus Augustine on the Psalter: *Rebuke me not, O Lord, in thy indignation; nor chastise me in thy wrath*; that is, so that I might not be one of those to whom it shall be said at the Judgement: 'Go, cursed ones, into everlasting fire'. *Nor chastise me in thy indignation*; that is, may it not be necessary for me to enter the refining fire, which is also called Purgatory: for it is more severe than all the pains that a person can suffer in this life] (*PL* 184.791). Both references are given by Oliger.
112–13 *Unde Beatus Gregorius*   Gregory is presented with this choice by an angel in his life in the *Golden Legend* (trans. Ryan, p. 179). The usual reading has him choosing lifelong 'infirmities and pains and aches' in preference to *two* days spent in Purgatory, rather than the three recorded in all manuscripts of the *Speculum*.
115–16 *Sancta ergo* [...] *soluantur*   2 Mach. 12:46.
118–19 *mouendo* [...] *moueant*   In **R**, *n* and *u* are usually distinguishable, and

in both instances the letter in question is clearly an *n*. Forms from *moneo* are possible, but I have emended on the basis of ME 'styre and meeue'.

121–2 *in uocacione qua uocati estis*   Cf. 1 Cor. 7:20 ('unusquisque in qua vocatione vocatus est in ea permaneat' [Let every man abide in the same calling in which he was called]).

122 *usque in finem*   Oliger compares Matt. 24:13 ('qui autem perseveraverit usque in finem, hic salvus erit' [But he that shall persevere to the end, he shall be saved]), which may be relevant.

I.iv

6 *est*   Oliger misread J's reading as 'ita', but conjectured an 'est' anyway.

6 *simplices*   See note to I.i.29.

10–11   The ME lacks the crucial 'includi cupiunt' from the main clause, 'pro securiore uacacione omnium huius periculorum includi cupiunt' [for þe moore syker eschewynge of alle þese periles *they desire to be enclosed*]. The omission must have happened at an earlier stage of transmission, because an attempt has been made (by supplying a new verb phrase, 'thei werkyn') to make sense of the sentence, though the result is weaker than the original.

12–13 *Prudenciam uoca amicam tuam*   Prov. 7:4.

ME 12 *ferue|ne|se*   For 'fervence', 'fervour' (cf. II.i.40).

18–19   For the story of Samson and Delilah, see Judges 16:4–15.

ME 21 *Dalyda*   H's 'dalyaunce' is an error of copying rather than of translation, thus providing evidence that H is not the archetype of *A Mirror*. See also ME I.i.40.

19–20   For Solomon's heart being led astray by his wives and concubines, see 3 Kings 11:1–8.

20–22   For David and Bathsheba, see 2 Kings 11:2–17. Though used here in a discussion of the sins brought in by the sense of sight, all three incidents are of course commonplaces of the antifeminist tradition.

22–3   For Achor's theft, see Joshua 7.

23–4   For the Fall, see Genesis 3, and especially 3:6, 'And the woman saw that the tree was good to eat, and fair to the eyes, and delightful to behold: and she took of the fruit thereof, and did eat, and gave to her husband who did eat.'

24–6   For the Israelites' turning to idols during the exodus, see Judges 2 and Ezekiel 20. In neither place, however, is it explicitly the *sight* of foreign peoples' religious practices that causes the Israelites' apostasy.

27–8 *Auerte oculos meos*   Ps. 118:37.

29 *suggerit*   From 'suggerere' (to bring or supply). The ME doublet 'souketh and receyuyth' (35) must derive from Latin 'su(g)git', from 'sugere' (to suck;

spellings with -gg- are well-attested in medieval Latin), either as a genuine variant or the result of missing the sign of abbreviation for -*er* after 'sugg-'. As Harley notes, the variant turns the ear into 'a greedy consumer'. Either reading could be original but, since **R**'s 'suggerit' makes good sense, I have let it stand.

33–5 *Factus sum*   Ps. 30:13–14.

ME 42 *circuyt or compas*   Emended to restore the doublet for 'circuitu'. The same phrase appears at II.ii.12.

ME 48–51   The ME expansion of 'de inclusis viuentibus sicut debent' is discussed in the Introduction. Harley punctuates differently, putting everything from '& naamly of anchoresses' to the end of the sentence in parentheses. She also emends, cancelling the second 'enclosed' as if it were an example of dittography. The effect is to make anchoresses' the most strictly enclosed form of religious life available (more so than that of male anchorites, perhaps). That may or may not be true, but I have interpreted the text rather to say that anchorites (and female anchorites in particular) are more strictly enclosed than other forms of enclosed religious life. Such a reading finds a corollary in William Lyndwood's contemporary gloss on *reclusi*: 'Understand this as those enclosed individually, as anchorites are with us; this should not be understood as those enclosed as a community, as all nuns are (or should be)' (*Provinciale*, iii.20.2). The passage also says (and again Lyndwood would concur) that a properly ordered anchoritic life ('viventibus sicut debent') can be lived only with one's superiors' permission.

41–4   As Oliger notes, there are echoes here of Romans 1: cf 1:26–7, 'Propterea tradidit illos Deus in passiones ignominiae nam feminae eorum inmutaverunt naturalem usum in eum usum qui est contra naturam. Similiter autem et masculi relicto naturali usu feminae exarserunt in desideriis suis in invicem masculi in masculos turpitudinem operantes et mercedem quam oportuit erroris sui in semet ipsis recipientes' [For this cause God delivered them up to shameful affections. For their women have changed the natural use into that use which is against nature. And, in like manner, the men also, leaving the natural use of the women, have burned in their lusts one towards another, men with men working that which is filthy, and receiving in themselves the recompense which was due to their error]. 'Deo odibilem' (44) directly recalls Rom. 1:30.

42 *uenerea*   **J**'s 'venena' ('poisonous') is possible, but the ME agrees with **R**'s more specific reading.

45   Marginal note in ME: 'nota de luxuria'.

ME 58 *ancresse*   The only instance in the *Mirror* where the Latin *inclusus* is translated not by the inclusive *recluse* but by a gender-specific term. Perhaps, given the context of the discussion here, his readers' gender was more to the forefront of the translator's mind than it usually appears to be. See also the Introduction.

45–8 The distinctions made here between consensual and involuntary, and waking and (by implication) sleeping, pollutions are standard. See the account by Dyan Elliott in *Fallen Bodies*, pp. 14–34.

49 *corporis uoluptuosa pollucio*   Marginal note, keyed to these words in text: 'Nota quod sit mollicies'.

50–2 *mollicies*   The quotation is from 1 Cor. 6:10. John Boswell reports that 'At least from the time of Aquinas on, all moral theologians defined "mollitia" or "mollicies" [...] as masturbation': *Christianity, Social Tolerance, and Homosexuality* (Chicago, 1980), p. 107 n. 55. The ME rather coyly retains the 'Latyn of þe Apostyl' for this vice that dare not translate its name.

62 *miles Christi*   On the *topos* of the *miles Christi*, see the Introduction.

69–70 *plures sanctorum patrum*   The reference is presumably to the Desert Fathers, though the ME 'oure olde fadres' (ME 86–7) does not make this clear.

74–5 *Non enim uocauit*   1 Thess. 4:7. The ME 'satisfaccion' for 'sanctificacionem' (ME 92) is an error.

I.v

3–4 *Uacate & uidete*   Ps. 33:9 ('gustate et videte quoniam suavis est Dominus') conflated (as it often is) with Ps. 45:11 ('vacate et videte quoniam ego sum Deus'). ME 'Taak heede' does not capture the implication of 'Uacate'. See also the next note.

ME 5 *entendynge*   In none of its recorded senses is this an obvious translation of 'uacacionem'. Nor does it seem to render the pre-correction reading of R, 'uocacionem'. (The senses gathered under *OED* INTEND III, 'To strain, direct, or bend the attention; to attend to; to attend' seem closest.) The appearance of 'entenden nat' in a doublet with 'medlen' ('busy themselves') in line 6 clarifies the translator's usage, in which the negative must be understood.

13–14 *in oracione, meditacione & leccione*   See the Introduction for this modified version of the monastic triad of reading, meditation and prayer.

15–19 The ME has misconstrued the Latin. A more accurate translation would be: 'First as to prayer. I believe that no-one doubts or is unaware how much the mind is distracted from the words that the tongue is speaking, when it thinks about, concentrates on, or pursues curious imaginings of other vain, voluptuous or irrelevant things. Who is not drawn towards those things that his innermost thought is set upon, whether of love or hate, sorrow or joy? And each of them *steriþ so gretly þe herte* [...]'

22–3 *Populus iste*   Isaiah 29:13, though the most exact correspondence is with Matt. 15:8.

ME 26 *wyttirly*   The usual meaning of 'witterly' is 'clearly [...] certainly [...] without doubt' (*OED*), but it occasionally overlaps with 'utterly' (*MED* WITTERLI 2c), and this is the sense required here (cf. Latin 'penitus'). The form appears again at ME III.i.75.

31–2 *Corpus*   Sap. 9:15.

33–5   The ME is corrupt. The manuscript reading 'þat drawith to hey or erþely þinges' corresponds to the Latin 'secum attrahit & retinet in terrenis'. Presumably 'hey' (see apparatus to ME 38) is an error for 'hem' ('secum'), but the omission of '& retinet' has left the sentence struggling to make sense. Properly translated, the sentence should say that the wit that is busily occupied with worldly things is so vexed and troubled by them that it attracts the affections (or desires) of the soul, which is bound to the body, to those earthly things, and holds it there.

47–8   For Paul's rapture (narrated in the third person) see 2 Cor. 12:2–4.

63–4 *uocat ea* [...] *infirma mundi*   Romans 4:17 followed by 1 Cor. 1:27.

69–70 *Predestinacio*   An expansion and gloss on Romans 9, esp. 11–2, 'cum enim nondum nati fuissent aut aliquid egissent bonum aut malum, ut secundum electionem propositum Dei maneret, non ex operibus sed ex vocante' [For when the children were not yet born, nor had done any good or evil (that the purpose of God, according to election, might stand,) Not of works, but of him that calleth].

II.i

4 *in edificatoria leccione*   On the *Mirror*'s alteration of this phrase to 'edificatyf spekynge' and its implications, see the Introduction. ME *edificatyf* ('Edifying; adapted to promote spiritual improvement', *OED*) is not recorded in either *OED* or *MED* earlier than Love's *Mirror*.

5–6 *Oracio* [...] *est ascensus mentis in Deum*   Aquinas, *Summa Theologica*, 2.2 q. 83 art. 1, quoting John Damascene, and art. 5. Aquinas's discussion lies behind most of the analytical material in this chapter, either directly or at some remove.

ME 10 *nedes*   The adverb, 'Of necessity, necessarily, unavoidably' (*OED* NEEDS), here modifying the doublet 'required & askyd' (ME 10–11). The addition of 'is' (to render the passive 'requiritur') is (*pace* Harley) necessary to complete the sense and syntax.

9 *succursum*   Cf. the doublet in the ME: 'relees & socour' (12–13). It is tempting to emend 'relees' to 'relief' by analogy with 'socour or relief' (ME I.ii.76, a passage with no parallel in the Latin), but cf *OED* RELEASE 4a:

'Deliverance or liberation from trouble, pain, sorrow, or the like; an instance of this'.

9–27   This discussion is related, sometimes quite closely, to Aquinas (as above, note to lines 5–6), art. 13, 'Utrum de necessitate orationis sit quod sit attenta'.

16 *actualis deuocio*   The distinction between 'habitual' devotion (arising from the general disposition of the soul) and 'actual' devotion (as exemplified in specific acts) is a characteristically scholastic one, though this particular statement is not to be found in the *quaestio* from Aquinas that this chapter otherwise seems to draw upon. The ME *Mirror* provides a periphrastic gloss for both terms.

30 *Videte, uigilate & orate*   Mark 13:33.

47 *Oracio Dominica*   The ME provides a gloss.

47–9 *Oracio Dominica*   Cf. Augustine, *Epistle* 130 (to Proba), c. 12: 'nihil aliud dicimus quam quod in ista dominica oratione positum est, si recte et congruenter oramus') [if we pray rightly, and as becomes our wants, we say nothing but what is already contained in the Lord's Prayer] (*PL* 33.502, trans. J. G. Cunningham (1887), rev. Kevin Knight, online at http://www.newadvent.org/fathers/1102130.htm).

49 *sentencialiter*   expressly (*DMLBS*). For ME 'sentencialy', the closest available definition is 'with regard to meaning or content' (*MED*).

51–6   Cf. Aquinas (as above, lines 5–6), art. 16, 'Utrum peccatores orando impetrent aliquod a Deo'. For lines 54–6 cf. 'Orationem vero peccatoris ex bono naturae desiderio procedentem Deus audit, non quasi ex iustitia, quia peccator hoc non meretur, sed ex pura misericordia, observatis tamen quatuor praemissis conditionibus, ut scilicet pro se petat, necessaria ad salutem, pie et perseveranter' and 'quamvis eius oratio non sit meritoria, potest tamen esse impetrativa' [On the other hand God hears the sinner's prayer if it proceed from a good natural desire, not out of justice, because the sinner does not merit to be heard, but out of pure mercy, provided however he fulfil the four conditions given above, namely, that he beseech for himself things necessary for salvation, piously and perseveringly ... And though his prayer is not meritorious, it can be impetrative].

ME 70 *fect*   For the emendation, cf. below II.i.134. Harley posits an aphetic form of 'effect' (translating 'effectum'). This is unrecorded, but seems most likely: cf. 'fect' for 'infect' (*OED*), 'fectif' for 'defectif' and 'fectualli' for 'affectualli' (*MED*). It would also be possible to interpret 'þe fect' as 'þ'efect' (the distinction being more one of orthography than pronunciation), but both here and in line 134 'þe' and 'fect' are written clearly as two words.

58–9 *Omnia quecumque*   Mark 11:24.

60–1 *Glossa*   This is not the *Glossa ordinaria* but Nicholas of Lyra's *Postilla super totam Bibliam*, completed 1331 (Strassburg, 1492). Found also in

Aquinas, *loc. cit.* art. 15: 'Et ideo ponuntur quatuor conditiones, quibus concurrentibus, semper aliquis impetrat quod petit, ut scilicet pro se petat, necessaria ad salutem, pie et perseveranter' [Hence it is that four conditions are laid down; namely, to ask for ourselves; things necessary for salvation; piously; perseveringly. When all these four concur, we always obtain what we ask for].

68 *miscere*   J's reading ('missere', send) could be viable, but ME 'medle' confirms that R's more idiomatic reading is correct.

71 *ineffabilem*   Note the periphrastic gloss in ME.

75–101   Marginal bracket against these lines, and the marginal note 'Orationis efficacia'.

75–8   Peter's threefold denial of Christ is narrated in all four gospels (see e.g. Matthew 26). David's adultery with Bathsheba and (indirect) murder of her husband Uriah is recounted in 2 Kings 11. The tradition that Mary Magdalene was a prostitute is not biblical, but derives from a later identification of her with the sinful woman who anoints Jesus's feet in Luke 7:36–50 (see Jansen, *Making of the Magdalen*, pp. 32–5). The parable of the penitent publican is in Luke 18:9–14.

78–85   For the sparing of Nineveh, see Jonah 3; for the plague against David, 2 Kings 24. The story of Ezechias (Hezekiah) is in 4 Kings 18–20.

85–7   The ten plagues of Egypt are in Exodus 7–11. For the victory over Amalech, see Exodus 17:8–13.

87–9   God causes the sun to stand still for Joshua in Joshua 10.

89–92   Elisha brings down blindness on the Syrian army in 4 Kings 6, and the siege of Samaria is in 4 Kings 7.

92–4   The drought prophesied and ended by Elijah is in 3 Kings 17–18. The precise duration of 42 months comes from James 5:17.

95   Solomon's prayer for wisdom is in 3 Kings 3:1–15.

96–9   The story of Alexander the Great confining his enemies behind two mountains near the Caspian Sea was transmitted by the Alexander Romance, and well-known in medieval England (Mandeville includes it, for example). The reference here is to the *Historia Scholastica* of Peter Comestor, Esther c. 5 (*PL* 198.1498).

ME 126 *mavmettres*   Emendation from 'mavmettes' (idols) is required by the sense ('idolaters', translating Latin 'ydolatras'). Cf. *OED* MAMMETER, *MED* MAUMETERE.

99–101   Ahab's penitence is in 3 Kings 21, as specified.

104–13   This question is considered by Aquinas (as above, lines 5–6), art. 14.

116–17 *quid infirmo sit utile*   Prosper of Aquitaine, *Sententiae ex Augustino delibatae*, c. 212 (*PL* 55.1877). Quoted by Aquinas (as above, lines 5–6), art. 15.

II.ii

16 *Hec autem*   Note the impassioned addition to the ME.

24–5 *Faciamus hominem*   Gen. 1:26.

26 *Filioque*   The doctrine that the Spirit proceeds from the Father and the Son, and not from the Father alone, was a source of controversy between eastern and western churches over much of the second half of the first millennium. The Roman insertion of the word *filioque* into the Nicene Creed was an important factor in the Schism of 1054. Given all of which, it is ironic that neither **R** nor **H** reproduce the text accurately at this point.

29–39   The doctrine of the created trinity in the human soul, and its relation to the Trinity itself, comes from Augustine, *De Trinitate*, lib. 10 (*PL* 42.971–84).

ME 30 *vndirstonde*   Harley emends to 'vndirstonynge', but this is unnecessary: cf. UNDERSTAND (n.), 'Understanding; knowledge' (*OED*); 'the capacity or ability to understand or comprehend something' (*MED*).

38–9   There is an omission in the ME, no doubt due to eyeskip on 'finaliter': 'referatur finaliter [ad Dei laudem, gloriam & honorem, ut sic omnia fiant finaliter] propter amorem Dei.' A correct translation would see all the workings of the soul or body referred 'in the final analysis to the praise, glory and honour of God, so that in this way everything may ultimately be done for the love of God'. The omission could have been the translator's, or it may have occurred in the transmission of the Latin text he used.

44 *Creatorem*   Note the expansion in the ME.

51   In the ME, the rhetorical question is answered in the affirmative.

62 *Videte opera Dei*   Ps. 66:4.

75 *tristis*   Matt. 26:38. Note the mistranslation of 'tristis' (sorrowful) in the ME: 'þersty'. The variant appears in other English texts. See for example the Harrowing of Hell play in *The Chester Mystery Cycle*, ed. R. M. Lumiansky and David Mills, vol. 1, EETS suppl. ser. 3 (London, 1974), line 108 on p. 329.

87–92   The description of the passion is firmly in the affective tradition. The details of Christ's limbs being stretched, and his body jarred and broken as the cross is dropped into its mortise, are familiar from the Mystery Plays, and are also reported by Love. See *Mirror*, ed. Sargent, p. 175.

ME 104 *stremees*   The ending '-ees' is unusual (not recorded in either *OED* or *MED*), but clearly so written in the manuscript here and on its other occurrence at II.ii.129, and cf 'profreed' (III.i.45).

96 *insensibiles creature*   Note the expansion in the ME.

96–102   The eclipse of the sun, the rending of the veil, the shaking of the earth, raising of the dead and splitting of rocks are from Matthew 27:45–53. The response of the Jews is from Luke 23:48.

103–4 *Attendite & videte*   Lam. 1:12.
105–37   The shedding of Christ's blood was a common subject of affective meditation. See for example *The .vii. shedynges of the blode of Ihesu cryste* (London, 1500; STC 14546). The seven occasions are linked to the seven deadly sins in a couple of Middle English lyrics (*NIMEV*, nos 1707 and 1708), but in neither case is the correspondence with the *Speculum* exact.
111–37   Marginal notes in **R** against each of the seven sheddings point up their opposition to the seven deadly sins: contra superbiam (94); contra inuidiam (98); contra cupiditatem (102); contra iram (105); contra gulam (107); contra concupiscenciam (111); contra accidiam (114). In the ME, sheddings two to six are highlighted with marginal numerals (ii[a] to vi[a]), though the first and last shedding go unnumbered.
138–9 *Lauare sepcies*   2 Kings 5:10.
142 *ineffabiliter*   Note the periphrastic gloss in ME.
143–6   A commonplace of the affective tradition. For a closely contemporary example see *Dives and Pauper*, 1.2: 'Take heid to the ymage how his heid is bowid doun to the, redy to kissyn the and comyn at on wyt the. See how hese armys and hese hondys been spred abrod on the tre in toekene that he is redy to fangyn the and halsyn the and kissyn the and takyn the to his mercy' (ed. P. H. Barnum, vol. 1:1, EETS orig. ser. 275 (London, 1976), pp. 84–5).
153 *primis parentibus*   The ME (though using the more arcane 'progenitoures') glosses this with their names, 'Adam & Eve'.
156–7 *Christi corporis & sanguinis*   The ME has only 'his body'. In the late Middle Ages, communion in both kinds was normally reserved to the celebrant, the laity receiving only the eucharistic bread.
175–9   The ME transposes these lines from the second into the third person.
209 *Videte opera Dei*   Ps. 65:5.
216–18   Augustine is so quoted by Aquinas (*Summa Theologica*, Suppl., Appendix, q. 2 art. 1): 'Ille ignis purgatorii durior erit, quam quidquid in hoc saeculo poenarum aut sentire, aut viderem aut cogitare quis potest' [This fire of Purgatory will be more severe than any pain that can be felt, seen or conceived in this world]; also (for example) by Thomas of Chobham, *Summa de arte praedicandi*, ii.488–91 (ed. F. Morenzoni (Turnhout, 1988), p. 33). This is not a direct quotation from Augustine, but cf. the ps.-Augustinian *De vera et falsa poenitentia* 18, 'Hic autem ignis etsi aeternus non fuerit, miro tamen modo est gravis: excellit enim omnem poenam quam unquam passus est aliquis in hac vita' [Even though the fire here is not everlasting, nevertheless it is extraordinarily severe: for it exceeds every pain that anyone could ever suffer in this life] (*PL* 40.1128), and the similar statement quoted above I.iii.111–12 and notes.
226–7 *Uide*   Jeremiah 2:19.

II.iii

1–3 Walter Hilton, in the *Epistola de leccione*, stresses the importance for his addressee (who is a priest as well as a solitary) of reciting the canonical hours as he is obliged to do, however keen he might be to move on to his own, less formal, prayers and meditations. See *Epistola de leccione*, ed. Clark and Taylor, lines 301–15 (pp. 235–6), and cf. Russell-Smith (trans.) 'Letter to a Hermit', p. 237.

17–19 For the story of Josiah, see 4 Kings 22 (not 21, as given in the text).

19–21 For this story, see Nehemiah 8, as specified here.

22–4 That Mary was reading a relevant prophecy (usually Isaiah 7:14, 'Behold a virgin shall conceive') when she was surprised by the entrance of the angel Gabriel was a standard feature of the late-medieval iconography of the Annunciation. It is not biblical, however, and does not feature significantly before the twelfth century.

24–7 For the story of Philip and the Ethiopian eunuch, Acts 8:26–40.

43–5 *Quecumque scripta sunt* Romans 15:4.

47 *Videte vosmetipsos* Mark 13:9.

56–7 For Peter and Mary Magdalene, see above II.i.75–8. For the thief crucified with Christ, see Luke 23:39–43.

64–7 An allusion to the story of the Flood, Gen. 6–9. The detail of 15 cubits is from Gen. 7:20.

67–9 For the destruction of Sodom and Gomorrah, see Gen. 19:1–29.

69–71 That Adam and Eve sinned in gluttony is conceded by Aquinas, who nonetheless argues that the first sin was pride. Gluttony is given special prominence by Ambrose (as Aquinas notes): 'Ambrosius dicit, super Luc., quod eo ordine Diabolus Christum tentavit quo primum hominem deiecit. Sed Christus primo tentatus est de gula, ut patet Matth. IV, cum ei dictum est, si filius Dei es, dic ut lapides isti panes fiant. Ergo primum peccatum primi hominis non fuit superbia, sed gula' (*Summa Theologica*, 2.2, q. 163, art. 1) [Ambrose says, commenting on Luke 4:3, 'And the devil said to Him,' that the devil in tempting Christ observed the same order as in overcoming the first man. Now Christ was first tempted to gluttony, as appears from Matthew 4:3, where it was said to Him: 'If thou be the Son of God, command that these stones be made bread.' Therefore the first man's first sin was not pride but gluttony].

71–2 Esau sells his birthright in Gen. 25:29–34.

72–3 Cf. Ezekiel 16:49, 'Behold this was the iniquity of Sodom thy sister, pride, fulness of bread, and abundance, and the idleness of her, and of her daughters.'

78–84   Note the hierarchy of three categories: one who knows Latin (the *literatus*), one who knows only the vernacular, and the *simpliciter illiteratus*.
85–6   Cf. *Rule of St Benedict*, c. 48, 'Otiositas inimica est anime'. See *RSB 1980*, p. 248. The phrase was a commonplace, but its context in Benedict's *Rule* is relevant: it is a discussion of reading and manual labour.
95–8   A textbook example of the *Ubi sunt* topos (from 'Ubi sunt qui ante nos fuerunt?', 'Where are those who were before us?'), a lament for the mutability of things that is ubiquitous in medieval culture.
102–3 *Inuisibilia Dei*   Romans 1:20.

III.i

2 *sicut superius*   Cf. II.i.3–4 (where manual labour is not mentioned) and II.iii.4–5 (where it is).
3   Marginal note: 'orare, meditare, legere'.
15 *absoluatur*   Emended with the sense of *DMLBS* ABSOLVERE 7, 'to complete, conclude'. This seems preferable to any of the recorded senses of R's 'obsoluatur', which all involve the idea of giving up or acquitting oneself of an obligation.
25–6 *Vtinam calidus esses*   Apoc. 3:15–16.
27–8 *Populus hic*   Matt. 15:8, where Christ is alluding to Isaiah 29:13.
ME 42   On margin: 'nota de coronacione Christi'.
45–6 *Videte Salomonem*   Cant. 3:11.
47–8 *Quid turbati estis*   Luke 24:38–9.
49–52   For the bronze serpent, see Num. 21:4–9. The typological connection with the passion is made by Christ himself, John 3:14–15.
ME 62 *knokke*   Emended from 'knowe' in order to translate 'pulsa'. The same error is made at ME 71.
55–6 *Ab occultis meis*   Ps. 19:13.
56–7 *Sana me Domine*   Jeremiah 17:14.
ME 87 *knokke*   Note, first, that the translation (of 'pulsanti', 74) is correct this time, and also the *Mirror*'s expansion.
89 *superfluum*   A periphrastic gloss in ME.
97 *militancium*   ME 'laboureres' is an error.
100 *lacrimis exorabit*   This clause ('he wells up with tears') is omitted in the ME.
ME 120–1 *acceptable*   In fact, the Latin is the superlative 'gratissima' but, constrained by such ME as is there, I have not been able to render that in my translation.

III.ii

8–9 *Sedebit solitarius*   Lam. 3:28.

14 *Gustate & uidete*   Ps. 33:9.

19 *flos & fructus*   Note that J follows the reading of R prior to its correction.

21–4   Cf. 'Si uis perfecte purgari a uiciis, in quantum preuales accende in te ignem diuini amoris. Si dulcedinem diuini amoris perfecte gustaueris, de temporali dulcedine non curabis' [If you want to be completely purged of vices, then as much as you are able you should kindle within yourself the fire of divine love. Once you have tasted fully the sweetness of divine love, you will set no store by the sweetness of this world], a *sententia* included in the florilegium *Manipulus florum* (s.v. *amor*, be), where it is attributed to Hrabanus Maurus 'in quodam sermone'. I have used Chris L. Nighman's 'Electronic *Manipulus florum* Project' at http://www.manipulusflorum.com. The source of the *sententia* has not been identified.

25–6 *Memoriam abundancie*   Ps. 144:7.

28 *prudencia circumspecta*   The ME offers a periphrastic gloss.

29–30   The topos of Satan transforming himself into an angel of light derives ultimately from 2 Cor. 11:14. See above I.iii.8–9n.

33–7   The desert tradition is much concerned with the discernment of angels from demons. In Athanasius's *Life*, St Antony recognises the initial fear that any supernatural apparition will cause, but then advises: 'Si igitur post timorem horrore conceptum, successerit gaudium et ad Deum fiducia atque ineffabilis charitas, venisse sciamus auxilium, quia securitas animae praesentis majestatis indicium est [...] Si autem incussa formido permanserit, hostis est qui videtur: quoniam nec refovere novit, ut Gabriel paventem Virginem ne timeat jubet; et sicuti pastores nuntio consolati sunt.' [If then the horror and trembling are replaced by joy and confidence in God and ineffable love, we know that help has arrived because calmness of the soul is proof of the presence of the holy power [...] But if the fear remains, it is the enemy who has appeared, since he does not know how to comfort as Gabriel did when he told the trembling Virgin not to fear and as the angels brought comfort to the shepherds] (c. 18 of Evagrius's Latin translation, *PL* 73.143; trans. Carolinne White, *Early Christian Lives* (London, 1998), pp. 31–2).

42–3 *Gracia Dei*   1 Cor. 15:10.

43–4 *omne datum*   James 1:17.

45–7 *Deo gracias*   A series of liturgical formulae. 'Non nobis Domine' derives from Ps. 113:9.

47–8   Gregory (not Augustine), *Moralia in Job*, lib. 34 c. 23 (*PL* 76.750).

49 *humilibus dat*   James 4:6.

49–50 *humilem spiritu*   Prov. 29:23.
55 *referatur*   The ME follows **R** rather than **J**'s 'reducatur'.
ME 64 *loue*   Emended from 'lawe' to translate the Latin 'amorem'.
56 *vero*   Note one of the minority of instances where a marginal insertion in **R** is incorporated in the text in **J**.
57 *Plenitudo legis*   Rom. 13:10.
58–9 *si affectus* [...] *aliqua creatura*   The ME is erroneous here, introducing an apparent relative clause ('þat a man hath') where all that is required is a translation of the verb 'ponat' ('should place'), thus: 'if the will fixes itself upon some created thing as the end of its delight'.
69 *Fides non habet meritum*   Gregory, *Homilia in evangelium*, lib. 2 hom. 2 (*PL* 76.1197). See the discussion of this popular tag in the Introduction.
72–3 *nulla persona est alia*   This somewhat awkward phrase (which clearly posed problems to the *Mirror* translator) is part of the vocabulary of trinitarian theology. Compare, for example, 'In qua tamen pluralitate non ponitur nisi simplex et indiuisa essentia, et tamen nulla persona est alia, nulla notio est alia, nulla forte similiter ratio est alia, et tamen haec omnia non sunt nisi una essentia' [But in that plurality there is contained nothing but a simple and undivided essence, and yet no person is the same as another, no *notion* (property) is the same as another, and similarly no reason is the same as another, but nevertheless all these things are nothing but a single essence] (Grosseteste, *De Libero arbitrio*, c. 8; ed. Ludwig Baur (Münster, 1912), online at http://www.grosseteste.com).
76 *quando voluit*   The ME offers a gloss.
86 *Credere* [...] *firmissime*   As pointed out in the Introduction, this echoes the first canon of the Fourth Lateran Council (1215).
94–125   These arguments and similitudes for eucharistic doctrine are commonplace. Most of those invoked here can also be found in the 'Treatise on the Sacrament' appended to Love's *Mirror* (see pp. 226–7 in Sargent's edition). The argument that likens transubstantiation to the Creation (lines 97–100); the analogies of the broken mirror (110–12) and of the dissemination of the human voice (115–16), and the statement that the body present in the host is the same as Jesus's historical body (117–19) are all to be found in Love.
ME 113 *diffyed*   'Digested' (*OED* DEFY v.2).
97   The rhetorical question is answered in the ME, as it was at II.ii.56.
100–4   As noted in the Introduction, this engages directly with the Wycliffite opposition to the doctrine of transubstantiation.
104–8 *Philosophum in fine 4 Metheorum*   Aristotle's *Meteora* or *Meteorologica*. (Oliger and Harley read this incorrectly as a citation of the *Metaphysics*.) The *vetus translatio* is ed. Pieter L. Schoonheim (Turnhout, 2000), but the

Notes to the texts: III.ii–IV.i

reference here is in fact to Avicenna's *De Congelatione*, which was attributed to Aristotle in the Middle Ages and regularly appended to Book 4 of the *Meteorologica* (see Schoonheim, p. xix). The argument that one metal can, by altering its accidents, be given the appearance of another, without however (*pace* the alchemists) effecting any change in its substance, is made at the end of the treatise: see *Avicennae de congelatione et conglutinatione lapidum*, ed. E. J. Holmyard and D. C. Mandeville (Paris, 1927), pp. 53–5. The analogy is not made in Love's 'Treatise'.
119 Jesus appears to the disciples though the doors are locked at John 20:19.
119–20 *State & videte* Exod. 14:13.
122–5 *Ego sum panis vite* John 6 (not 5, as stated):48, 52, 56.
ME 133 The words supplied at the foot of the leaf have no counterpart in the Latin, and were presumably added after the succeeding quire(s) had been lost.

III.iii

23 *Uacate & videte* Ps. 45:11.
28–30 *diligentibus Deum* Rom. 8:28.
40–1 For the thorn in Paul's flesh, see 2 Cor. 12:7.
41–3 For Paul's avowed unworthiness, see 1 Cor. 15:9.
43–9 The examples of Mary Magdalene and David have already been cited in a similar context at II.i.75–8. See the references there given.
49–51 For the blindness and other afflictions suffered by Tobit (Tobias senior), see the Book of Tobit passim.
51–6 See the Book of Job, passim.
60 *Quis coronabitur* Cf. 2 Tim. 2:5.
71 *temptacio sit uita hominis* Cf. Job 7:1, 'militia est vita hominis super terram.'
83 Marginal note: 'de opere manuali approbata'.
84–8 This passage is discussed in the Introduction.

IV.i

4–5 For the hundredfold reward, see Matt. 19:29.
5–6 The phrase 'stola glorie' is biblical, being used repeatedly in Ecclesiasticus (e.g. 'stolam gloriae indues eam et coronam gratulationis superpones tibi', 6:32); it was also used in a number of liturgical rites of investiture. The twin robes of glory, denoting the perfection of the resurrected body and soul, were a commonplace. See e.g. Bernard, *In Festo omnium sanctorum*, Sermo 3.1: 'Stola enim prima ipsa est, quam diximus, felicitas et requies animarum:

secunda vero immortalitas et gloria corporum' [And so the first robe is, as we have said, felicity and rest for the soul; and the second is immortality and glory for the body] (*PL* 183.469).

6 *accidentale gaudium*   A reference to the common scholastic distinction between the essential joy of the blessed, which consists in their state of bliss and the beatific vision, and the accidental joy that derives (as stated here) from created things. See for example Bonaventure, *Commentaria in quatuor libros sententiarum*, Lib. II, d. xi, art. 2, q. 2; online at http://www.franciscan-archive.org/bonaventura/opera/bono2285.html.

19 *incerta*   Note J's particularly unfortunate error.

31–2 *ibant gaudentes*   Acts 5:41.

33–6 *Beati eritis*   Matt. 5:11–12.

38–41 *Omne gaudium*   James 1:2–4.

45   It is not obvious to which passage the author is alluding here. Oliger suggests 2 Cor. 1:5, 'quoniam sicut abundant passiones Christi in nobis ita et per Christum abundat consolatio nostra' [For as the sufferings of Christ abound in us: so also by Christ doth our comfort abound].

48 *idem propheta*   This is an odd reference, unless 'idem' is being used purely for emphasis (a usage unrecorded in *DMLBS*). The word 'propheta' usually denotes an Old Testament author, but all the citations in this chapter so far have been to the New Testament.

48–9 *Fuerunt* […] *mihi lacrime*   Ps. 41:4.

49–51 *Secundum* […] *multitudinem dolorum*   Ps. 93:19.

59–61   Cf. 1 Cor. 3:8, 'unusquisque autem propriam mercedem accipiet secundum suum laborem' [And every man shall receive his own reward, according to his own labour].

64–5   Cf. John 3:8, 'Spiritus ubi vult spirat' [The Spirit breatheth where he will].

66–7 *Gustate & videte*   Ps. 33:9.

77–85   As noted in the Introduction, this sounds like an account of the experiences recorded by Richard Rolle. Note especially the reference to 'dulcor' (83), one element of the characteristic Rollean triad *fervor, dulcor, canor*.

85–6   Again, see the Introduction for this typically cautious response to Rolle's account of his experiences.

87–94   The error in the title of Ailred's work (it should be *De oneribus Babylonis*) is shared by both manuscripts of the *Speculum* and the *Mirror*. This is an abridgement of an anecdote that Ailred tells concerning a nun of Watton. She would, he recounts, exclude from her breast all love for the world, all carnal desires and all the demands of her body, and desire only heavenly things. On one occasion when she was thus occupied 'mira quaedam suavitas superveniens omnes animi motus, omnes cogitationum excursus, omnes insuper spirituales, quos circa amicos habebat, exstinxerit affectus: moxque anima ejus, quasi oneribus quae in mundo sunt valedicens, rapitur supra se, et ab ineffabili quadam et incomprehensibili luce excepta, nihil aliud videbat, nisi quod est, et quod omnium esse est [...] In hoc igitur excessu cum ei hora non parva praeteriisset, pulsata a sororibus, vix potuit ad corporales, quos reliquerat, sensus redire' [a marvellous sweetness came over her, extinguishing all stirrings of her spirit, all movements of her thought, and also all spiritual attachments that she had towards her friends; and presently her soul, as if bidding farewell to all the burdens that exist in the world, was ravished above itself and, caught up by some ineffable and incomprehensible light, saw nothing but that which [simply] is, and which is the being of all things [...] After she had remained in this rapture (*excessus*) no little time, when she was summoned by her sisters, only with difficulty did she bring her senses back to those bodily things that she had left behind]. See *Sermo III*, *PL* 195.370–1.

103 *Videte magnalia Dei*   Exodus 14 (not 9, as given here):9.

108–15   The unprepared introduction of a third degree of love here suggests an allusion to a source with which the readers of the *Speculum* are supposed to be familiar. For a man to love himself only for God's sake is the *fourth* degree of love in Bernard's *De diligendo Deo* (c. 10), but this remains the closest parallel that I have identified. Bernard agrees that it is virtually impossible to experience this degree of love in our present life: 'Beatum dixerim et sanctum, cui tale aliquid in hac mortali vita raro interdum, aut vel semel, et hoc ipsum raptim, atque unius vix momenti spatio experiri donatum est. Te enim quodammodo perdere, tanquam qui non sis, et omnino non sentire teipsum, et a teipso exinaniri, et pene annullari, coelestis est conversationis, non humanae affectionis' [I should call him blessed and holy to whom it is given to experience even for a single instant something which is rare indeed in this life. To lose yourself as though you did not exist and to have no sense of yourself, to be emptied out of yourself and almost annihilated, belongs to heavenly not to human love] (*PL* 182.990; trans. G. R. Evans in *Bernard of Clairvaux: Selected Works* (New York, 1987), p. 195).

117–18   Cassian's *Collations* are in *PL* 49. For 3.7, see cols 566–70; for 4.3, 586–7; for 6.9, 655–7; for 9.25, 801–2; for 10.5, 824–6, and for 10.7, 827–8.

123–4 *Deus in adiutorium*   Ps. 69:2, a verse that also occurs often in the liturgy. Its frequent use by the desert fathers is reported by Cassian, *Collations*, 10.10 (*PL* 49.833).

IV.ii

11–13 The four gifts (or dowries) of the glorified body are listed briefly by Aquinas, *Summa Theologica* 3, q. 45 art. 1 (obj. 3), and treated in turn Suppl. qq. 82–5. His order is impassibility, subtlety, agility, clarity. For the development of the doctrine, see further A. Challet, 'Corps glorieux', *Dictionnaire de théologie catholique*, vol. 3, ed. A. Vacant et al. (Paris, 1938), cols 1879–1906.

19–21 For this and the parallels drawn later in this chapter, see Innocent III, *De Sacris altaris mysterio*, c. 12: 'Singula sibi Christus singulatim accepit antequam resurgens a mortuis naturam glorificati corporis induisset. Subtilitatem cum nasceretur ex Virgine; claritatem, cum transfiguraretur in monte; agilitatem cum incederet super mare; impassibilitatem cum manducaretur in coena' [Christ took on each and every single one of these properties [even] before he assumed the nature of a glorified body when he rose from the dead. Subtlety when he was born of the Virgin; clarity when he was transfigured on the mountain; agility when he walked upon the sea; impassibility when he was eaten at the Last Supper] (*PL* 217.864). Quoted by Hugh Ripelin with ascription to Hugh of St Victor in the *Compendium theologicae veritatis* (Lyon, 1649), VII.27 (p. 556). The final chapters of this ubiquitous compilation (hereafter, *Compendium*) may have served as a handy reference for the *Speculum*-author in this and the next chapter, as succeeding notes will demonstrate. Aquinas argues that such parallels should not be made, 'quia dos nominat quandam qualitatem immanentem corpori glorioso' [because the gifts are immanent qualities of a glorified body] (*Summa Theologica* 3, q. 45 art. 2).

22 Marginal note against the second gift: 2^a dos; followed by 3^a dos (line 31), 4^a dos (line 41).

22–4 *iusti fulgebunt* Matt. 13:43, also quoted in this context by Aquinas, Suppl. q. 85 art. 1.

31 *subtilitas* The term is impossible to render entirely satisfactorily in normal modern English. It incorporates both the physical quality of fineness and mental capacity of discrimination, but with none of the connotations of insidiousness that the word often bears today. (See *OED* SUBTLETY 4 and 5, both senses 'now rare'.) Since the term is still used in theological discourse, however, and there is no ready alternative, I have retained it.

35–6 *simul in loco* Aquinas presents philosophical arguments against this position in Suppl. q. 83 art. 2.

37–8 Jesus comes in to the disciples even though the doors are shut at John 20:19.

Notes to the texts: IV.ii–IV.iii

50–5   *De Similitudinibus*, c. 57 (*PL* 159.634).
54–5   *torrente uoluptatis Dei*   Cf Ps. 36:9; 'spiritualiter' (55) is a sobering addition to the biblical text, not present in the text of Anselm in Migne.
57–8   *non uidemus*   Cf. 1 Cor. 13:12, 'videmus nunc per speculum in enigmate tunc autem facie ad faciem' [We see now through a glass in a dark manner; but then face to face].
59–60   *Voca operarios*   Matt. 20:8.
75–7   Cf. Luke 11:9–10, 'et ego vobis dico petite et dabitur vobis quaerite et invenietis pulsate et aperietur vobis; omnis enim qui petit accipit et qui quaerit invenit et pulsanti aperietur' [And I say to you, Ask, and it shall be given you: seek, and you shall find: knock, and it shall be opened to you. For every one that asketh, receiveth; and he that seeketh, findeth; and to him that knocketh, it shall be opened].
79–83   *Osculetur*   Cant. 1:1–3.

IV.iii

1–7   For the three gifts and their appropriation to the three powers of the soul, see Aquinas, *Summa Theologica*, Suppl. q. 95. All authorities agree that the first gift of the soul is vision or cognition; for gifts two and three different authors choose (as Aquinas notes) from among love, delight, fruition and comprehension. See also *Compendium*, VII.25 (p. 551).
4   Note on margin: 'prima dos anime'.
10–15   This completes the argument presented in III.ii that the teachings of the Church should be believed despite any conflict with human reason.
16   Note on margin: '2ª'.
19–20   *Oculus non vidit*   1 Cor. 2:9.
21–3   *Merces sanctorum*   Hugh of St Victor (?), *Allegoriae in novum testamentum libros novem complectentes*, 2.1 (*PL* 175.766). Quoted with the ascription to Bernard, *Compendium*, VII.31 (p. 567).
24–6   *minus sunt omnes delicie*   William Perault (Peraldus), *Speculum religiosorum*, VI.xxxii. Printed (with the frequent attribution to Humbert of Romans) in Margarin de la Bigne, *Maxima bibliotheca veterum patrum* (Lyon, 1677), xxv.753.
28   Note on margin: '3ª'.
30   Folio numbers are discontinuous here due to the miscopying/binding of R described in the Introduction. As a consequence, J omits from here to line 103.
34–6   *nichil [...] aderit*   Augustine, *De Trinitate*, 13.7 (*PL* 42.1020–1). Quoted *Compendium*, VII.31 (p. 567), just after the quotation attributed to Bernard noted above, 21–3.

Notes to the texts: IV.iii 141

37–41 *Tanta est   De Libero arbitrio* 3.25 (*PL* 32.1308–9). As specified, this is almost the end of Augustine's treatise.

45–52 For the distinction between the essential and accidental joy of the blessed, see above IV.i.6n. The distinction between the *intensive* and *extensive* augmentation of that joy (51–2) is also a scholastic one. It is stated succinctly by Bonaventure (as above, IV.i.6n): 'Extensive dicitur crescere, quando quis de pluribus gaudet; intensive vero, quando affectus eius de aliquo copiosius gaudet' [It is said 'to grow' extensively when anyone rejoices from more (things); but intensively when his affection rejoices from something more copiously]. Though using the technical terms, the *Speculum* also glosses their meaning sufficiently, as well as providing an illustrative example.

55–63 For the three aureoles, see Aquinas, *Summa Theologica*, Suppl. q. 96, art. 11: 'Quidam vero distinguunt tres aureolas secundum tres vires animae, ut dicantur tres aureolae respondere potissimis trium virium animae actibus. Potissimus enim actus rationalis est veritatem fidei etiam in aliis diffundere; et huic actui debetur doctorum aureola. Irascibilis vero actus potissimus est etiam mortem propter Christum superare; et huic actui debetur aureola martyrum. Concupiscibilis autem actus potissimus est a delectabilibus maximis penitus abstinere; et huic debetur aureola virginum' [Some, however, distinguish the three aureoles in accordance with the three powers of the soul, by saying that the three aureoles correspond to the three chief acts of the soul's three highest powers. For the act of the rational power is to publish the truth of faith even to others, and to this act the aureole of doctors is due: the highest act of the irascible power is to overcome even death for Christ's sake, and to this act the aureole of martyrs is due: and the highest act of the concupiscible power is to abstain altogether from the greatest carnal pleasures, and to this act the aureole of virgins is due]. The irascible and concupiscible powers together make up the sense appetites of the soul, from which the passions derive. The aureoles are also included in *Compendium*, VII.29 (p. 561).

64–5 *magis satagite*   2 Pet. 1:10.

69–70 *Beati qui*   Apoc. 19:9.

81–6 *Compendium*, VII.31 (p. 566). Gloating over the punishment of the damned (85–6) is not part of the catalogue there given, though it is numbered among the traditional joys of the blessed.

94–5 For Ailred's *De Institutione*, see the Introduction.

101–5 Note the recollection of the outline of the treatise given in the Prologue (Prol. 13–17).

103 Copying of R returns to sequence, and J resumes. See above IV.iii.30n.

106–7 *dum uobis bene fuerit*   Cf. Gen. 40:14. The formula has already been used in I.iii.97–8.

Appendix to the Notes to the Texts: annotations to base manuscripts

R

Notae and other annotations and marginalia are relatively sparse in **R**, and they are detailed in the Notes to the Text.

In addition to these are the appearances of James Grenehalgh's characteristic J. G. and J. G. S. monograms. See the brief discussion in the Introduction. The following table summarises their occurrence.

fol. 46r	J. G. S.	*beside* I.v.71–5 (on the discernment of a solitary vocation)
fol. 47r	Grenehalgh cart' Ia. Io. Sewell' *at foot of leaf* (near a discussion of perseverance in prayer)	
fol. 51r	J. G. S.	*beside* II.iii.39–41 (on the rewards for withstanding temptation)
fol. 51v	J. G.	*beside* II.iii.60–2 (the profits of tribulations)
fol. 53r	JG. .	*beside* III.i.81–5 (tribulations increase our merit)
	J. G. S.	*beside* III.i.88 (ask for nothing in prayer that is against God's will)
fol. 53v	J. G.	*beside* III.i.93–8 (those who should be prayed for – the initials apparently aligned with 'exiles and prisoners')
fol. 55v	J. G.	*beside* III.iii.7–10 (happy acceptance of tribulations)
fol. 57r	J. G. S.	*beside* IV.i.24–32 (put up with temporary tribulations, remembering the eternal reward)

H

H, at least from fol. 8v onwards, is much more frequently annotated than R. (I have found no rationale for the absence of annotation from fols 1r–8r.) Such annotation most often takes the form of a simple *nota* (which appears in its abbreviated form, *no^a*). There are a few more detailed *notae*, and some manicules.

It is not always entirely clear precisely to which part of the text the annotator was trying to draw attention. The following table lists all the marginal annotations and attempts to identify the passage in the edited text they indicate.

Some coincide with paraph marks within the text, or otherwise with the beginning of a new thought. Some highlight the citation of an authority or biblical source, or a technical term (actual and habitual devotion at fols 17v–18r, for example). Others seem to have been placed in recognition of a rhetorical flourish or impassioned turn of phrase, more often than not of a devotional character likely to induce compunction (above all, the Passion). Certain other subjects appealed to the annotator: spiritual battle; Judgement, purgatory and hell; and matters of doctrine (e.g. the Trinity).

The annotations are summarised in the following table.

6r	marginal bracket	I.iii.17–24
8r	marginal bracket	I.iii.76–9
8v	*nota*	I.iii.89–90
	manicule	I.iii.93–4
8v–9r	*nota* + marginal bracket	I.iii.95–104
9r	*nota*	I.iii.101–2
	nota	I.iii.110
9v–10r	*nota* + marginal bracket	I.iii.116–131
	[within which, further *notae*	I.iii.122, 127
	and *Gregorius*	I.iii.129]
10v	*nota, tercia capitulum*	I.iv.1
11r	*nota*	I.iv.13
	nota + marginal bracket	I.iv.16–27
	[within which, further *notae*	I.iv.23–4]
11v	*nota* + marginal bracket	I.iv.32–40
12r	*nota*	I.iv.43
	nota	I.iv.52–3
12v	*nota de luxuria*	I.iv.57–8

Appendix to the Notes to the Texts 145

13r	*narracio*	I.iv.68
	nota	I.iv.79
13v	*nota*	I.iv.89
14r	*nota*	I.v.10
	nota	I.v.14
15v	*nota* + bracket to next *nota*	I.v.46–7
	nota	I.v.54–5
16v	*nota* + bracket	I.v.79–85
17r	*nota*	II.i.2–3
17v	*nota*	II.i.20
18r	*nota* + marginal bracket	II.i.29–35
	nota	II.i.39
18v	*nota*	II.i.50
19r	*nota* + marginal bracket	II.i.66–7
	nota	II.69–70
19v	*nota* + marginal bracket	II.i.71–5
	manicule	II.i.84
20r	*nota*	II.i.86–7
	nota + marginal bracket	II.i.94–5
	manicule + bracket to next *nota*	II.i.99
20v	*nota*	II.i.112
21r	marginal bracket	II.i.114–16
	nota	II.i.119
	nota + marginal bracket	II.i.123–7
21v	*nota*	II.i.130
	manicule	II.i.132–3
	nota + manicule	II.i.140
22r	*nota*	II.i.144–5
	manicule	II.i.148
	nota	II.ii.1
22v	*nota* + marginal bracket	II.ii.5–8
23r	*nota*	II.ii.27
23v	*nota*	II.ii.37
24r	*nota*	II.ii.48
24v	*nota*	II.ii.62
25r	*nota de passione christi*	II.ii.73
	nota contra desperacionem	II.ii.81
25v	*nota*	II.ii.87

	nota	II.ii.94
26r	*nota*	II.ii.99
	nota	II.ii.110
26v	*nota*	II.ii.113–14
	nota	II.ii.119
28r	*nota*	II.ii.155
	nota de helisea propheta	II.ii.160
29r	*nota*	II.ii.181
29v	*nota*	II.ii.195
30r	*nota*	II.ii.208
	nota	II.ii.212–13
	nota	II.ii.220–1
30v	*nota*	II.ii.229–30
31r	*nota de coronacione Christi*	III.i.42
31v	*nota*	III.i.59
32r	*nota*	III.i.69
32v	*nota*	III.i.83–4
33r	*nota*	III.i.93–4
	nota	III.i.102
33v	*nota*	III.i.109–10
34r	*nota*	III.ii.27
	marginal bracket	III.ii.29–33
	nota	III.ii.35
34v	*nota*	III.ii.38–9
	nota	III.ii.41
	nota	III.ii.45
35r	*nota*	III.ii.53–4
35v	*nota*	III.ii.69
36r	*nota*	III.ii.81
	nota	III.ii.85
36v	*nota*	III.ii.93
	marginal bracket	III.ii.95–6
37r	*amen*, written vertically	III.ii.108–10
37v	*amen*, written vertically	III.ii.128–30

Bibliography

Catalogues and other works of reference

A Catalogue of the Harleian Manuscripts in the British Museum, 2 vols (London, 1808–12).

Bernard, Edward, *Catalogi librorum manuscriptorum Angliae et Hiberniae in unum collecti cum indice alphabetico* (Oxford, 1697/8).

Bloomfield, Morton W., et al., *Incipits of Latin Works on the Virtues and Vices, 1100–1500 A.D.* (Cambridge MA, 1979).

Boffey, Julia and A. S. G. Edwards, eds, *A New Index of Middle English Verse*, (London, 2005).

British Library online Catalogue of Illuminated Manuscripts at http://www.bl.uk/catalogues/illuminatedmanuscripts.

British Library online Manuscripts Catalogue at http://www.bl.uk/catalogues/manuscripts.

Catalogue of Stowe Manuscripts, 2 vols (London, 1895–6).

Coxe, H. O., *Catalogus codicum MSS. qui in collegiis aulisque Oxoniensibus hodie adservantur*, 2 vols (Oxford, 1852).

Dictionary of Medieval Latin from British Sources (London, 1975–).

Hanna, Ralph, *A Descriptive Catalogue of the Western Medieval Manuscripts of St John's College, Oxford* (Oxford, 2002).

McIntosh, Angus, M. L. Samuels, Michael Benskin, *The Linguistic Atlas of Late Medieval English* 4 vols (Aberdeen, 1986).

Middle English Dictionary. Online edition, University of Michigan, 2006, at http://quod.lib.umich.edu/m/med/.

Oxford Dictionary of National Biography. Online edition, Oxford University Press, September 2012, at http://www.oxforddnb.com/.

Oxford English Dictionary. Online edition. Oxford University Press, September 2012, at http://www.oed.com/.

Pollard, A. W., and G. R. Redgrave, eds, *A Short-Title Catalogue of Books*

Printed in England, Scotland and Ireland, and of English Books Printed Abroad 1475–1640, 2nd ed. rev. W. A. Jackson, F. S. Ferguson and K. F. Pantzer (London, 1976–91).

Sharpe, Richard, *A Handlist of the Latin Writers of Great Britain and Ireland before 1540* (Turnhout, 1997).

Walther, H., *Proverbia sententiaeque Latinitatis Medii Aevi: Lateinische Sprichwörter und Sentenzen des Mittelalters in alphabetischer Anordnung* (Göttingen, 1963).

Warner, G. F., and J. P. Gilson, *Catalogue of Western Manuscripts in the Old Royal and King's Collection*, 4 vols (London, 1921).

Manuscript sources

Bristol, University of Bristol, Special Collections, DM 1590/I–III (papers of Basil Cottle/Rotha Mary Clay).
Cambridge, St John's College Archives, D 91.13.
——, D 91.20.
Lincoln, Lincolnshire Archives Office, Episcopal Register XIII (Register of Henry Beaufort).
——, Episcopal Register XVII (Register of William Gray).
London, British Library, MS Cotton Otho B. XIV.
——, MS Harley 2372.
——, MS Royal 5 A v.
Norwich, Norfolk Record Office, NCC Hyrning.
Oxford, Bodleian Library, MS Rawlinson C.258.
——, MS Rawlinson C. 72.
Oxford, St John's College, MS 177.
Winchester, Hampshire Record Office A1/14 (Register of William Waynflete II).

Primary sources

Allen, Hope Emily, ed., *English Writings of Richard Rolle* (Oxford, 1931).
Anon., *The .vii. shedynges of the blode of Ihesu cryste* (London, 1500).
Aquinas, Sancti Thomae Aquinatis, *Opera omnia iussu impensaque Leonis XIII P. M. edita, t. 4–12: Summa theologiae* (Rome, 1888–9).
——, *Sancti Thomae de Aquino Opera omnia iussu Leonis XIII P.M. edita cura et studio Fratrum Praedicatorum. Tomus XLI B–C: De perfectione spiritualis vitae, Contra doctrinam retrahentium a religione* (Rome, 1969), online at http://www.corpusthomisticum.org/ocr.html.

——, *The Summa Theologica of St. Thomas Aquinas* (1920), rev. Kevin Knight (2008) and available online at http://www.newadvent.org/summa/.
Archer, M., ed., *Register of Bishop Philip Repingdon, 1405–1419*, vol. 1, Lincoln Record Society 57 (1963).
Bannister, A. T., ed., *The Register of Thomas Spofford, Bishop of Hereford (1422–1448)*, Canterbury & York Society 23 (1917).
Barnum, P. H., ed., *Dives and Pauper*, vol. 1:1, EETS orig. ser. 275 (London, 1976).
Baur, Ludwig, ed., [Robert Grosseteste] *De Libero arbitrio* (Münster, 1912), online at http://www.grosseteste.com.
Bazire, Joyce, and Eric Colledge, eds, *The Chastising of God's Children and The Treatise of Perfection of the Sons of God* (Oxford, 1957).
Bliss, W. H., and J. A. Twemlow, *Calendar of Entries in the Papal Registers Relating to Great Britain and Ireland, Papal Letters, Volume 4: A.D. 1362–1404* (London, 1902).
——, *Calendar of Entries in the Papal Registers Relating to Great Britain and Ireland, Papal Letters, Volume 5: A.D. 1398–1404* (London, 1904).
——, *Calendar of Entries in the Papal Registers Relating to Great Britain and Ireland, Papal Letters, Volume 6: A.D. 1417–1431* (London, 1906).
Bonaventure, *Commentaria in Quatuor Libros Sententiarum* (Quaracchi, 1882), online at http://www.franciscan-archive.org/bonaventura/opera/bon02285.html.
Calendar of the Close Rolls Preserved in the Public Record Office, A.D. 1377–1381 (London, 1914).
Calendar of the Patent Rolls A.D. 1381–1385 (London, 1897).
Calendar of the Patent Rolls A.D. 1416–1422 (London, 1911).
Clark, J. P. H., and R. Dorward, trans., *Walter Hilton: The Scale of Perfection* (New York, 1991).
Clark, John P. H. and Cheryl Taylor, *Walter Hilton's Latin Writings* (Salzburg, 1987).
Cunningham, J. G., trans., [Augustine], 'Letter 130' (1887), rev. Kevin Knight, online at http://www.newadvent.org/fathers/1102130.htm.
David of Augsburg, *De exterioris et interioris hominis compositione libri III* (Quaracchi, 1899).
[Denys of Ryckel] *Doctoris ecstatici D. Dionysii Cartusiani Opera Omnia*, vol. 40 (Montreuil, 1911), pp. 51–71.
Dunstan, G. R., ed., *The Register of Edmund Lacy: Bishop of Exeter, 1420–1455. Registrum commune, Vol. I*, Canterbury & York Society 60 (1963).
Emery, Kent, Jr., *Dionysii Cartusiensis opera selecta* (Turnhout, 1991).
Evans, G. R., trans., *Bernard of Clairvaux: Selected Works* (New York, 1987).

Forshaw, Helen P., ed., *Edmund of Abingdon: Speculum Religiosorum and Speculum Ecclesie* (Oxford, 1973).
Foster, C. W., ed., 'Lincolnshire Wills Proved in the Prerogative Court of Canterbury 1471–1490', *Associated Architectural Societies' Reports* 41 (1932–3), pp. 61–114 and 179–218.
——, *Lincoln Wills Registered in the District Probate Registry at Lincoln, Volume I: 1271–1526*, Lincoln Record Society 5 (1914).
Fry, Timothy, ed. and trans., *RB 1980: The Rule of St. Benedict* (Collegeville MN, 1980).
Furnivall, Frederick J., and I. Gollancz, eds, *Hoccleve's Works: The Minor Poems*, rev. Jerome Mitchell and A. I. Doyle, EETS extra ser. 61+73 (Oxford, 1970).
Gibbons, Alfred W., ed., *Early Lincoln Wills*, Lincoln Record Society 1 (1888).
Harley, Marta Powell, ed., *The Myrour of Recluses: A Middle English Translation of* Speculum Inclusorum (Madison, 1995).
Hingeston-Randolph, F. C., ed., *The Register of Bishop Stafford* (London, 1886).
Hodgson, Phyllis, ed., *The Cloud of Unknowing, and Related Treatises on Contemplative Prayer* (Salzburg, 1982).
Hogg, James, ed., 'Richard Methley: To Hew Heremyte: A Pystyl of Solytary Lyfe Nowadayes', *Analecta Cartusiana* 31 (1977), pp. 91–119.
——, *The Speculum Inclusorum, Vol. 2: St. John's College, Oxford, Ms. 177 of the Speculativum Clausorum*, Analecta Cartusiana 59:2 (1981).
Holmes, T. S., ed., *The Registers of Walter Giffard, Bishop of Bath and Wells, 1265–6, and of Henry Bowett, Bishop of Bath and Wells, 1401–7*, Somerset Record Society 13 (1899).
Holmyard, E. J., and D. C. Mandeville, eds, *Avicennae de congelatione et conglutinatione lapidum* (Paris, 1927).
Hoste, A., and C. H. Talbot, eds, *Aelredus Rievallensis: Opera Ascetica* (Turnhout, 1971).
Hudson, Anne, ed., *The Testimony of William Thorpe, Two Wycliffite texts*, EETS, orig. ser. 301 (1993).
Loserth, J., ed., [Wyclif] *Tractatus de Ecclesia* (London, 1886).
Lumiansky, R. M., and David Mills, eds, *The Chester Mystery Cycle*, vol. 1, EETS suppl. ser. 3 (London, 1974).
Lyndwood, William, *Provinciale (seu Constitutiones Angliae)* (Oxford, 1679).
MacCracken, Henry Noble, ed., *Minor Poems of John Lydgate, Volume II, Secular Poems*, EETS, orig. ser. 192 (London, 1934).
Macpherson, Mary Paul, trans., 'A Rule of Life for a Recluse', in *Aelred of Rievaulx: Treatises & Pastoral Prayer*, ed. David Knowles (Spencer MA, 1971).
Migne, J.-P., *Patrologia Latina cursus completus*, 221 vols (Paris, 1844–65).

Millett, Bella, ed., *Ancrene Wisse: A Corrected Edition of the Text in Cambridge, Corpus Christi College, 402, with Variants from Other Manuscripts*, 2 vols, EETS, orig. ser. 325–6 (Oxford, 2005–6).
——, trans., *Ancrene Wisse: Guide for Anchoresses* (Exeter, 2009).
Morenzoni, F., ed., *Thomas de Chobham: Summa De Arte praedicandi* (Turnhout, 1988).
Nicholas of Lyra, *Postilla super totam Bibliam* (Strassburg, 1492).
Oliger, Livarius, ed., 'Regula reclusorum angliae et quaestiones tres de vita solitaria', *Antonianum* 9 (1934), pp. 37–84 and 243–68.
——, 'Regulae tres reclusorum et eremitarum angliae saec. xiii-xiv', *Antonianum* 3 (1928), pp. 151–90 and 299–320.
——, *Speculum Inclusorum Auctore Anonymo Anglico Saeculi XIV*, Lateranum n. s. iv/i (Rome, 1938).
Perault, William (Peraldus), *Speculum religiosorum*, in Margarin de la Bigne, *Maxima Bibliotheca Veterum Patrum* (Lyon, 1677), vol. 25.
Procter, John, trans., [Aquinas] 'Contra doctrinam retrahentium a religione' (1902), rev. Joseph Kenny, online at http://dhspriory.org/thomas/ContraRetrahentes.htm.
Ripelin, Hugh, *Compendium theologicae veritatis* (Lyon, 1649).
Rogers, Alan, ed., *The Act Book of St Katherine's Gild, Stamford, 1480–1534* (Bury St Edmunds, 2011).
Russell-Smith, Joy, trans., [Walter Hilton] 'A Letter to a Hermit', *The Way* 6 (1966), pp. 230–41.
Ryan, William Granger, trans., *Jacobus de Voragine, The Golden Legend: Readings on the Saints*, 2 vols (Princeton, 1993).
Sargent, Michael G., ed., *Nicholas Love. The Mirror of the Blessed Life of Jesus Christ* (Exeter, 2005).
Schoonheim, Pieter L., ed., *Aristotle's Meteorology in the Arabico-Latin Tradition* (Leiden, 2000).
Sicard, P., et al., eds, *L'œuvre de Hugues de Saint-Victor, I: De institutione novitiorum; De virtute orandi; De laude caritatis; De arrha animae* (Turnhout, 1997).
Smith, Lucy Toulmin, ed., *The Itinerary of John Leland in or about the Years 1535–1543*, 5 vols (London, 1906–10).
Watson, Nicholas, and Jacqueline Jenkins, eds, *The Writings of Julian of Norwich: A Vision Showed to a Devout Woman and A Revelation of Love* (Pennsylvania, 2006).
Weaver, F. W., ed., *Somerset Medieval Wills. Second Series: 1501–1530*, Somerset Record Society 19 (1903).
White, Carolinne, trans., *Early Christian Lives* (London, 1998).
Windeatt, Barry, ed., *The Book of Margery Kempe* (London, 2000).

Secondary works

Anon., 'Anchorites in Faversham Churchyard', *Archaeologia Cantiana* 11 (1877), pp. 24–39.
Anon., *Collegium Divi Johannis Evangelistae, 1511–1911* (Cambridge, 1911).
Ayto, John, and Alexandra Barratt, eds, *Aelred of Rievaulx's De Institutione Inclusarum*, EETS orig. ser. 287 (1984).
Beckett, Neil, 'St. Bridget, Henry V, and Syon Abbey', in *Studies in St Birgitta and the Brigittine Order*, ed. James Hogg, 2 vols, Analecta Cartusiana 19 (Salzburg, 1993), pp. 125–50.
Boswell, John, *Christianity, Social Tolerance, and Homosexuality* (Chicago, 1980).
Catto, Jeremy, 'After Arundel: The Closing or the Opening of the English Mind?', in Gillespie and Ghosh, *After Arundel*, pp. 43–54.
——, 'Religious Change under Henry V', in *Henry V: The Practice of Kingship*, ed. G. L. Harriss (Oxford, 1985).
Challet, A., 'Corps glorieux', *Dictionnaire de théologie catholique*, vol. 3, ed. A. Vacant et al. (Paris, 1938), cols 1879–1906.
Clay, Rotha Mary, 'Further Studies on Medieval Recluses', *Journal of the British Archaeological Association*, 3rd ser. 16 (1953), pp. 74–86.
——, *The Hermits and Anchorites of England* (London, 1914).
Cloake, John, *Palaces and Parks of Richmond and Kew*, vol. 1: *The Palaces of Shene and Richmond* (Stroud, 1995).
——, 'The Charterhouse of Sheen', *Surrey Archaeological Collections* 71 (1977), pp. 145–98.
Cohen, Jeffrey Jerome, and Bonnie G. Wheeler, eds, *Becoming Male in the Middle Ages* (New York, 1997).
Cré, Marleen, *Vernacular Mysticism in the Charterhouse*, The Medieval Translator 9 (Turnhout, 2006).
Cullum, P. H., and Katherine J. Lewis, eds, *Holiness And Masculinity in the Middle Ages* (Cardiff, 2005).
D'Evelyn, Charlotte, 'Instructions for Religious', in *A Manual of the Writings in Middle English*, vol. 2, ed. J. Burke Severs (New Haven, 1970), pp. 458–81.
Darwin, Francis D. S., *English Mediaeval Recluse* (London, n.d., c. 1944).
Dohar, William J., '"Since the Pestilence Time": Pastoral Care in the Later Middle Ages', in *A History of Pastoral Care*, ed. G. R. Evans (London, 2000), pp. 169–200.
Doyle, A. I., 'Carthusian Participation in the Movement of Works of Richard Rolle Between England and Other Parts of Europe in the 14th and 15th Centuries', in Hogg, *Kartäusermystik und -Mystiker*, ii.109–20.

———, and see under Gillespie.
Elliott, Dyan, *Fallen Bodies: Pollution, Sexuality, and Demonology in the Middle Ages* (University Park PA, 1998).
Elm, Kaspar, 'Vita Regularis Sine Regula: Bedeutung, Rechtsstellung und Selbstverständnis des mittelalterlichen und frühneuzeitlichen Semireligiosentums', in *Häresie und vorzeitige Reformation im Spätmittelalter*, ed. František Šmahel (Munich, 1998), pp. 239–73.
Engen, John van, 'Friar Johannes Nyder on Laypeople Living as Religious in the World', in *Vita Religiosa im Mittelalter: Festschrift für Kaspar Elm zum 70. Geburtstag* (Berlin, 1999), pp. 583–615.
Friedman, John B., *Northern English Books, Owners, and Makers in the Late Middle Ages* (New York, 1995).
Gieben, Servus, 'Robert Grosseteste and Medieval Courtesy-Books,' *Vivarium* 5 (1967), pp. 47–74.
Gillespie, Vincent, 'Cura Pastoralis in Deserto' in *De Cella in Seculum*, ed. Michael G. Sargent (Cambridge, 1989), pp. 161–81.
———, 'Dial M for Mystic: Mystical Texts in the Library of Syon Abbey and the Spirituality of the Syon Brethren,' in Glasscoe, *Medieval Mystical Tradition* VI, pp. 241–68.
———, '*Lukynge in haly bukes: Lectio* in some Late Medieval Spiritual Miscellanies', *Spätmittelalterliche geistliche Literatur in der Nationalsprache* 2, ed. James Hogg, Analecta Cartusiana 106 (1984), pp. 1–27.
———, *Syon Abbey*, with A. I. Doyle, *The Libraries of the Carthusians*, Corpus of British Medieval Library Catalogues 9 (London, 2001).
———, and Kantik Ghosh, eds, *After Arundel: Religious Writing in Fifteenth-Century England* (Turnhout, 2011).
Glasscoe, Marion, ed., *The Medieval Mystical Tradition: England, Ireland and Wales*, Exeter Symposium VI (Cambridge, 1999).
Gougaud, Louis, *Ermites et recluses* (Vienne, 1928).
Gransden, Antonia, 'The Reply of a Fourteenth-Century Abbot of Bury St. Edmunds to a Man's Petition to be a Recluse', *English Historical Review* 75 (1960), pp. 464–7.
Hadley, Dawn M., ed., *Masculinity in Medieval Europe* (London, 1999).
Hanna, Ralph, 'John Dygon, Fifth Recluse of Sheen: His Career, Books and Acquaintance', in *Imagining the Book*, ed. Stephen Kelly and John J. Thompson (Turnhout, 2006), pp. 127–41.
Hill, Nick, and Alan Rogers, *Gild, Hospital and Alderman: New Light on the Founding of Browne's Hospital, Stamford 1475 to 1509* (Bury St Edmunds, 2013).
Hirsh, John C., *Hope Emily Allen: Medieval scholarship and feminism* (Norman OK, 1988).

Hogg, James, ed., *Kartäusermystik und -Mystiker*, Analecta Cartusiana 55 (Salzburg, 1981).
Hughes-Edwards, Mari, 'Anchoritism: The English Tradition', in McAvoy, *Anchoritic Traditions*, pp. 131–52.
——, 'Hedgehog Skins and Hairshirts: The Changing Role of Asceticism in the Anchoritic Ideal', *Mystics Quarterly*, 28:1–2 (2002), pp. 6–26.
——, '"How Good it is to be Alone"? Sociability, Solitude and Medieval English Anchoritism', *Mystics Quarterly*, 35:3–4 (2009). pp. 31–61.
——, *Reading Medieval Anchoritism* (Cardiff, 2012).
——, '"Wrapt as if to the Third Heaven": Gender and Contemplative Experience in Late-Medieval Anchoritic Guidance Writing' in McAvoy and Hughes-Edwards, *Anchorites, Wombs and Tombs*, pp. 131–41.
Jansen, Katherine Ludwig, *The Making of the Magdalen: Preaching and Popular Devotion in the Later Middle Ages* (Princeton, 2001).
Johnston, F. R., 'Syon Abbey', in *The Victoria History of the County of Middlesex*, vol. 1 (Oxford, 1969), pp. 182–91.
Jolliffe, P. S., *A Check-List of Middle English Prose Writings of Spiritual Guidance* (Toronto, 1974).
Jones, E. A., 'A New Look into the *Speculum Inclusorum*', in Glasscoe, *Medieval Mystical Tradition* VI, pp. 123–45.
——, 'Anchoritic Aspects of Julian of Norwich', in *A Companion to Julian of Norwich*, ed. Liz Herbert McAvoy (Cambridge, 2008), pp. 75–87.
——, 'Ceremonies of Enclosure: Rite, Rhetoric and Reality', in *Rhetoric of the Anchorhold*, ed. Liz Herbert McAvoy (Cardiff, 2008), pp. 34–9.
——, 'Hermits and Anchorites in Historical Context', in *Teaching Anchorites and Mystics*, ed. Roger Ellis, Dee Dyas, Valerie Edden (Cambridge, 2005), pp. 3–18.
——, 'Hidden Lives: Methodological Reflections on a New Database of the Hermits and Anchorites of Medieval England', *Medieval Prosopography* 29 (2013, at press).
——, 'Langland and Hermits', *Yearbook of Langland Studies* 11 (1997), pp. 67–86.
——, 'Rites of Enclosure: The English *Ordines* for the Enclosing of Anchorites, s.xii–s.xvi', *Traditio* 67 (2012), pp. 145–234.
——, 'Vae Soli! Solitaries and Pastoral Care', in *Texts and Traditions of Medieval Pastoral Care*, ed. C. Gunn and C. Innes-Parker (Woodbridge, 2009), pp. 11–28.
Jones, Michael K., and Malcolm G. Underwood, *The King's Mother* (Cambridge, 1992).
Ker, N. R., *Medieval Libraries of Great Britain*, 2nd ed. (London, 1964).
Lees, Clare A. et al., eds, *Medieval Masculinities: Regarding Men in the Middle Ages* (Minneapolis, 1994).

Leyser, Conrad, 'Masculinity in Flux: Nocturnal Emissions and the Limits of Celibacy in the Early Middle Ages', in Hadley, *Masculinity in Medieval Europe*, pp. 103–20.
L'Hermite-Leclercq, Paulette, 'La réclusion volontaire au moyen âge: une institution religieuse spécialement féminine', in *La condición de la mujer en la edad media* (Madrid, 1986), pp. 135–54.
Licence, Tom, *Hermits & Recluses in English Society, 950–1200* (Oxford, 2011).
Lindenbaum, Sheila, 'London after Arundel: Learned Rectors and the Strategies of Orthodox Reform', in Gillespie and Ghosh, *After Arundel*, pp. 187–208.
Logan, F. Donald, *Runaway Religious in Medieval England* (Cambridge, 1996).
Malden, H. E., 'House of Carthusian Monks: Priory of Sheen', in *A History of the County of Surrey: Volume 2*, Victoria County History (London, 1967), pp. 89–94.
McAvoy, Liz Herbert, ed., *Anchoritic Traditions of Medieval Europe* (Woodbridge, 2010).
———, 'Gender, Rhetoric and Space in *Speculum Inclusorum*, *Letter to a Bury Recluse* and the Strange Case of Christina Carpenter', in Liz Herbert McAvoy, ed., *Rhetoric of the Anchorhold: Space Place and Body within the Discourses of Enclosure* (Cardiff, 2008), pp. 111–26.
———, *Medieval Anchoritisms: Gender, Space and the Solitary Life* (Woodbridge, 2011)
———, '"Neb … sumdeal ilich wummon & neddre is behinden": Reading the Monstrous in the Anchoritic Text' in *The Medieval Mystical Tradition in England*, Exeter Symposium VII, ed. E. A. Jones (Cambridge, 2004), pp. 51–67.
———, and Mari Hughes-Edwards, eds, *Anchorites Wombs and Tombs: Intersections of Gender and Enclosure in the Middle Ages* (Cardiff, 2005).
Millett, Bella, 'Can There Be Such a Thing as an "Anchoritic Rule"?', in *Anchoritism in the Middle Ages: Texts and Traditions*, ed. C. Innes-Parker and N. Kukita Yoshikawa (Cardiff, 2013), pp. 11–30.
Murray, Jacqueline, 'Masculinizing Religious Life: Sexual Prowess, the Battle for Chastity and Monastic Identity', in Cullum and Lewis, *Holiness and Masculinity*, pp. 24–42.
Nixon, H. M., *Five Centuries of English Bookbinding* (London, 1978).
O Clabaigh, Colman, 'Anchorites in Late Medieval Ireland', in McAvoy, *Anchoritic Traditions*, pp. 153–77.
O'Brien, Robert, 'The "*Stimulus Peccatoris*" of William of Rymyngton', *Cîteaux: Commentarii Cistercienses* 16 (1965), pp. 278–304.
Owen, H., and J. B. Blakeway, *A History of Shrewsbury*, 2 vols (London, 1825).
Page, William, 'Religious Houses: Introduction', in *A History of the County of Sussex: Volume 2*, Victoria County History (London, 1973), pp. 45–7.

Patterson, Lee, *Negotiating the Past: The Historical Understanding of Medieval Literature* (Madison, 1987).
Pevsner, Nikolaus, *Lincolnshire*, rev. John Harris and Nicholas Antram (New Haven CT, 2002).
Raine, James, ed., *Testamenta Eboracensia*, vol. 1, Surtees Society 4 (1836).
Robbins, R. H., 'Medical Manuscripts in Middle English', *Speculum* 45 (1970), pp. 393–415.
Rogers, Alan, *Noble Merchant: William Browne (c1410–1489) and Stamford in the Fifteenth Century* (Bury St Edmunds, 2012).
Rymer, Thomas, 'Rymer's Foedera with Syllabus: June 1415', *Rymer's Foedera Volume 9*, online at http://www.british-history.ac.uk/.
Sargent, Michael G., 'Contemporary Criticism of Richard Rolle' in Hogg, *Kartäusermystik und -mystiker*, i.160–205.
——, *James Grenehalgh as Textual Critic*, 2 vols (Salzburg, 1984).
——, 'The Transmission by the English Carthusians of Some Late Medieval Spiritual Writings', *Journal of Ecclesiastical History* 27 (1976), pp. 225–40.
Smith, David M., 'Suffragan Bishops in the Medieval Diocese of Lincoln', *Lincolnshire History and Archaeology* 17 (1982), pp. 17–27.
——, *The Heads of Religious Houses: England and Wales, III. 1377–1540* (Cambridge, 2008).
Smith, Eustace J., 'In Memoriam: Livarius Oliger, O. F. M., 1875–1951', *The Americas* 7 (1951), pp. 475–80.
Smith, Katherine Allen, 'Saints in Shining Armor: Martial Asceticism and Masculine Models of Sanctity, ca. 1050–1250', *Speculum* 83 (2008), pp. 572–602.
Storey, Anthony, *Mount Grace Lady Chapel: An Historical Enquiry* (Beverley, 2001).
Swanson, Robert, 'Angels Incarnate: Clergy and Masculinity from Gregorian Reform to Reformation', in Hadley, *Masculinity in Medieval Europe*, pp. 160–77.
Thompson, E. M., *The Carthusian Order in England* (London, 1930).
The Town of Stamford, Royal Commission on the Historical Monuments of England (London, 1977).
Turner, E., 'Domus Anchoritae, Aldrington', *Sussex Archaeological Collections* 12 (1860), pp. 117–39.
Warren, Ann K., *Anchorites and their Patrons in Medieval England* (Berkeley, 1985).
Watson, Nicholas, 'Censorship and Cultural Change in Late-Medieval England: Vernacular Theology, the Oxford Translation Debate, and Arundel's Constitutions of 1409', *Speculum* 70 (1995), pp. 822–64.

Bibliography 157

Web resources

This section is reserved for resources available exclusively on the web. Print sources that I have consulted online will be found listed in the appropriate section elsewhere in the Bibliography.

'The French of England': www.fordham.edu/frenchofengland/.
'Electronic *Manipulus florum* Project': http://www.manipulusflorum.com.
'Piccard-online', Landesarchiv Baden-Württemberg, Hauptstaatsarchiv Stuttgart, J 340: http://www.piccard-online.de.
'Manuscripts of the West Midlands': http://www.hrionline.ac.uk/mwm/.